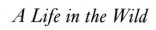

A Life in the Wild

A Life in the Wild

ÉAMON DE BUITLÉAR

Gill & Macmillan

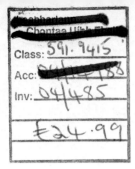
Do Laillí

Gill & Macmillan Ltd
Hume Avenue
Park West
Dublin 12
with associated companies throughout the world
www.gillmacmillan.ie

© 2004 Éamon de Buitléar

0 7171 3615 9

Index compiled by Gráinne Farren
Print origination by Carole Lynch
Printed by MPG Books, Cornwall

The paper used in this book is made from the wood pulp of managed forests. For every tree felled, at least one tree is planted, thereby renewing natural resources.

A catalogue record is available for this book from the British Library.

3 5 4 2

Contents

Acknowledgments

Writing a book is not unlike filming wildlife; it can be a lonely occupation. One important difference in this instance was that all those hours were not spent cramped up in an uncomfortable bird hide. Working from home had the added advantage of being able to check dates of past events with my wife Laillí, who like many women possesses a wonderful way of connecting the months and years with children's births. Thanks are due to our children, especially Róisín and Cian, for their encouragement, and to my sister-in-law Nóra for reminding me of various events during the making of the early *Amuigh Faoin Spéir* wildlife TV series.

Details regarding some of the characters living in the Bray area were confirmed for me by local man Tony Sutton. The few years that my American friend, Sid Neff, spent fishing in Ireland obviously left a lasting impression on him. He could relate in great detail his angling experiences on various rivers with Ned Maguire, whom he liked to refer to as his piscatorial friend. I am also grateful to him for the photographs which are included of Ned and himself. Ronnie McShane was most helpful in jogging my memory in relation to our days with Ceoltóirí Chualann, and both Nicholas Carolan and Órla Henihan were never too busy to respond to my queries with regard to traditional music.

My thanks to my scientist friends, Ken Whelan and Rory Harrington, who were as usual more than willing to supply me with up-to-date information in relation to the environment and wildlife. Joe Saunders and Emer Colleran kindly filled me in on the history of the Burren saga.

Were it not for Bryan Deegan, who first suggested it, the thought would not have occurred to me to write this book. My thanks to Michael Gill, who finally persuaded me by offering to publish it, for his invaluable advice throughout.

Creating a book is much like filmmaking, where the editor's handling of a large amount of material can either make or break a production. I owe my editor Eleanor Ashe a debt of gratitude for her patience in handling the endless pages I kept sending her and for her skill in finally getting it all into order. Deirdre Nolan, as managing editor, remained hidden away somewhere in the background, while she expertly gave the material that essential final polish before sending it on its way for publication.

Éamon de Buitléar

1

Beginnings
1930s

Hillsbrook – My mother's people – Father, a Gaelgeóir – A busy household – St Brigid's school – Living by the river – The river in flood – Poaching time – The river baliffs – Great anglers – Our neighbours

Hillsbrook

The noisy procession passed by our gate on the first Monday of every month. We could hear it coming as we played along the banks of the River Dargle where our family lived. We clambered up excitedly to watch the spectacle from our garden wall. Flocks of sheep, groups of cattle and a few horse-carts carrying litters of piglets and young lambs all had to pass down our road on their way to the fairground near Bray. We were very small boys, my two brothers and I, and we weren't sure where these animals came from, but we wouldn't miss the excitement for anything.

Those were the pre-war days of the early 1930s when there was little or no motor traffic. Space was not a problem on the roads, and the animals heading for the fair could spread themselves across both sides, bellowing and bleating as they made their way down the valley. In later years we were to learn that the men driving the sheep and cattle had come from beyond Enniskerry and from the mountainous area of Glencree, eight or nine miles upstream from where we lived. They were hardy hill farmers and they thought nothing of walking that long distance every month with their animals.

I was born in 1930 and named after my father, Éamon, but in order to avoid confusion I was called Éamon Óg. Father was Commanding Officer of the 1st Battalion based in Galway. When I was about two and a half years old, he received word that he was to be transferred back to

Dublin. In preparation for the move, he travelled over to the east coast to look at houses in the Co. Wicklow area. He took a fancy to a small, one-story house called *Hillsbrook*, situated a mile or so from the town of Bray in the Dargle Valley. It stood beside the river, which came tumbling down over a weir and had an acre of unkempt garden running right down to the water's edge. This was an idyllic location and my parents were quickly convinced that it was just the place to rear a family.

They could only afford to rent the house at first and it was quite some time before they gathered enough money together to buy Hillsbrook and carry out some badly needed home improvements. The house consisted of four rooms and a lean-to wooden kitchen, to which was attached another small room. Outside was a yard surrounded by a high wall, an outside tap and a small shed, part of which housed a lavatory. There was no bathroom and no running water inside the house.

My mother's people

It seemed to us children that we were surrounded by aunts and uncles, and in fact my maternal grandfather, Tom O'Brien, actually lived with us for some time. He was a good gardener and looked after the vegetable patch, but he could be crusty at times and I don't think he had much time for children. My grandmother died when my mother, Nóra O'Brien, was only twelve years old. My mother was the eldest of six and it was her responsibility from then on to look after her brothers and sisters. I think they found it hard to let her go when she married, which is probably why aunts and uncles were still around when we were small.

Life must have been difficult for my mother as a young girl growing up in Passage East, Co. Waterford. She had to manage the house and all her siblings, not to mention an impatient father. One day when she had cooked a duck for their dinner, her father decided that it had not been left long enough in the oven. He promptly opened the window and threw the roast duck into the street! My aunts and uncles regarded Nóra as if she were their mother and, being the eldest, she handed out advice to them even when they were well into their adult years. She was a very strong woman with a sharp turn of wit, and was quick to give a reply to anybody

2

who criticised what she believed to be right. She built up confidence in her children by constantly emphasising to us that we were at least as good as anybody else.

She had a busy time with us – seven in all. Déaglán was more than two years older than me, and Ruairí a year younger. Lochlann was born in 1935, the first sibling to be born in Hillsbrook. Then the girls followed on: our sister Deirbhile was born in 1937, Ailbhe a few years later and our youngest sister Colma in 1942.

Father, a Gaelgeóir

My father was born in Clanbrassil Street in Dublin in 1902. Later the family moved to 12 Heytesbury Street and it was from there that my father attended the Christian Brothers school at Synge Street. After he left school he became very interested in the Irish language. He worked initially as a clerk in Brooks Thomas hardware merchants and at the same time began to study Irish. He then attended a course at the College of Modern Irish in Dublin, qualifying as a teacher of the language. He taught Irish in various branches of the Gaelic League and worked in the *Freeman's Journal* translating Dáil speeches from Irish into English.

My father and mother met in the Gaelic League and when they married they decided that their family should be reared speaking Irish. My mother also had a love of Irish language and music, having lived close to the Ring Gaeltacht as a girl. Many of the songs she taught us came from happy holidays spent in Ring. She cared little for the rules of grammar, however, and tended to use the future tense when she was actually referring to the present. Whatever about this particular grammatical peculiarity, my mother was certainly ahead of her time and as somebody once suggested, perhaps this construction on the language might have had the effect of making us more forward-looking!

My father was a perfectionist and when it came to learning Irish, he studied the dialect spoken in the West Cork Gaeltacht of Béal Átha an Ghaorthaidh. The Irish scholar Seán Ó Cuiv had invented his own phonetics in the dialect of the West Cork Gaeltacht and a series of books prepared by him included a translation of *Aesop's Fables* and the well-known Irish story of Séadhna. My father knew these off by heart. His

3

Irish was fluent and his diction accurate. When he joined the army and was posted in Galway he came into contact with Gaelgeóirí from the Aran Islands and thus further developed his appreciation of all things Irish.

Bray had once been a garrison town and the British Legion still held their annual remembrance marches there when we were young boys. There were few if any Irish speakers around Bray at the time and the sight of children growing up speaking Irish must have seemed very strange indeed to many of the locals. Bray was a mile or two from our house and when our mother went shopping, we usually accompanied her. During one of those shopping trips to Bray, our younger brother Ruairí was sitting in what we used to call a go-car. My elder brother Déaglán and I walked along, holding on to each side of the go-car, chattering away to each other in Irish. As we made our way along the Dargle Road towards the town, we passed a row of small houses known as St Brigid's Terrace. A local woman, wearing a long blue and white apron, was leaning over one of the small garden gates, with her bare folded arms. She missed nothing of what was going on and every passer-by received a greeting. As my mother came along she was greeted in a flat Bray accent: 'Good mornin' mam! Cool kind of day!'

It was at this point that the woman heard what must have seemed to her to be a very strange babble, coming from the three of us. 'Excuse me, mam!' We had by now gone past the gate and my mother continued to push the buggy along, as she made her way down the road towards Bray. 'Excuse me mam!' the woman called after her, unfolding her arms and pointing a finger at us. 'Excuse me, mam! But were they born that way?' she asked in utter astonishment. (She would have been even more astonished if she knew that the elder of us, Déaglán, would eventually become Chief Fire Officer of the London Fire Service!)

A busy household

Being older than the girls, the boys became experts at house cleaning and polishing. My mother believed that boys should do at least as much, if not more, housework than girls. This resulted in both Ruairí and I becoming such experts at dusting and polishing that we would automatically inspect the dust situation in other houses. We usually regarded other people's shelves and mantelpieces as inferior to the standard demanded of us by our mother. There was a long strip of linoleum in our hallway that glittered from our special polishing technique. It was Ruairí's idea to put on two or three pairs of old woollen stockings on our feet and after laying down the polish, we would both take short runs and slide up and down the hallway until you could almost see your reflection in the linoleum. This method succeeded both in getting superior results as well as saving us a lot of elbow grease. Making beds was a chore we did not care too much about, but you daren't take a shortcut when my mother was around. Making a bed meant removing all the blankets and sheets every time and there was no such thing as just pulling up the bedclothes in one go. On one occasion she made me remake a bed no less than five times.

We could all swim at an early age and the easiest way for us to learn was to adapt the dog's paddle, the canine method of staying afloat. We also learned to swim underwater with our eyes open and I had the experience once of meeting a salmon face to face in the pool. I surfaced pretty quickly on that occasion!

Being able to swim ensured that we would be less likely to get into trouble if we fell into the river, and as long as we stayed back from the bank during those really heavy floods, we were probably not in any real danger. As often happens with large families, the older ones usually looked after the youngsters.

St Brigid's school

School began for me at the age of five when I went with my elder brother, Déaglán, to St Brigid's, a small private school in Bray. Miss Brayden, a stern lady, ran the school and we were all quite shy of her. I had not yet learned much English, and Miss Brayden did not know much Irish. The lack of English did not seem to be much of a disadvantage to me at that particular age, but Miss Brayden's lack of Irish caused a problem for her at times. Eventually Déaglán progressed onwards and then my brother Ruairí and myself attended each day. Things became somewhat critical during this period.

St Brigid's was a small school, catering for children aged between five and ten years. It had both girls and boys and there were only three small classrooms. On one occasion a girl in class promised me a fountain pen if I kissed her little red-haired companion. The challenge was so tempting that I said I would be quite prepared to kiss her plus all the other girls in the class for such a reward. I was only about seven years of age and as I set to work grabbing each one of the girls in turn, there were shrieks from the unfortunate victims as well as from the onlookers. Miss Brayden came rushing in as soon as she heard the commotion and was quite shocked at the sight of her little darlings bawling their eyes out.

Eventually Miss Brayden wrote to my mother asking that Ruairí and I should both be taken out of the school as we were becoming unruly, adding that whenever she tried to correct either of us, our mutterings in Irish went well beyond her knowledge of the language. I think we were probably at the age when we would have had to leave anyway and this we did.

Living by the river

Most children did not have a wristwatch in those days but, living by the river, we always knew when it was lunch-hour and teatime, even if we weren't hungry. A very loud whistle would echo all the way down the valley that could be heard as far away as Bray. The one o'clock whistle was to inform the workers in the Dargle & Bray Laundry that it was time for lunch. At a quarter to two, the whistle lasted several minutes, calling the workers back to their duties. The two o'clock whistle was the signal to resume work. The laundry was a few hundred yards from our house and we could see the long line of women workers walking up the road every day on their way to and from the laundry.

The laundry was owned by Wallace's Coal Merchants and was well known for its high standards. The spotless white sheets billowed in the wind as they hung on lines outside the building. The delivery and collection of clothes in large baskets was by horse-cart. These were two-wheeled, varnished vehicles drawn by fine animals with shiny coats. The horses were kept in the laundry's stables at night but on Saturdays they were brought across a bridge to fields on the other side of the river.

The laundry used a great quantity of water in carrying out its various operations. One of the strangest sights of the week, and one that often puzzled visitors to our house, was the flotilla of brown paper bags that frequently floated down the river. This was part of the laundry's refuse and in those days the easiest way to get rid of waste was to throw it straight into the river!

Living in a house with the river just outside the kitchen window must have been a constant worry for my mother. The pool at the edge of the garden was quite deep and she had to keep a constant eye on us while we played outside. Yet none of us ever got into difficulties in the water. The worst that happened was either getting our clothes wet or receiving a cut foot while paddling in the river.

There were brown trout in the River Dargle as well as a very good run of salmon and sea trout. Anglers were seen regularly on our stretch of river and my father became interested in teaching himself how to fish. After reading about the various techniques in relation to the sport, he eventually decided that fishing with a dry-fly was angling at its best. The angler watches to see what insects are being taken from the surface of the water by the trout. He then attempts to match that particular insect with an artificial imitation. The artificial fly is made of feathers and fashioned in such a way that it floats dry on top of the water. It actually imitates an insect sitting on the water in preparation for take-off, just after it has emerged from its nymphal stage.

Anglers who practise the art of fishing exclusively with the dry-fly are usually regarded as purists and tend to use the very best of tackle available. My father, in his usual systematic way, went through a selection of catalogues of all the best-known manufacturers and finally chose Hardy's of Alnwick. They were based in Northumberland and were famous as the makers of Palakona split-cane rods. Their fishing tackle was known all over the world. The sole agents for Hardy's tackle in Ireland were Hely's of Dame Street in Dublin.

My father knew the woman in charge of the fishing tackle department at Hely's. I remember him coming home with a selection of Hardy's fly rods, which he had been allowed to take home to test out on the river. The rods were in neat cloth cases, some in three sections and others in two sections. They were made of seasoned Chinese tonkin cane and each one had the name written in script, under a shiny coat of varnish. The brand names included titles such as 'Perfection', 'Pope', 'Knockabout', 'Gold Medal', and there was one named after a famous dry-fly angler called 'Halford'. There were many more models, all of different lengths and weights, but my father chose the 'Knockabout' – a two-piece, nine-foot dry-fly rod that had an action that suited him.

Following my father around as he went fly-casting out on the river awakened my interest in fishing. It was not long before he made me a wooden fishing rod of my own. Rather like the grey heron that we often watched from the kitchen window, I would stand at the water's edge with my new rod, patiently waiting for a hungry fish. The heron seemed to stand for hours, day after day, crouched and motionless in this very same spot, watching for some unwary eel to wiggle on to the wet slab in its attempt to cross over the weir. Depending on the run of fish and the level of the water, the heron's long wait was often richly rewarded.

One day when there was a fresh flood on the river, I stood in my favourite spot and had my line in the water as usual. Goodness only knows what I was expecting to catch, because when I lifted my rod there was a lively fish at the end of my line that startled me so much I ran in terror up the dry slope of the weir. Looking over my shoulder, I could see that the fish was still following me, tumbling and jumping on top of the water, and it continued to wriggle as I unknowingly pulled it after me on to dry land. The reluctant fish had no choice; I was still clutching on to my rod as I retreated further and further up the slope of the weir.

My father and Déaglán watched all the excitement unfold from the kitchen window. They almost knocked over the breakfast table in their scramble to reach the door and arrived down at the weir in record time to save a five-and-half-year-old angler, who in his own mind was about to be devoured by his catch, a fine one-pound trout!

The river in flood

In common with other rivers, the Dargle has many moods, which it continues to express in a variety of ways. During those warm days of summer the river was at its laziest, with one half of the weir often drying up completely and the other half disgorging, as best it could, its rationed share of water into the thirsty pool below. Long hours of sunshine and slow-moving currents created ideal conditions for the growth of algae. The river-bed gradually became covered in a brown and green moss-like

substance, bits of which regularly popped to the surface with the continuation of the dry spell. The river did not look its most attractive during
this period but it was a safer playground for us as we paddled in the
warm water, using our nets to catch sticklebacks, minnows and elvers. We
occupied ourselves by making dams from loose stones, building a series
of special little pools to hold our catch.

During the big autumn floods the mood changed dramatically. Two
days of non-stop rain and the river turned from a meandering, oversized
stream into a raging brown torrent. We watched the river rising inch by
inch until eventually it had risen several feet. The weir disappeared
completely under the huge volume of water that rushed headlong down
towards the sea, sweeping away all in its path.

The drama could be seen from the kitchen and we cheered whenever a
big tree, carried down by the flood, sailed past the window. During one of
these autumn floods, we spotted an unwilling passenger sitting among the
branches of a large tree. An adventurous waterhen had very unwisely
taken refuge in the branches and was now clinging on like some ancient
mariner, high up in the rigging of his ship's mast as his vessel headed
towards disaster. Our final sighting was of the beleaguered bird struggling
to keep a foothold on one of the highest branches, as the tree and its
passenger quickly passed downriver.

These spectacularly heavy floods dramatically transformed the river's
landscape. New pools, faster or slower runs, large rocks where there had
been none or huge boulders carried down from much further upstream,
could appear overnight in a completely new location. It was exciting to
find these changes after the huge rush of water had subsided and there
were now new areas waiting to be explored. Having spent so much of my
youth on the river, I was very familiar with the feeding haunts of the trout
in the various traditional runs and pools. Changes to those habitats caused
by a recent flood always added to the excitement of another fishing safari.

Poaching time

A large, well-built granite bridge carried the main street of Bray over the
River Dargle. It was a favourite spot from which to keep a watch for
fresh-run salmon on their way upstream from the sea. The trained eye of

the local poachers could see what the ordinary passers-by were sure to miss, and the sight of some of the 'old reliables' hanging around in the vicinity as soon as the floodwaters had subsided was a sure sign that the fish were moving.

Heavy floods late in the year could produce spectacular views of fresh-run salmon and sea trout, throwing themselves at the torrents of white foamy water tumbling down the weir. Although there were no anglers fishing on the river after September, poacher Harry Christian could never stay away for long, even during the closed season. He knew every rock and pool on the Dargle. He would make a mental note of the number of fish and their movements as they struggled to get over the weir. The fish were on their way to the spawning beds further upstream. Some would swim several miles up as far as the Powerscourt Estate. Others would branch off into the Cookstown River and others into smaller tributaries. Their final location would always be in a stretch of the river where they themselves had been spawned.

Harry practised the art of poaching with pride. He showed taste in the way he captured his prey, and a salmon landed would carry no ugly gaff mark on its side. It was Harry who taught me how to fashion trout flies from a selection of silks, feathers and tinsels. He was also an expert at making by hand fine devon minnows from old copper gas tubing.

Salmon that have spent about a year at sea are known as grilse, but Harry Christian always referred to them as peal and we never knew them as anything else. It was a name used in many parts of Ireland and the word may have come from the Irish word *píl*, meaning something big. If you hooked one while fishing for trout, you would certainly regard it as big! The grilse, or peal, were about six pounds in weight and usually ran into the river from late summer to autumn. The bigger fish that had spent two winters at sea and weighed between ten and twenty pounds were known simply as salmon, and they began arriving in the Dargle in late spring.

Angling was not one of my mother's priorities but she did catch a salmon once. It was during one of those heavy autumn floods when the fish were attempting to make their way upstream. My mother happened to look out the window just as an over-anxious salmon leapt too far to the right and landed on a patch of dry land beside the weir. Without hesitation, she grabbed a big towel from a chair beside the stove, ran down to the edge of the water, and threw the towel over the struggling fish. She grappled with her valuable catch for a minute or two before eventually enveloping it and rushing back with it to the kitchen while at the same time putting her faith in the Almighty that she hadn't been spotted by the bailiffs.

The river bailiffs

The Earl of Meath controlled the fishing rights on the lower reaches of the Dargle, including the stretch of water from Bray Bridge down to the sea. Above the bridge, the area under his control included about a mile of river that ran up to within a hundred yards or so of the weir at Hillsbrook. The Earl had two or three bailiffs who patrolled this stretch of the river and they kept a constant eye out for any activity in the area by local poachers. The run of fish during those years was considerable and the Dargle was regarded as the best river on the east coast for both salmon and sea trout.

When a large crowd gathered on Bray Bridge it was usually a sign that the salmon had arrived in from the sea and that Lord Meath's men were below in the river, working with their nets. Each of the bailiffs wore body-waders that made it possible for them to wade in water up to their chests. The anglers, in contrast, wore ordinary rubber thigh-waders. The bailiffs each had a large, long-handled hoop-net and as they waded up along the river they prodded the nets under the bank in their attempts to corner the salmon. It was during heavy floods that most of the salmon entered the river but catching them with pole nets in conditions of very high water was almost impossible.

The bailiffs had most success immediately after a flood, before the fish moved far up the river. They were not permitted to operate any closer than a distance of about one hundred yards of the weir. The pool at the weir was an important resting-place for fish and as salmon were an extra source of revenue, it was in the estate's interest to protect them. Once my Aunt Annie's boyfriend, Gerry Penny, acted as a bailiff, with embarrassing results. Gerry was a stylish dresser and played the saxophone. Living in the heart of Dublin, my father's family had no experience of life in the country. It was a great new adventure for them to have a brother living away outside of Dublin, whom they could now visit at weekends. The acre of garden by the river at Hillsbrook must have seemed like a big estate to my father's brothers and sisters. Whenever Gerry arrived at Hillsbrook, he would gain great satisfaction from walking up and down the riverbank, as if he were an official bailiff. If some unfortunate angler happened to wander across the river and on to our piece of land, Gerry was sure to challenge him and inform him that he was trespassing. On one occasion he noticed a fisherman wading across the river and he immediately headed down to the riverbank to intercept the intruder. 'Are you aware that you are on private property?' began Gerry. The somewhat surprised angler had just reached the bank. 'Oh, I'm sure it's quite all right,' he replied, in a pronounced English accent. 'I'm Captain Jameson,' he added, 'the Earl of Meath's agent.'

Gerry didn't believe the captain and in fact thought he was having him on. 'Is that so now,' he countered. 'Well if you're Captain whatever yeh said yer name was, I'm Napoleon, and you're on private property!' The captain didn't answer but just stood spellbound staring at this strange-looking individual in a striped suit, speaking with a strange accent. Gerry of course was totally unaware that Capt. R.J.A. Jameson's boss, Lord Meath, owned a very large estate that extended outwards from the very bank on which he was actually standing and for which Captain Jameson happened to have full responsibility!

Fortunately my father, who was up at the house, happened to see that something was not quite right and he quickly appeared on the scene. The poor captain was saved from any further embarrassment and was informed that he could fish away to his heart's content when and wherever he wished. Meanwhile, Gerry, the self-appointed Estate Manager, was discouraged from doing any more patrolling along the riverbank.

Great anglers

There were various characters who regularly fished on the Dargle, and as I grew older I got to know many of them. The two anglers who in those days were regarded as the best fishermen on the Dargle were Johnny Keith and Ned Maguire. Johnny Keith, a Wexford man, was a car mechanic whose clothes were always oily and, although he had big hands, he could make the most delicate, tiny dry-flies. Even though we were young children, we liked to see Johnny arriving at our pool. His box of flies, which had little compartments with pop-up windows, always fascinated us and we longed for him to choose another fly to try out on some wily trout, so that we could get another opportunity to see the fly-box. When he chose one of these feathered imitations, he could thread the gut-cast through the eye of the hook, tie on the fly in a matter of seconds and then bite off the piece of surplus gut with his teeth.

Ned Maguire was a native of Stonyford in Kilkenny, but he worked for most of his life as a chemist in Hayes, Conyngham and Robinson's shop in Bray. Ned was an excellent fisherman, an accomplished fly-tyer, a good naturalist and an imaginative storyteller. He had great admiration for Johnny as an angler, and in describing his fly-tying skills he remarked to one of his fishing friends, 'With the shovels of hands that Johnny has, I don't know how he can make such beautiful flies!' Ned's father had been a steward on Major McCalmont's Estate in Co. Kilkenny, so Ned could fish on the stretch of the Nore that ran through the estate when-ever he wished. His knowledge of nature and his expertise in fishing all originated there. When he moved to Co. Wicklow, he spent his leisure hours fishing on the Dargle and on the North and South lakes in Roundwood.

Night fishing is a popular sport with some anglers, as it offers the opportunity to catch some of those bigger fish that don't feed so readily during daylight. There is little to see on a riverbank in the dark, but on these occasions the challenge is to use senses other than one's eyes. Ned was so familiar with the sounds of the wild that, simply by listening, he was aware of what the creatures of the waterside were up to. He would get a great thrill from pinpointing an otter's movements even when it could not be seen. He did this by noting the location of the loud 'kurruk' warning calls of various waterhens at different points along the river.

The first call would begin in the distance downstream, where a lone waterhen had become alerted to an otter moving into its territory. Each call echoed from one waterhen's haunt to the next as the otter gradually worked its way towards where Ned was fishing. Ned would remain motion-less, watching for a glimpse of the animal and listening for the sounds that would tell him that the otter had moved on to continue its hunting further upstream. I suppose it is a skill that observers of wildlife would learn naturally from being close to nature. Most people on hearing those waterside sounds would never even guess at the exciting adventures being played out along the river either during the night-hours or in daylight!

Our neighbours

The farm next door to our house was an education in itself. There were three cows, two plough-horses, a turkey or two, ducks and a dozen hens or so. Old May Barton was the owner of the farm. She shared the holding with a relative, Willie Staunton, and had a live-in help, Mary Ormond, who was of similar age, and there was also George, the workman. We children spent a lot of time on Barton's farm, where we became familiar with daily chores that included everything from feeding farmyard hens, guinea fowl and ducks, to milking cows.

Heading off to the hayfields on a hay bogey was for us one of the highlights of summer. The large, flat, wooden float was only about two-and-a-half feet above the ground, with two iron wheels and no sideboards. The farm's strongest cart-horse was yoked-up between the wooden shafts to pull the hay bogey a quarter mile up to the fields along a narrow road called the Blind Lane. There were three small cottages on the Blind Lane. The 'Dogger' Byrne lived in one of the cottages. People would bring their puppies to him to have their tails docked, which he did by biting them off. Others in the locality used more conventional methods! The Cullen family lived next to him. Mickey Cullen was unmarried and lived with his sister. He often wheeled out his sister's two little children and we would see them with him on his way down to Bray. My mother asked him one day why the children had a brown paper bag tied around each of their necks. Mickey replied that they had the whooping cough and that he had put some hairy mollies into each of the bags in order to ease their coughing! The hairy molly is another name for the larvae, or hairy caterpillar, of the garden tiger moth. Reading a book on folklore recently, I came across a list of old Wicklow cures that included a cure for whooping cough. The cure was exactly as Mickey Cullen described that day, with the hairy mollies and the brown paper bags.

A little way up the road beyond Barton's farmyard and just across the road from the Dargle River lived a family of gypsies who spoke with an English accent. Gypsy Smith, as everyone knew him, lived in a horse-drawn caravan. He owned a black-maned, coffee-coloured jennet, which was used to pull a light, two-wheeled cart. The cart was Gypsy Smith's only means of transport to and from Bray. The jennet was a lively animal and always seemed to travel at a very fast trot with its owner sitting sideways, nicely balanced on the cart, his legs dangling over the edge. The gypsy's wife, 'Madame' Smith, told fortunes along the seafront in Bray. She was a tanned woman with big gold earrings and she wore a brightly coloured silk scarf on her shoulders.

The Smiths' caravan was located upstream from our house and was quite close to the river. They had two boys and their eldest son, Hubert, whom I knew best, used to fish for trout on the Dargle. Hubert showed me how he made snares out of hairs plucked from a horse's tail. With these he was able to catch starlings. Feathers from starling wings have always been a popular material in a variety of trout fly patterns, and several of the anglers on the Dargle were glad to have them when making their own flies.

In the field behind the caravan and just beyond a stone wall, Hubert set the six newly made small horsehair nooses in a line close to the ground. He then staked each end down with two wooden pegs and laid some pieces of bread in the grass around where the almost invisible snares were. We hid behind the wall and waited for the return of a flock of starlings that Hubert had earlier seen feeding in the field. The birds were back in no time and they glided down and landed close to the snares, just where Hubert had thrown the bread. At first there were some minor battles, as individual starlings noisily argued with each other for the biggest bits of the feast. As I was trying to keep out of sight, it was difficult for me to see what exactly was happening in the grassy patch beyond. But before I could say anything, Hubert suddenly clapped me on the back and shouted in glee: 'I've caught the little beggars!' Six of the birds had unwittingly stuck their heads into the invisible horsehair nooses and were fluttering frantically in their attempts to escape. This was the signal for Hubert to run out into the field and put the unfortunate birds out of their misery.

2

The Call of the Wilds
1940s

Pet birds and animals – Visiting the Áras – War years – Sights and sounds of Bray – Willow Park school – Summer holidays – First trip to the Gaeltacht

Pet birds and animals

From my earliest years I developed a love of nature. I was fascinated by the river and by the world of beauty that lay all around us in Hillsbrook. I wanted to be close to animals, close to nature. When I was about nine years of age my mother asked me what I would like to be when I grew up. We were all out walking at the time and I replied without hesitation, 'How would I own the zoo?'

Animal stories were my favourite reading material and I can still remember the excitement of following the adventures of *Ivan and the Wolves* or looking at exotic species of wildlife in *The Wonder Book of Animals*. Whenever I asked for books, at Christmas or on birthdays, they always had to be about animals.

My first attempt at having a pet was when I found a baby song thrush in the garden. It must have been injured when I found it and I did my best to nurse it for the rest of that day. Next morning when I looked into its temporary home in the cardboard shoebox, it was lying quite still on its side. I cried so much at the loss of what I thought would be my very first pet that my mother promised she would get me a real pet bird some day soon.

When my father arrived home a few weeks later carrying a small box with holes in it, I could hear the chirping inside even before he handed over the mysterious parcel. There were two birds in there – the woman who sold the birds to my father had said that it would be better to have a

16

pair rather than one on its own. It was the first time I had ever seen budgerigars, and I was delighted at the sight of the two parrot-like little birds. One of the budgies was yellow; this, according to the breeder, was the cock, and the hen was a lovely green colour with a striped yellow back. The two birds were carefully released into a chrome cage that my father had bought in a pet shop on his way home. Both budgies settled down immediately and a great deal of their time was taken up by chirruping to each other.

I spent a lot of time looking after my new pets, making sure that the seed holder and the water container were kept full and that the inside of the cage was clean. I had the birds for only a week and I was carrying out my usual cleaning operations, when both escaped from the cage and flew straight out through the kitchen window! I was devastated. For days afterwards I walked around the nearby fields, holding up a small dish of mixed budgerigar seed and calling to the birds. Whenever a wild bird chirped in a hedgerow, I was sure it was one of the budgies. But my feeble attempts at imitating their calls were of no avail. They didn't respond and I never saw either of my budgies again.

One of my earliest pets from the wild was a jackdaw, which I found as a nestling. I began training the jackdaw by repeating its name, 'Bill', every time I fed it, and before long it would answer 'Caw' and immediately fly to me. I then trained him to sit on the handlebars of my bicycle and he would accompany me whenever I cycled down to Bray. I was really showing off and I would go down to the town with him more often than was necessary. On one of my trips to Bray a smart little townie called out 'Good *crowface!*' as I passed him by. I knew that this colourful remark was meant for me and not for the jackdaw.

It was fortunate that I was on my own that day, because had my brothers heard the little townie's comical remark, they would have grabbed at the opportunity and I would forever have had to live with the nickname. The thought of having my real name replaced by an ornithological one such as 'Crow-face' didn't appeal to me, and I was not willing to take the risk of ever allowing any of my brothers to hear that particular greeting. Much as I liked to have my pet travel to town with me, I made an immediate decision to give up my showing off and cancel all future cycle rides to Bray with Bill the jackdaw.

Visiting the Áras

In 1938 Dr Douglas Hyde, linguist, collector of folk songs, one of the founders of the Gaelic League and author of *Love Songs of Connaught*, among many other books, retired from the chair of Irish at University College, Dublin. To his surprise he was then invited by the rival parties in Dáil Éireann to become Ireland's first President under the 1937 Constitution. The President requested the army to appoint my father as his *aide-de-camp*. As he was now to be the President's personal officer, my father would have to live at Áras an Uachtaráin, which of course meant that my mother would see even less of him.

My father must have been telling the President about my interest in fishing because he invited me to come and fish in the lake at Áras an Uachtaráin. I sat on the bank under the trees, fishing away happily until I eventually landed five or six small rudd, which I brought up to show to the President. When I entered the room he came out from behind his big desk to meet me, a jovial man dressed in tweeds and sporting a big walrus moustache. He admired my meagre catch and praised me for being a good fisherman!

There were other times when Ruairí and I were brought up to the Áras and allowed into the kitchen, where the whole staff were Irish-speaking. Most of the women were from the Donegal Gaeltacht. One night we were allowed to stay overnight. It was our first time being in a lift and we got great value out of making it endlessly go up and down, until our father found out what we were at and chased us to the bedroom.

The President enjoyed the outdoors and liked to go fishing but he was not a serious angler and was happy enough to go bait-fishing for pike. He also liked to go on shooting trips, and my father accompanied him on these excursions into the countryside. After President Hyde became ill in 1941, my father returned to General Army Headquarters and our trips to the Áras were over.

War years

As schoolboys we had our own views regarding the war, but it was something that seemed to us to be happening very far away. At night-time we would sometimes hear Lord Haw-Haw broadcasting from Germany and contradicting what the announcer on the BBC had said in relation to the success of the Allied Forces. At the beginning of the war many of us schoolboys wore small swastikas that we manufactured from penny coins. After placing the penny on a tram-track we would wait for a passing tram to flatten it; the image would then be cut out with a hacksaw and polished to the coin's original copper colour. A pin was soldered on to the back of the swastika and the finished badge was proudly attached to our jumper or jacket. We became expert badge-makers. Today the mention of anyone wearing swastikas in Ireland comes as quite a shock, but at the time we were only schoolboys of nine or ten years of age. As the horrors of the war became more evident, the swastikas were eventually rejected.

During the war, my father worked in Army Intelligence. With his facility for languages he had in fact been sent by the army to Berlin University in 1934 to learn German. Some of our school friends came to the conclusion that he was a German spy! During the war, at least ten German agents landed in Ireland. The most senior Nazi agent to be captured was Major Hermann Goertz, who was held in Arbour Hill barracks. In prison, he was still able to receive messages from Germany and send replies. My father was very involved in trying to break Nazi codes, including the one being used by Goertz. Dr Richard Hayes of the National Library, whom the Germans knew only as Captain Grey, worked closely with my father.

They arranged to see Goertz and informed him that they would like to see the code being written out; he had often boasted that nobody would ever succeed in cracking it. As Goertz was under the impression that neither of his two visitors knew anything about codes, he agreed to their request. Dr Hayes had the gift of remembering every detail of anything he read. My father's memory was not quite as good, so whenever Goertz was not looking, he scribbled the information on his hand. After spending about a half-hour with Goertz, they left and arranged to meet in the morning.

The following day when they met, my father asked, 'Have you worked out Goertz's cipher, Richard?' To which Dr Hayes replied, 'I have!' 'I have cracked it too!' my father exclaimed. Before going further they agreed to write down the result of their hard night's work. They then looked at each other's pieces of paper and the wording on both was exactly the same. Each had written 'United States Navy'! Even though they had used completely different methods they had come up with the same solution, and Goertz's code had finally been broken. The messages coming to and from Germany from then on could be read both by my father and by Richard Hayes. The system that Goertz had used, and which MI5 were also attempting to break, was a complicated one, as he substituted figures for letters. Generally speaking, if an alphabet were used in a code you would have, for instance, ABCD and a figure and then FGHI and so on. But Goertz had a figure for each letter and he split the figure in two halves, which made it extremely difficult to decipher.

Goertz was never told that his code had been broken and he was allowed to continue sending secret messages from his prison to his contacts outside. Army Intelligence doctored the messages going out as well as those coming in, and Goertz was never the wiser as to what was going on. It was his intention to eventually have the Germans land in Ireland, at which point he would take full command!

Sights and sounds of Bray

Cars were few and far between during and after the war. Horses and carts, cabs and pony-traps were the common means of transport, and there was a big demand for horseshoes. There were three or four blacksmiths working full-time in Bray. Andy Devitt's forge was just beyond the church in the main street and we loved to stand at the big open doors and watch Andy as he shaped the horseshoes from pieces of red-hot iron. Sometimes we slipped inside and watched him working the long handle up and down, pumping the huge bellows underneath the fire. Eventually the fire became extremely hot and it heated the pieces of iron until they turned completely red. Andy was a muscular man in an under-vest and a leather apron over his trousers. When he had the horseshoe shaped he removed it from the red-hot embers. He then held it on the anvil with an iron thongs and hit the shoe a few more smacks, sending sparks flying in all directions around the forge. He dipped the horseshoe into the water-trough and it would sizzle and change colour. Finally, gripping the horse's hoof between his knees, he carefully placed the hot iron shoe on to the upturned hoof and it too would sizzle, giving off a very distinctive but not unpleasant smell. He explained to us that it didn't hurt the horse because the hoof was made of the same material as our fingernails, only much thicker.

Down beyond Bray Bridge in Castle Street, the Foley brothers had a saddler's shop, and the big attraction there was the stuffed pony that took up the whole of the front window. It was once a real live pony and even as it stood motionless in the window it still looked very life-like. It had a saddle on its back and a bridle and reins and if you were small enough, one of the Foleys would lift you up and let you sit for a moment on the pony's back. We would never miss a visit to Foley's window and if we had a schoolbag that needed stitching, we had a really good excuse to go inside and stay for a while.

Itze Barnes played the bass drum in St Kevin's Pipe Band. The drum was almost as big as himself and when he carried it on his chest, all one could see from the front were two skinny legs supporting a large drum! The members of St Kevin's Band wore a saffron kilt and a black tunic with silver buttons. As a small boy I was allowed to act as mascot, and on St Patrick's Day I marched, in my saffron kilt, at the front of the band alongside the Pipe Major. I must have looked quite comical walking like a goose in my efforts to keep in step with the Pipe Major. It was only when my first parade was over and I was on my way home that I saw a local boy imitating me for the benefit of his mother.

The only person in the band who was dressed differently to the rest of the members was Itze. It was the tradition in pipe bands for the person carrying the big drum to wear a leopard skin over the tunic as a protection against the wear and tear of the drum. Itze was small and wore spectacles but in spite of this the leopard skin earned him the unlikely name of 'Tarzan'!

The bass drum is an awkward instrument to transport and has to be carried on a leather harness that comes up across the shoulders and is attached to the drum by a swivel-clip. Itze had discovered that apart from holding the drum on to his chest, the swivel could serve another purpose. If he were in form he hit the drum at a particular point in the performance, causing the instrument to give a quick spin on the swivel before he came in on the next beat. This was a tricky manoeuvre and sometimes had its pitfalls. It was during the St Patrick's Day parade that Itze decided to give the large crowd lining the main street extra value for their money. The parade had begun at Bray's Town Hall and, as it came down towards the church, the street echoed to the sounds of bagpipes, tenor drums and side drums. The band was playing 'When Malachy Wore the Collar of Gold'. It was a favourite march and one that was played quite early in the parade and again on the way home.

The Pipe Major leading the band had just given his long staff a twirl when Itze decided that this was an opportune time to make his own special contribution. He waited until the pipers had come to the end of the first sixteen bars of the tune. It was then that 'Tarzan' hit the bottom edge of the big drum with the lambskin-covered drum-stick, while with the other hand he gave the top edge of the drum a quick push. This was designed to give the drum a spin, but the swivel holding the instrument seemed to jam. Poor Itze, who was caught completely off balance, was pulled by the weight of the drum and he rolled in under the feet of the pipers.

There was confusion among the band members, accompanied by a squeal of pipes and a groan of drones as the pipers momentarily lost their grip on the chanters. The onlookers, obviously not realising that Itze was almost being choked to death by the harness on his big drum, laughed and clapped at this most unexpected display of gymnastics.

Bray was very popular as a holiday seaside resort in the 1940s. It was close to Dublin and had a railway line running direct to the city. This made it possible for families to come and spend the day at the seaside. On fine days during the summer the beach was thronged with visitors, and a line of horses and cabs waited outside the railway station for those who didn't feel inclined to walk the short distance to the beach. There were dozens of B & Bs along the seafront. Notices outside many of the houses advertised 'Teas, ^{1}/$_2$d' and 'Teas, ^{1}/$_4$d' (one shilling and four-pence). You could buy a kettle full of boiling water to make a cup of tea, or go inside and have something more substantial to eat.

On a Sunday morning as we walked along the seafront, we passed some of the B & Bs and my brother Déaglán asked my father why the houses were all selling 'heat' for ^{1}/$_2$d and ^{1}/$_4$d. Déaglán was reading what he thought was the Irish word 'teas' (pronounced 'tass'), meaning 'heat' in Irish. As we continued on our walk along the promenade and up towards Bray Head, we stopped when we heard music and saw an old man sitting on a wooden seat, playing a fiddle. It was my first meeting with a blind person. It was also the very first time I had seen anybody play a fiddle. As soon as the tune ended my father put some money in the musician's tin box. He spoke in Irish to the old fiddle player and I felt that they must have met somewhere before. As we made our way home I learned that the blind fiddler came from Co. Cork and that he made the journey to Bray every summer to play music near the sea.

Willow Park school

My mother's youngest brother, Turlough O'Brien, was studying for the priesthood in Rockwell College, Co. Tipperary. The Holy Ghost Fathers run both Rockwell College and Blackrock College in Co. Dublin, and it was because of Turlough's connection with that order of priests that we were sent to Blackrock's Preparatory School, Willow Park. My younger brother Ruairí and I started on the same day. Déaglán had already been attending the school for a year or two. It was a strange experience to go from a small mixed school, where there were no facilities for games, to an all-boys' school with large fields where they played rugby.

Although Déaglán played a lot of rugby at Willow Park, I don't remember being on a team during my time there. Togging out in rugby gear to play games was far less attractive to me than getting back home to the river and to my various pets. Ruairí wasn't in the least interested, but one memorable day, when the Willow Park team was short of a player for what we were told would be an important schools' match, a prefect decided to put a good sturdy fellow on as a substitute and rather unwisely he happened to pick Ruairí. It was an occasion when lots of parents were coming to watch the match and we were instructed by the Dean, Fr Maguire, to be on our very best behaviour. If Ruairí was familiar with the rules of rugby, which I doubt, they would take second place to upholding the honour of the school and that meant only one thing to Ruairí: the opposing side must be prevented from winning at all costs!

The match began with both teams fairly evenly matched. Then, without warning, a player from the other team broke away with the ball. He had come around on the blind side and was streaking away across the field, with nobody between him and the Willow Park score-line. The visitors went wild and they cheered and clapped, urging on their hero. But the crowd had yet to see Ruairí in action and he immediately took off in pursuit as if he were the country's 100-yard reigning champion. It was obvious to him that they were in immediate danger of losing this important match and Willow Park would be in disgrace. He could feel that the school was now depending on him to save the day!

As Ruairí closed in on his quarry, he could see that his chances of making a successful tackle and preventing a crucial score before the line was reached could not be guaranteed. There was only one option left to him: he shot out his foot and tripped up the player, sending him flying to the ground on his ear. There was a big 'Aaaww' of disappointment from the crowd, and the Dean, who was surrounded by parents, groaned with embarrassment and glared in my direction as I stood with my classmates watching from the sideline. It was a memorable match for all the wrong reasons and Fr Maguire, who was never too fond of either of us, but especially not of Ruairí, grew to like the de Buitléars even less after that eventful day!

Willow Park at that time was a small school and the staff consisted only of the Dean, two lay teachers and two or three clerical students. The lay teachers wore gowns and the clerics, like the priests, wore long black soutanes and Roman collars. The clerical students took classes and were called prefects, but they were not in the least like the prefects we used to hear about in English public schools and they didn't administer corporal punishment, which was the responsibility of the Dean. The prefects were kind men and could be fun, but the lay teachers, who were older, were more serious, especially Mr O'Beirne, who was a good maths teacher but very strict. If you were in his good books, you could have an easy enough time with him but if you were what he would term a 'slacker', life could be less enjoyable. When Mr O'Beirne heard some of the boys mention that I sometimes wore a kilt, he dared me to wear it to school. I came in the next day in my outfit, and when class was over he told me I was a better man than he had thought. He then organised a number of the boys as bodyguards, just in case some of the others might be tempted to pull the kilt off me.

Sending four boys to school at Willow Park and later to Blackrock College must have been quite an expense for my parents. My mother, however, was born of a country tradition in which it was customary never to pay the marked price for anything. She was also quite liable to give people who were completely unfamiliar with country ways the benefit of this ancient custom. I am quite sure that she would have bargained over the years with the college bursar, in much the same way as she did on a weekly basis with the local shopkeepers in Bray.

My experience of seeing her in action with one innocent individual began on a morning when I complained that I had pains in my eyes whenever I tried to look sideways. My mother's reaction was to whisk me down to Bray and into Dublin on the train. We walked from Westland Row Station to Merrion Square, where, according to my mother, the best doctors had shining brass plates on their hall doors. The one we were to visit was an eye specialist, Dr Dwyer-Joyce. He was a small man with a high forehead, dressed in what looked to me to be a morning suit. After examining my eyes and giving me a reading test, he informed my mother that my eyes were perfect and that I was probably just getting chicken-pox. My mother was not too pleased when Dr Dwyer-Joyce asked for a fee of three pounds, which to us was a fortune. She didn't argue about the price, however, as she had her own way of dealing with the matter. While the good doctor stood at the door of his consulting room awaiting his fee, my mother rooted in her handbag as she made towards him. As soon as she reached him she pushed one pound and ten shillings into his hand, it being exactly half the amount requested. And then, muttering a parting, 'That will do you!', she hurriedly dragged me out the front door after her and into Merrion Square, in the direction of the train.

I can still see that poor man in his black and grey striped trousers, standing at the door in disbelief, blinking through rimless glasses at the thirty shillings my mother had placed in the palm of his hand. As I sat on the train to Bray it occurred to me that here was one specialist I would never visit again, regardless of what eye complaint might afflict me in the future. The following morning I was confined to bed with chickenpox.

Summer holidays

The best part of school days were the long summer holidays. The school term finished in June and then we were free for almost three months. We had a wooden raft, and on fine summer days we floated it on the long flat stretch of water above the weir. Tall trees formed the edge of a mixed woodland on the bank opposite our side of the river and we could pole the raft upstream and imagine that we were exploring the banks of the Amazon. I seemed to be the one who sailed it and enjoyed it the most and I spent endless hours on the river.

By being extra careful I could sail the raft very quietly and perhaps surprise a skulking waterhen or get close to a pair of nesting wagtails. I could also take a closer look at the bank where a pair of kingfishers had their nest and, on a clear day, when the sun was at a certain angle, I could peer under the raft where views of an underwater world could be seen. Although I had never been to the Amazon, my feeling in those days was that sailing my raft up the Dargle was every bit as good.

Ruairí had a school friend, Séamus Reilly, whom he invited to come sailing up the river on the raft. My mother liked Séamus but she used to say that Séamus and Ruairí were 'two opposites'. Séamus was always very well dressed and usually wore his school blazer and short grey flannels, which were always spotless. Ruairí wasn't particular about his appearance, at least not at that age. Mrs Reilly would say 'if only Séamus were a little more like Ruairí', while at the same time my mother would wish that Ruairí were a little more like Séamus!

The trip that Séamus took on the raft was really his first and last attempt to 'explore the Amazon' with us. As he innocently stepped on to the raft in his blue blazer and grey flannels, he was cruelly advised that the best place to stand would be on the very edge of the board. The raft was no sooner underway than it suddenly lurched to one side, throwing its passenger headlong into the water. Poor Séamus had to be pulled from under the raft and brought into the house for a change of clothes. By the time he had dried out he actually looked a little more like Ruairí!

Harvest-time was between August and September and we prayed that the threshing on Fisher's farm would begin before we returned to school in September, or that we would at least be allowed to miss a few days. Fisher's was where our milk came from and it was delivered on a milk float at seven o'clock in the morning. The float, with two large churns, was drawn by a very sprightly pony that ran non-stop the three miles from Enniskerry to our house in the Dargle Valley. It also had to run the three miles back in the afternoon.

When the threshing machine arrived at Fisher's, we could hear the whistle more than three miles away as the big steam engine gave the signal that they were ready to begin the threshing. Men from neighbouring farms worked with each other at the threshing during the war years, and girls from the Solus factory in Bray were sometimes recruited to give a helping hand.

First trip to the Gaeltacht

My first trip to a Gaeltacht was with my father, to Baile Mhúirne in West Cork. We stayed in a small farmhouse while we were there. The River Sullane was nearby and my father would do a bit of fishing there every other day. The man of the house kept hens and ducks, and every morning before he set them free he would place two separate dishes on the ground, at some distance from each other. When the door was opened, the hens rushed out to one dish of food and the ducks to the other one. I was very impressed at how well he had trained them all.

Some years later my father arranged for me to holiday in an area a few miles further west, in Cúil Aodha. I stayed at the house of a great traditional singer, Pádraig Ó Tuama, or Peaití Thaidhg Pheig as he was known locally. Many years later, the composer Seán Ó Riada would become a neighbour of Peaití's. Peaití had a great store of songs and was greatly admired by Ó Riada. I often wonder if my father had detected at that early age that I might have had more of an interest in the songs and the music than my brothers would have had. Or was it as a result of having been to the Gaeltacht that I then became more aware of this richness of our culture? Perhaps it was a bit of both, but whatever the reason, a love of traditional songs and music would always remain with me and become part of my life.

3

New Projects
1940s

My first breeding project – Blackrock College – Holy matters –
More life by the river – Goats and gardens – Drums and drumsticks –
Naming birds

My first breeding project

The first mammals I kept as pets were two guinea pigs, and my big
ambition at the time was to begin breeding from them. The problem was
that they were both sows, which meant that my next assignment would
be to find them a boar as a mate. My mother had heard a friend, Mr
McGannity, mention that he had an aviary in his garden and she
suggested that I contact him as he would surely know a lot of people who
owned pets. Mr McGannity lived in Bray and was the Managing
Director of Vigzol Oils. His way of relaxing from the stresses of business
was to breed canaries. When he brought me into his back garden I was
delighted because not alone had he dozens of beautiful birds in his aviary,
he owned a collection of prize pet rabbits and three or four guinea pigs
as well. I found him to be extremely kind and very knowledgeable about
various pets and he was more than willing to give advice. Mr McGannity
was also president of the Fur & Feather Club. He informed me that they
held an annual show in the Mansion House every year and that I might
enter a guinea pig sometime. I was very pleased with the guinea pig boar
he gave me on loan as part of my new project.

Observing newly arrived youngsters can be fascinating and the sudden
appearance in the hutch one morning of a couple of baby guinea pigs was
for me a huge thrill. Unlike the young of some mammals, guinea pigs are
perfectly formed and fully furred when born and I found them a real

delight to watch. Each of my females had two babies, which had an attractive mixture of their parents' colours. My favourite was a little black and white one that had similar markings to a Dutch rabbit. It had two black patches around the eyes, a white flash from its forehead to its nose and a wide white band around its middle. This was the one that I would surely enter for the following year's show!

The Fur & Feather Show was very exciting and quite a number of guinea pigs had been entered, all of which would be competing for the top prize. Rabbits such as the ones I had seen in Mr McGannity's collection were also taking part in the competition, and in fact there were quite a number of classes catering for the various breeds. They included Dutch rabbits with straight regulated markings, Chinchilla rabbits in their overall silvery grey colour, English rabbits with the essential butterfly pattern on the nose and a dotted pattern on the body, and Rex rabbits with their unusual velvet like coat. On the day of the show, all the competitors had to have their animals in place at the Mansion House by half-past nine. Nobody was allowed into the hall until after lunch, when the judging would be completed. Some of us younger members peered in through the window and we could see a number of judges in white coats, working their way in among the various exhibits. Several of the judges were English and had been invited over especially for the show. I had entered my black-and-white guinea pig with Dutch markings and when I came back in the afternoon I was thrilled to see a card on its cage marked *First Prize*!

Breeding guinea pigs was one way of making some pocket money and I had an arrangement with Dublin Zoo to buy them from me on a regular basis. I would put them in a carrying basket and bring them with me into school in the morning, and I had permission to keep them in the classroom while they were in transit. It would have been difficult to get rich quickly with my first breeding project. Apart from anything else, guinea pigs have a 65 to 70 day gestation period, and for a boy wanting to make some money, this breeding period is quite long. I would have had to breed hundreds of guinea pigs to make a real profit. As it was, the wooden hut that I built for them in the garden had been christened *Shanty Town* by my mother and I doubt if I could have got away with providing more breeding space for my pets by putting up more of those architectural monstrosities!

Blackrock College

When I moved on from Willow Park Preparatory School to Blackrock College, our Dean of Discipline was Fr Mattie Harkins. He was a nice man, but if he had a sense of humour none of us was prepared to explore that particular aspect of his personality. I had no problems with him apart from one memorable incident. I had recently received as a birthday present from my mother my first natural history book on animals, *A Beast Book for the Pocket* by Edmund Sanders. Apart from describing the wild mammals, it included good colour drawings of the various domestic farm animals, including different breeds of cattle, pigs and horses. It also described the many breeds of pet rabbits, and the section on rodents had some useful information on the guinea pig.

I brought the book to school with me and I was reading snippets from it on my way down the corridor to the classroom, when coming in the opposite direction was Mattie. He noticed the book in my hand and asked me if he could borrow it. I was delighted that he might be beginning to take an interest in wildlife and I told him he could have a loan of the book for a day or two. It wasn't long before I was to find out that there was not even a remote possibility of Fr Harkins becoming a wildlife enthusiast! He called me into his office on the following morning and told me that I shouldn't have the book because 'it classified man in the same order with apes, monkeys and lemurs'. My impression was that he didn't want me to have the book because in the section on humans it mentioned 'there is no special mating season, though perhaps a greater inclination thereto appears in spring'. Whatever about the apes and monkeys, this section must have been a little too much for Mattie to accept. Having read the section he must have decided that it would be better not to run the risk of having one of his pupils scandalised by such dangerous reading. My mother was less than pleased when I told her that my birthday present had been confiscated. Fr Harkins had never met her and I was never told about their encounter, but she must have created a right old fuss because I had my *Beast Book* returned intact to me in no time.

Holy matters

There was a great emphasis on religion at school, which is hardly surprising as the majority of teachers were either priests or men preparing to be priests. Fr Harkins' pride and joy was the Holy Angels Sodality, and, as angels have wings and schoolboys have fertile imaginations, it was only natural that the sodality would eventually become known as 'Mattie's Airforce'.

The religious atmosphere in the school mirrored that in the community. The yearly mission was a feature of every parish, and two or three visiting priests would be invited by the parish priest to come and give sermons, hear confessions and encourage the parishioners to live better lives. The mission would be arranged for every evening of that special week, with the grand finale being held on the Friday. The most dramatic missionaries were the Redemptorist Fathers, whose fire and brimstone sermons rarely failed to terrify the more timid members of the community. My angling friend Ned Maguire told me about a visit by the Redemptorists to his own parish of Stoneyford in Co. Kilkenny. One of the local characters, Patsy Brennan, an old man who everyone knew had not been inside a church for decades, was somehow or other persuaded by one of the villagers to turn over a new leaf, attend the mission and atone for his sins. The parishioners were surprised and delighted when they noticed Patsy arriving every evening, almost ten minutes before the sermon began. Most of them had never seen Patsy Brennan within a mile of the church, let alone inside God's house and on his knees.

On the last day of the mission it was customary for the missionary priest to encourage the faithful to renew their baptismal vows. The church was packed on that last and final night of the mission and all the faithful were provided with candles for the occasion. As the members of the congregation held hundreds of lighted candles aloft, the church glowed in a beautiful warm light and one could almost feel the great sense of devotion among the people. The priest then called out in a loud voice from the pulpit; 'Do you renounce the devil?' To which the congregation answered, as with one voice, 'We do!' Patsy Brennan had reached a stage where he had atoned for all those years away from the church, and he was now more passionate even than the missionary himself. After his week of prayers and sermons, coming to the church before anyone else, and spending so much time on knees that were now very sore, he was brimful of eagerness and enthusiasm. The priest's voice rang out loud and clear: 'Do you renounce the devil?' Patsy, who now regarded the devil as his arch-enemy, lost the run of himself and shouted in a voice that could be heard above all the others, and presumably by the devil himself, for whom it was really meant: 'We do, the hoor!'

There was a mixture of boarders, day pupils and scholastics at Blackrock College and the majority of scholastics would progress to the seminary after they had finished in sixth year. The scholastics' quarters, both for sleeping and eating, were separate from those of the boarders. Perhaps the college authorities felt that the road to the seminary would have fewer twists and turns if the scholastics were kept away from the rest of the boys. A feeling of 'holiness' in those who were not scholastics often came about during the annual retreat at the college. It didn't last long for most boys, but it stayed with me for quite some time. It came to an abrupt end when I consulted with Fr Roche, my Latin teacher, who very wisely advised me to forget all about it. I am sure he could see through my feeling of holiness better than I could and he jokingly added that what I should really do was to 'look for a rich widow who might have a good piece of land!' My mother was bitterly disappointed when I told her that I definitely was not going to be a priest. Having confided in some of her close friends that one of her sons was going in that direction, she was doubly downcast.

I always had a good deal of respect for the priests I met at Blackrock, and later in life, while filming in Africa, I came to realise the tremendous work that priests and nuns do in the Third World. Fr John Roche had been in Africa for many years, where he travelled in the bush on a motor-bike. He had a good sense of humour and was very popular with those of us who were fortunate enough to know him. He confiscated my mouth organ one day when he heard me playing it as he came into the classroom. I knew he played one himself, which is why he delayed so long in return-ing it. Somebody tried to console me by telling me that he was without a mouth organ of his own at the time and he needed to do a bit of practice! Fr Roche was the only priest with whom I was friendly enough to go and visit after I left Blackrock. The last time I saw him I brought him in a brand new mouth organ, with which I hope he enjoyed many hours entertaining the community.

The Gilbert & Sullivan Operettas, under the direction of Fr Corless, were annual events every December at the college. Fr Corless, whom we all knew as 'Bing', directed his first operetta in 1934 when he was a prefect, and he continued with this work when he returned to Blackrock as a young priest. We had *H.M.S. Pinafore, The Gondoliers, The Pirates of Penzance* and *The Mikado*. The Gilbert & Sullivan Operettas were really the extent of our musical education at Blackrock, unless one took individual piano lessons as an extra class, for which there was a fee. Early in the school year, Fr Corless auditioned the pupils for a part in the operetta. We were called up to the concert hall in twos and threes, and each boy would be invited to sing the scale while Bing accompanied on the piano. My younger brother Ruairí and I went for an audition but were told that we were not musical enough. We must have made a really good impression on Bing because we were never invited to audition again or to take part in any further productions! I don't think it worried either of us, as taking part in the operetta meant a lot of time spent at school, and we had more than enough to keep us occupied at home by the river.

More life by the river

During the summer holidays we looked for excuses to go to Jubilee Hall, where our schoolmates, the Hernons, lived and where there were ponies to be ridden and an orchard full of a whole variety of apples that we could sample until we could eat no more. At the back of Jubilee, we chased hares with dogs up around 'Cathy Gollagher' Mountain, but we never succeeded in catching one. On really hot days we swam in the river at home or paid a visit to Bray seafront, where we were members of Bray swimming club. It was an open sea club, which meant a boarded walk out from the promenade to a diving board but no pool – if the tide was out there was no water. The swimming club often held what was known as a 'smoking concert', which the committee organised in the Royal Hotel in Bray. A musician, a singer and a comedian would be hired to entertain the guests, who sat at tables around the large room. Drinks were available from the bar and every table had a dish-full of cigarettes that were free of charge. You could puff cigarettes until the smoke came out of your ears; in fact there was so much of a haze in the room that it looked liked a cowboy saloon in an old western movie.

Although we always had one or two dogs at Hillsbrook, my mother never paid for any of these canine friends. She felt that money shouldn't change hands for a dog. Her view was that there were always people looking to find a good home for a dog and all one had to do was to make a few enquiries. Strangely enough, all those 'free' dogs she was given down through the years had very good pedigrees. The very first dogs I remember at Hillsbrook were a black-and-white cocker spaniel called Timmy and a red setter called Kerry. The cocker spent most of its life sleeping in the shed and the setter spent all day watching for trout in the stream at the side of the house. He would stand motionless in the water for hours, with one forepaw raised at the ready to scoop out an unwary fish. Kerry always chose the same spot in the stream – where the footbridge threw a shadow on the water. The deeper part here had less of a ripple and the shadow thrown by the bridge made it easier to see any movement in mid-stream. Although he could clearly see the trout, he didn't have the gift of being able to use his paws like a grizzly bear does when scooping out salmon. I don't think he ever caught anything. Kerry had only half a tail, the result of one of those rare visits to dry land, when he backed into the push mower as my grandfather was mowing the lawn.

In later years we had a dog whose name was Nip, a cross between a bull-terrier and a bulldog. A friend from my mother's native village of Passage East brought Nip to us one weekend. It was the only non-pedigree dog we ever had, but my mother's excuse was that both its parents had pedigrees. Nip was hopping with fleas the evening he arrived and it was only after he was thoroughly washed that we could see the true whiteness of his coat. He was as ugly a dog as ever I saw but Mother just loved him. Nip was heavy-chested, mean-eyed and built like a small tank, with more of the bull-terrier look about him than that of the bulldog. Apart from his looks, he was otherwise good-natured. I had been under the impression that every dog could swim, but once when I pushed Nip into the weir pool, he was so heavy he just sank and I could see him trying to walk on the bottom, with bubbles coming out of his nose. I was really afraid he was going to drown and I had to jump into the water and pull him out.

My mother loved playing poker, which for her was a way of enjoying an evening with friends, but more importantly, it brought in some badly needed extra cash to run the house. She had the reputation of rarely being the loser, which is probably why she could afford to play with those friends of hers who were much better off financially. A number of them were successful business people. The card games were played at our house and at the houses of the other members.

Whenever a poker game was played locally, my mother cycled to her destination. On one particularly dark night after arriving home, she was wheeling her bike across the small footbridge where the red setter used to fish, when her handbag slipped off the handlebars and fell into the stream. In the darkness she could not see where the bag had gone, and, rather than risk falling in herself, she decided to wait until morning. Looking into the brook in broad daylight, however, didn't solve the problem for her, as the handbag was nowhere to be seen. The Dargle River was only about twenty yards downstream from the footbridge and the probability was that the bag fell into the brook and had floated for a while before being carried down into the main waterway. What most worried my mother was that, having had a very successful poker game the night before, all the proceeds from the game were in the handbag! Ruairí and I waded up and down the brook but we could find no trace of the bag. My mother then directed that Ruairí, who was the better swimmer, should search the deeper water in the river.

If the bailiff had arrived he would surely have got the impression that what he was seeing was a poacher at work. Ruairí was using a stick and poking under the bank at short intervals as he waded down the river. In fact he looked very much like a poacher trying to locate a salmon. After about half an hour's wading and searching, he unexpectedly discovered the bag stuck under the bank about a hundred and fifty yards below where the stream entered the river. My mother was both relieved and delighted, as her winnings of fifteen pound notes were in the handbag and, apart from being soggy and wet, they were otherwise intact. Fifteen pounds at that time was a considerable sum of money.

Goats and gardens

I didn't really have finance in mind when I acquired my first goat. She was a white female and I was delighted that I now had something approaching a real farm animal. I was used to milking the cows next door in Bartons, so minding a goat, I felt, would not be very difficult. There was a big white puck goat a mile up the road from us, on Major Hudson's farm, and you could actually smell the animal from a few hundred yards before reaching the gate! I wanted to find out as much as I could about goats and I began buying a weekly newspaper called *The Smallholder*, which gave some information on goat breeding in Britain. It was probably at the back of my mind at that stage that earning a living in the future would preferably be outdoors.

The two kids born to my white female goat in the spring were delightful. I bought a few more animals and my herd gradually increased to six goats in all. I was now supplying the house with milk daily, and I began to tot up the figures in hopes of getting paid for all the pints being consumed by the family. I milked the goats before setting off for school in the morning and again when I returned in the late afternoon. As time went on I was beginning to lose any hope of getting rich on selling goat's milk to my mother. Although she didn't say it, she probably felt we all owed her money by now! In other words I was in debt and I could forget about doing my milk tots.

My brother Ruairí, who was very fond of gardening, was fighting a losing battle with the goats – there was hardly a tree in the garden that had not been stripped of its bark. As the animals were changing the landscape to such a degree and I was wasting time and money, I eventually decided to bring the goat-farming venture to an end, much to Ruairí's relief.

Drums and drumsticks

At school, Aloysius Flood and myself, after finishing our sandwiches, would play music until the bell rang for class at two o'clock. Aloysius was a talented pianist and had an extensive repertoire of tunes that he could play by ear. I accompanied him, playing rhythm with a pair of drumsticks on the plywood seat of a bentwood chair. It was not quite the kind of drumming I was learning with the Dalkey Pipe Band at the time, but we had great fun and the boys seemed to enjoy it. Aloysius Flood eventually went on to become a Holy Ghost father and was Dean of Studies at St Michael's Boys' School for a number of years.

Playing the side drum with the Dalkey Pipe Band was enjoyable and although we never quite reached the standard of the Fintan Lawlor or the St Laurence O'Toole Pipe Bands in Dublin, the quality of the music was good. The St Kevin's Pipe Band in Bray wore the same uniform as the Dalkey Band, and this made it possible for members to fill in for either band whenever there was a shortage of players.

My introduction to Breton music was by a piper who was not a member of the band and who was to become known around the country, not as a musician but as a sculptor and a painter. When Yann Renard-Goulet arrived in Ireland he had no money, and in order to earn a living he had to work on the roads using a hand shovel. Yann was an active member of the Breton national movement, which has close underground links with its Basque counterpart. He was sentenced to death by the French for collaboration with Germany and was on France's 'Most Wanted' list. After escaping from France he landed in Ireland and made his way to Bray, where he lived for the remainder of his life. We did not know very much about his political life but we found him an interesting character.

Yann founded a youth movement in Bray whose dress was a Breton style beret, white shirt with red neckerchief and navy pants. He and I would march at the head of these dozens of young fellows with Yann playing Breton music on the war pipes, to my accompaniment on the side drum. My mother used to refer to the movement as The Hitler Youth but, in fairness, none of the members were politically minded and even if they had been, most of these young locals probably didn't understand the half of what Yann was saying because of his heavy French accent!

A year or two after I had left the youth movement, the parish priest of Bray informed Yann that he should disband the group. The youth movement included girls by that stage and it seems that the parish priest felt there was insufficient attention being paid to supervising these young people. Yann Goulet practised his art very successfully in Bray, where he worked on many important commissions and gained international recognition. He taught day and night classes in which his students learned sculpting, painting and pottery.

Naming birds

One of my big interests during those years, birds and birds' names, had an interesting spin-off for my father. It began with my very first picture bird book, which I got for Christmas in 1943, when I was thirteen years of age. The book was in *The Young Naturalist* series, and its title was *How to Recognise British Wild Birds*. It had colour pictures of three or four birds to every page and my father added in the Irish names in black ink, to match the original names in English. Quite a number of the birds did not appear in Ireland but books on Irish birds were not available in those days, so it took me a while to figure out what species were unlikely to be found in the Irish countryside.

My father continued collecting and translating bird names after he left the army. He used sources such as Dineen's Irish/English Dictionary, Dwelly's Gaelic/English Dictionary, McKenna's and de Bhaldraithe's English/Irish Dictionary, as well as other bird lists. Checking the meaning and derivation of a number of bird names revealed misnomers in English uncritically carried over into Irish equivalents such as: Redpoll, *gleoisín cúldearg*, meaning little red-backed chatterer. In fact the bird is greyish and dark-streaked and has a red fore-crown. Another example was: Redstart, *ceann deargán*, meaning reddish head. In fact this bird has an ash-grey back and crown with a black throat and has a rusty-red tail but not a red head. 'Start' derives from old English *steort*, a tail. In my father's list the redpoll has been renamed *an deargán* (red forehead) and the redstart has been renamed *an t-earrdheargán* (redtail). A full dictionary was eventually compiled of English/Latin/Irish bird names that included all the bird names occurring in a number of field guides.

Some years after my father had completed the dictionary, the Department of Education formed a committee to classify bird names in Irish, and both of us were invited to be among the panel. One or two of the members had been appointed solely because of their knowledge of ornithology and had little or no knowledge of the Irish language. This led to some of the bird names being unimaginative, particularly when they were direct translations from English. My father was naturally very unhappy with some of these choices.

A warbler known as the blackcap is one example of this situation. The committee decided the bird should be named a*n caipín dubh*. This is a direct translation from the English name and obviously a native Irish speaker would deal differently with it. The cap from which the bird gets its name is black in the male but reddish-brown in the female. It reaches only to the upper part of the eye in both male and female and in fact looks quite like a monk's cap. A more imaginative name, according to my father, might have been *an manach*, the monk. His second choice for the blackcap would have been *an ceolaire ceanndubh*, which, translated into English, means blackheaded warbler. The male, as in most birds, is the one that sings!

My father's extensive list of bird names continues to be used by various government departments and others, but sadly the dictionary itself, which he had hoped to see published one day, remains gathering dust on some shelf in An Gúm, the government's publication office.

4

First Job
1940s

Garnetts & Keegan's – Fishing hats out of the Liffey – Some regular customers – Stocktaking – Turning to the Gaeltacht – Rugby days

Garnetts & Keegan's

In the 1940s, Dublin had two upmarket fishing tackle shops: Garnetts & Keegan's of Parliament Street and Hely's of Dame Street. These establishments were on a par with the original famous Brown Thomas store in Grafton Street, which specialised in expensive clothes, and Callaghans of Dame Street, where one could purchase equally expensive horse-riding gear. Although there are now very many fishing tackle shops around the country, I do not know of any that has the old-world atmosphere one felt in either Garnetts & Keegan's or Hely's.

Jobs were extremely scarce during the late 1940s and early 1950s but it was essential that, after leaving Blackrock, I should begin earning a wage in some way or other. I wanted to work at something that I really enjoyed. My first choice would have been a job in the open air but such a job was far easier to imagine than to find.

I loved angling and even while at school I knew how to make flies and do simple repairs on rods. It was not surprising then that my footsteps strayed towards Garnetts & Keegan's. One day I took a bus into Dublin and walked down the quays to Parliament Street. I enquired of the lady behind the counter if 'the boss' was around and was informed that Mr Harris was out but was expected back in an hour. I returned twice and asked the same question of the lady (whom I would shortly come to know as Evelyn Monaghan) before eventually meeting Mr Harris.

It was fortunate that I seemed to have got the timing right on that particular day. Mr Harris's first question to me was, 'How did you know that there might be a vacancy here?' Of course I didn't know, as I had just come in on chance. I was later to learn that the lad who had been working in the job I was now seeking had been fired the previous day for helping himself to some of the shop's exclusive fishing tackle! In fact I had seen him on the river a week or so previously when some of the anglers had pointed him out, remarking on how well equipped he was.

As I stood outside the counter Mr Harris gave me some flies to attach to a cast, by way of a test, he said. Whether Mr Harris was going to give me the job or not, it was a useful way of fulfilling a hurried customer's order in a shop that was having a busy afternoon and where nobody had time to attach flies on to lengths of nylon monofilament. It wasn't much of a challenge for me, as tying flies on to a cast was an activity I practised every time I went fishing. The rest of the interview, which was really more of a chat, took place in the pub next door. I was informed that I could begin on the following Monday. I had landed a job and even though I would not be out in the open spaces, I would at least be dealing with people who spent all their spare moments enjoying themselves in the countryside.

J.R. Harris, or 'Dick' as he was known to his friends, was making a name for himself as an entomologist specialising in freshwater aquatic insects. I had heard anglers on the Dargle mentioning his name. He was a pioneer in the field of entomology where it related to aquatic insects and angling, and his work was recognised overseas. His book *A Fly Fisher's Entomology* became a classic. He had worked in the fishing department of Elvery's Sportshop in O'Connell Street, and he joined Garnetts & Keegan's when it was taken over by a well-known business-man, John Hanlon, a director of Pollicoffs, the large Dublin clothing wholesalers. John Hanlon spent most of the working week at Pollicoffs and we only saw him at the shop on Saturday mornings. He was well-to-do and his family owned the pub at Hanlon's Corner.

Fishing hats out of the Liffey

Garnetts & Keegan's customers came from a cross-section of the community, a significant number being of Anglo-Irish descent. Many of them who had served in the British army were majors and colonels and a few were brigadiers. There were others who had titles and quite a few were eccentric characters straight out of a Sommerville and Ross story. They had 'beautiful manners' and lived for their hunting and fishing. One day a small, thin man rushed into the shop. He was dressed in a well-tailored grey suit and carried a rolled umbrella. 'My hat blew off!' was his anxious reply when I asked if there was anything I could do for him. 'I beg your pardon?' I said, not quite believing what I had heard and at the same time having no idea what this worried-looking customer might be trying to tell me. He spoke in an upper-class English accent. He repeated what he had said the first time, 'My hat blew off!' and then added, 'I was crossing the bridge when a gust of wind lifted my hat and blew it straight into the river!' He looked quite lost as he waited for my response.

'Oh, I'm sorry to hear that,' I replied, at the same time wondering why he had taken the trouble to come into the shop and tell me he had lost his head-gear. Perhaps he was under the impression that we stocked a range of hats and was hoping to buy a replacement. 'The policeman on point's duty on the bridge,' he continued, 'he advised me that I should call in here and borrow a rod to try and fish my hat out of the river.' He stood there, about a metre out from the counter, waiting for me to take immediate action. I pointed towards the back of the shop, 'That's Mr Harris down there,' I said. 'He's the boss and he might be able to help you.' I wasn't sure what Mr Harris's reaction might be to this lost soul's unusual request, or indeed how he might help him, but Dick listened to his story with interest and some amusement. 'B-b-b-but, surely your hat has been swept d-d-d-downstream by now?' queried Dick, who always had difficulty with words beginning with 'b' or 'd'. 'Well, I watched it for quite a while and it was floating around close to the wall, just below the bridge structure,' answered the worried customer.

'All right then,' replied Dick, turning and looking in my direction. 'Éamon!' he called, 'you're well used to poaching salmon on the Dargle. Assemble a rod and reel, put a big treble hook on the end of the line and go out and show this gentleman how good a poacher you are!' It was not really the time or the place to argue with Dick that I was not a poacher of salmon, so I quickly assembled the required tackle and headed out into the street. As my hatless customer followed me down towards Capel Street Bridge, I felt like a Scottish gillie leading his old 'Laird' to a favourite fishing haunt. The bridge was only about twenty metres from the shop, so thankfully we did not have far to travel.

'Look, there it is down there, close to the edge!' he pointed, as we peered over the stout iron rail of the bridge into the river. He hadn't mentioned that it was a bowler hat. Luckily it had landed upside down on the water and was floating around in a small backwash between the wall and the inner upright of the bridge. The incoming high tide was helping to keep the hat from being carried away by the current. As I lowered the large treble hook down towards the water, a crowd gathered to watch the excitement. The garda had temporarily suspended his involvement with the traffic and was requesting the onlookers to 'leave room now and give the fisherman a chance!' I gently lowered the treble hook until it was just over the bowler, manoeuvred it until it was well inside the crown and then flicked the rod sideways, catching the hook on the inside band of the hat. It was well hooked and I knew it was safe to reel in my line and lift out the soaking bowler from the clutches of Anna Livia. My prize catch no sooner appeared over the parapet of Capel Street Bridge than there was a big cheer from the crowd of onlookers and shouts of 'How are ye goin' to cook it, Mister? Are ye goin' to fry it?' Whatever about the future of the bowler hat, it was a good introduction to what would be a most interesting few years in the fishing tackle trade.

The mention of a garda being full-time on point's duty probably sounds strange to the younger generation today, but at a time when there were no traffic lights in Dublin, or in any town in Ireland for that matter, these well-trained 'special duty' gardaí were a common sight. Besides wearing white gloves, they wore a white over-sleeve from the wrist to the elbow, which helped to make them more obvious to drivers. Some of them had their own very particular style of directing traffic. The garda on Capel Street Bridge who had sent the hatless customer into Garnetts & Keegan's was a joy to watch. Whenever he was on duty people came and stood to observe his skill. The particular technique he had was brought to a fine art. The white gloves he wore were never pulled up completely but left so that the ends, where the tips of the fingers would normally be, were left limp. Unlike most of his colleagues, he scarcely used any arm movements and the extended loose parts of the gloves gave a certain emphasis to the quick gestures he made with his palms and fingers.

Some regular customers

Working in Garnetts and Keegan's was the next best thing to having a job in the open air. The customers were people who spent a lot of their spare time on a river or a lake or at the edge of the sea. Most of them were only too willing to share information about their favourite stretch of water. As a result, I soon became familiar with rivers and lakes I had never even seen. Eventually, I was able to recommend a particular fly or bait for a fishery I came to know just by listening to a customer describing his favourite fishing spot. I was often in a position where I could even suggest what to use on a specific stretch of water on a particular river! I was very familiar, for example, with the Ridge Pool on the Moy years before I had even been to the area.

One of our regular customers was a distinguished-looking, silver-haired man who had the pleasant habit of humming a traditional piping tune while he made a selection from the tray of sea trout flies. I soon learned that he was Colm Ó Lochlainn, owner of The Sign of the Three Candles, a small printing and publishing firm situated a few hundred yards from us, down Fleet Street. Colm had a great interest in folklore and it was said of him that he had to hear a tune only once and he would have it off by heart. He had collected and published a large amount of traditional music and songs. The piper Jim Ennis, father of the piper and folklore collector Séamus Ennis, used to give him weekly lessons on uilleann piping. Colm, in return, would give his tutor lessons in Irish. He had already taken lessons from another great piper, Nicholas Markey. His publishing firm was probably best known for two publications, *Irish Street Ballads* and *More Irish Street Ballads*. Ronnie Drew of The Dubliners says it was these two books that first started him singing. Colm later purchased the Casla Fishery in Conamara, which had been previously owned by Bruce Ismay of *Titanic* fame (it was said of Ismay that he escaped from the *Titanic* by dressing up as a woman).

The contrast between the range of customers regularly visiting the shop was marked. Chief Justice Kingsmill-Moore was a very experienced angler and author of that fine book *A Man May Fish*. I would not have expected to hear him humming a traditional piping tune in the manner of Colm Ó Lochlainn! Whenever the Chief Justice paid us a visit, he always sought out Mr Harris, with whom he would have regular discussions on the art of angling. He was a very knowledgeable man and extremely courteous. One particular spring morning, both men were enjoying one of those piscatorial meetings at the back of the shop. Dick had placed a tray of flies on the counter between himself and his eminent customer while they discussed the merits of the various feathery imitations and compared the various tyings. Evelyn and I were at the upper end of the shop. The door suddenly opened with a flourish. Lady Kennedy-Kish's entrance was always dramatic as she swept in with her customary 'Good morning!' to whoever happened to be behind the counter!

The good lady was a small bouncy woman who spoke with quite a grand accent. Her usual attire was a tweed skirt and jacket. Her chauffeur, Fred, who dressed in a uniform and leather knee-boots, drove her large saloon car and usually pulled up right outside the front door of the shop. Lady Kennedy-Kish had, as usual, come up from her home in Bunclody, Co. Wexford, to see Mr Harris. But when she saw the Chief Justice, she called out in a loud husky voice, 'K.M., you darling, I didn't expect to see you here!' As she continued on her way down to the end of the shop, she noticed the tray of flies on the counter between the two men. 'Do you know, K.M.,' she exclaimed excitedly, 'I had a whole box of these lovely salmon flies and a jolly old moth came and ate them all up!' The Chief Justice took all of this in his stride. He regularly fished on the River Slaney, close to where Lady Kennedy-Kish lived, and he had probably heard her utterances on many occasions.

Another of our customers was the famous gillie Laurie Gaffey. Laurie was a comical man who spoke with a shaky voice and had a distinct North of Ireland accent. A British firm of rod-makers did him the honour of naming one of their series of trout fly rods 'The Laurie Gaffey'. Laurie also had a small book of fishing poems published, which we regularly stocked on the bookshelves at Garnetts & Keegan's.

An angling store is in many ways a regular chat shop. During the winter, when the fishing season was over, it was common enough for an angler to arrive at the counter in Garnetts & Keegan's, asking to be shown a tray of trout or salmon flies. In the next breath he would more than likely add apologetically, 'The season is closed so I've only come in to chat about the fishing,' and then admit, 'I have such a vast collection of flies I could in fact sell dozens of them to you!' These visits by the fishermen during the off-season were always welcome, especially as we were rarely busy during that time of year. Indeed, a chat about a particular river or lake was often a pleasant relief from that most boring of winter occupations called stocktaking.

Stocktaking

Counting all those artificial flies was a task none of us enjoyed. Three of us shared the job – Evelyn, Nora and myself. There were hundreds of different patterns in special display trays in the fly-cabinet and there was an even larger amount stored in the overflow boxes. Their numbers amounted to thousands, and in winter, during stocktaking time, every fly had to be counted individually. Having spent all day counting under fluorescent lights, we were beginning to see stars by the time we were ready to go home and I cannot imagine any modern store doing a similar exercise in this day and age. Up above us on the third floor of the shop, a team of nine young women worked at tying a whole range of fishing flies. This in itself was unusual, as almost all other angling shops bought in their stocks of trout and salmon flies. There was a steady demand for Garnetts & Keegan's fishing flies all over the country and we stocked an extensive range of patterns. This was good for our customers but it also meant there was no shortage of flies for us to count at stocktaking time!

The exotic-looking salmon flies were tied by Josie Gibbons, the most experienced of the fly-tyers upstairs. The old-style, mixed-wing patterns were quite complicated and Josie used a whole range of highly coloured feathers, threads and tinsels to produce a real work of art. Each pattern of fly had a specific name and I can remember many of those regularly asked for: Thunder and Lightning, Black Doctor, Dusty Miller, Durham Ranger, Fiery Brown, Jock Scott and many more. Today, simpler hair-wing tyings are in fashion and the colourful traditional patterns are seldom used by modern anglers.

Turning to the Gaeltacht

All during my years at school and later when I began to work, there was constant pressure to speak English rather than Irish. In some respects it would have been easier to forget about using two languages, but at some stage I had made a conscious decision not to let the stronger language take over. This was probably at a time when traditional Irish music and song was beginning to absorb my interest. I had heard that an Irish-speaking club held weekly meetings near the railway station in Bray. When I explored the matter further, I found that it was an Irish-speaking branch of the Legion of Mary! The evenings consisted of singing Irish songs, playing music and reading poetry. Apart from a short prayer at the beginning and end of the proceedings, no other duties were imposed on those of us who wanted to remain on the fringes of the organisation. What was really important for most of us was that we were making contact with people who had an interest in the Irish language.

At the end of the 1940s there was a growing awareness among a small number of Bray people regarding the language. One of the most enthusiastic members of this group was Diarmuid Breathnach, with whom I struck up a friendship that has lasted to the present day. Diarmuid, his widowed mother and his sister Cáit lived on an estate at the top end of Bray town, in an area known as the Vevay. His father had been an Irish language teacher and it was from him that Diarmuid and Cáit had received a love of the language. Diarmuid's mother was from Upper Church, a small village in Co. Tipperary. She was a generous woman whose village upbringing never seemed to have been affected by the many years spent living close to the capital city. Although she never admitted to being able to speak the native language, her everyday speech consisted of a surprisingly wide range of Irish words. The loss of her husband created financial hardship for Mrs Breathnach and her family, but it did not seem to dampen her spirits or her interest in Diarmuid's or Cáit's friends, whose relationships – current or impending – were a constant source of curiosity for her. She was really a matchmaker at heart.

My first visit to the Conamara Gaeltacht was on a fishing trip with a friend whose father drove us all the way down to where we set up camp close to a lake. My friend's sole interest was in fishing for sea trout. Although the locals were speaking Irish all around us, he took no interest in it whatsoever and seemed unimpressed by the language. As he was not able to understand it, he seemed to have made up his mind to cut himself off from it altogether. The holiday was enjoyable but I felt that there must be more to the Conamara Gaeltacht than just fishing for sea trout!

The next opportunity I had of travelling west was when a group of us decided to hitch-hike to Conamara on a bank holiday weekend. We took a bus to the village of Lucan in Co. Dublin and, as there were six of us, we split up into pairs and began 'thumbing' our way. People were generous and in those days drivers did not regard picking up a stranger as a risk. We would probably not have attempted to travel to the west were it not for the kindness of so many car owners, since the train fare was too expensive for young people.

We had decided to meet at a place called An Cnoc (Cnoc na hAille) just beyond An Spidéal, about sixteen miles west of the city of Galway. We were offered seats by a number of cars travelling only part of the way and as a result the journey was slow. By the time my travelling companion Diarmuid Breathnach and I reached Galway, it was far too late to hitch the rest of the way to An Cnoc. Our four friends had probably already reached their destination, as we saw no sign of them on the way. There was almost no traffic and the two of us walked as far as Salthill, just outside the city. There was little hope of a lift at that stage so we decided to sleep on the hard benches along the seafront. It was the weekend of Diarmuid's twenty-first birthday, which is probably the only reason I can remember that the year was 1951! The benches were cold and uncomfortable and when we woke just before five o'clock in the morning, we decided to begin walking the rest of the journey. We were just in time for eight o'clock mass at An Spidéal and then continued on our way to Cnoc na hAille, six miles further west. By the time we reached our destination we were in good form for a big breakfast.

Hitch-hiking to various locations in the Gaeltacht became a regular occupation during long weekends. Eventually we decided to make An Cheathrú Rua our regular holiday base. Its situation thirty miles or so west of Galway added to the problem of actually getting there, but the richness of traditional songs and language made the extra effort well worth it. The most enjoyable evenings were those that we spent at gatherings in the homes of local people. Here a melodeon player invariably supplied the music for set dancing, and traditional singers were invited to perform between the dances. All the fun took place in a stone-floored kitchen, where the young women occupied one side of the room and the young men grouped together across from them, near the door or just beneath the stairs. Whenever a man wanted someone to dance with him, he didn't walk across and politely invite, he just caught her eye from across the room. The usual signal was a sideways jerk of the head, which simply meant 'Come on out on the floor!' I never noticed any young women remaining in their corner after being given 'the nod'. Most of the men wore peaked caps and it was common practice for them to keep wearing them while dancing or singing.

Rugby days

These trips to the Conamara Gaeltacht usually took place during bank holiday weekends, as we all had jobs and the distance was too great for just one night's stay. The five-and-a-half-day working week at Garnetts & Keegan's began at nine o'clock on Monday morning. We finished each day at half past five except on Saturdays, when we closed shop at one o'clock. Although I enjoyed the work, the weekends were never long enough, as there were so many other things to do whenever I had free time. My rugby had improved and I was now playing on the Blackrock Club's Seconds team. My brother Déaglán had made a name for himself in the position of hooker while playing on the various school's cup teams and after leaving school he played for the army. I had begun taking an interest in the game at quite a late stage and I never thought about playing in any position other than the one in which my elder brother had excelled.

My maximum weight at that time was only eleven stone and my height was five foot nine, which even in those days was regarded as far too light for a rugby forward. It seems that I earned my place on the team because of my ability to win the ball in the scrum with some regularity. The hours spent practising with my friend Johnny Hartnett during lunchtime at school must have eventually borne fruit. Johnny and I used to face each other on the parallel bars, swinging as if in a scrum and timing each other to see who could tip the ball fastest with our feet. Pity the poor student who would be coaxed and cajoled to act as scrumhalf for us two rugby lunatics, swinging like monkeys from those bars for most of the lunchtime break!

The rules of the game in those days were very different and the hooker, who was supported by his two front-row forwards, was allowed to swing right into the opposing team's side of the scrum in an effort to retrieve the ball with his feet. In performing this technique there were certain advantages in my being much lighter than the rest of the forwards, especially as my two front-row props did not have much weight to support while I was specialising in my acrobatics! But swinging in the scrum was a dangerous practice and I am glad to say that in recent years the rules have been altered and this technique is no longer allowed. The game has changed very much since those days, both with regard to the physique of the players and the way in which the game of rugby is played. Today, a person of my build and weight trying for a place as a forward on any senior club team would hardly even be considered.

After a season or so on the Seconds team, I went on to play regularly for Blackrock's First team, until a dislocated shoulder finally ended my rugby career. The prospect of becoming just a viewer instead of a member of an active team did not hold any attraction for me, and I soon lost interest and had no further involvement with the club.

There was, however, yet another de Buitléar hooker on the way. My young brother Lochlann joined the Blackrock Club soon after leaving school. In about two years he had won his place on the First team, in the same position in which I had played before I got injured. He eventually went on to win an international cap when he was picked to play for Ireland against Wales. As the position of hooker on the Irish team seemed to be held permanently by Ronnie Dawson, it was Lochlann's one and only time to be capped. He travelled with the Irish team on the Australian tour in 1967 and was listed so often as the substitute hooker, he used to say that he was the most widely travelled sub in the world.

After his retirement from rugby he acted as liaison officer to successive touring teams, including the All Blacks, Wallabies, the USA and the Springboks. Having been struck down twice by serious illness, Lochlann died in 1995 at the age of fifty-nine. Losing a member of one's family is always painful and one does not really expect the youngest brother to die first, especially a brother who was larger than life itself. A photograph that still hangs in the hall of Lochlann's home illustrates his mischievous sense of humour, which was well known to his large circle of rugby friends. The picture includes himself, Mick Doyle, Fergus Slattery and Willie John McBride. The caption he had inscribed under the picture said *Between us we have won 145 caps*. There was no mention, of course, that McBride won 63, Slattery 61, Mick Doyle 20 and Lochlann the remaining one!

5

Moving On
1950s

Meeting Laillí

The Saturday night céilí at Barry's Hotel in Dublin's city centre was a
regular haunt for our group. We usually travelled in from Bray by bus and
this was also our only means of transport home. As the last bus to Bray
left from Burgh Quay at 11.20 pm, we would be faced with a long walk of
fifteen miles or so if we happened to miss it. During the 1950s, O'Connell
Street was completely empty of traffic and people by half-past midnight.

The Kincora Céilí Band, under the direction of Mrs Harrington, a
dignified, grey-haired lady who played the fiddle, supplied the music for
the Saturday night céilí at Barry's. The majority of the regulars were
country people and they included native Irish speakers from the various
Gaeltachtaí. For us it was an opportunity to meet up with friends we had
met during the summer holidays or the long weekends in Conamara.

One autumn Saturday several of us had arranged to meet at Barry's.
Diarmuid Breathnach's sister Cáit had just returned from the west,
where she had gone at the end of summer to improve her Irish. While
there she became friendly with a local girl who had been helping her with
some of the intricacies of the language. Her new-found friend had come to
Dublin that week to begin studying hotel management at the College of
Catering in Cathal Brugha Street and it was now Cáit's turn to introduce
her to some of the fun at Barry's. Laillí was a beautiful-looking girl and,

being from the Gaeltacht area of An Cheathrú Rua, she had fluent Irish, which she spoke with a soft Conamara accent. I found her to be extremely attractive and kept inviting her out on to the dance floor as often as I could that night.

Changing jobs

After about three and a half years of working at Garnetts & Keegan's, I felt the urge to move on. I liked the job but I wanted more. Dick Harris was the manager and as he had never given any indication that he might leave and go somewhere else, there was no other position available to those of us working at the sales counter. It was time to change course. My brother Déaglán had moved on from a job he had as a commercial traveller for Kevin Hilton & Co. in Grafton Street, and he suggested that I might apply for the position. I had seen Kevin Hilton on occasions when he came to Bray where he entertained audiences at the famous swimming club smoking concerts. He was a semi-professional comedian and his performances were very popular. His firm, Kevin Hilton & Co., sold large quantities of brown wrapping paper, tissue paper, paper bags of countless sizes and balls of string.

I got the job, but quickly realised that it bore no relationship whatso-ever to fishing or to anything else I was familiar with. I was given a leather case in which I carried samples of the various papers and string stocked by Hiltons, and, as I had no transport, it meant that the long hard road from one establishment to another had to be covered on foot. My feeble attempts to convince shopkeepers and store managers to give me an order were for the most part unsuccessful. Soon I realised that it was a world of back-handers and that it was all sown up. I decided to part company with the paper trade forever. I can safely say that walking my shoes off in an effort to sell paper to unmannerly shopkeepers was, without doubt, the worst job I ever had!

There were several more adventures into areas of employment that for me were not wildly exciting. They included a spell in a solicitor's office in South Leinster Street, and a job in the stores at the Famor Biscuits factory in Santry, which had me getting up very early in the morning, six days a week. I had to catch the seven o'clock bus from Bray to Dublin to connect with another bus out to Santry. Following on from that was a short period working for Novum in Lower Abbey Street, when I travelled around the country trying to sell washing machines out of a mini-bus. That was also a pretty awful occupation but work was scarce and I had made up my mind that I would work at anything rather than follow the thousands of Irish people who were forced to leave Ireland in the hope of finding a better future in some other part of the world.

Laillí had been introduced to my own family and had been made very welcome at Hillsbrook. As I had fallen very much in love with her, I tried to have her invited out for Sunday lunch whenever she was free. Having completed her course in hotel management at Cathal Brugha Street, she was now working in Dublin and was free every second weekend.

The lure of music

Although money was scarce, people were all more or less in the same boat and as television had not yet arrived in Ireland, the scourge of consumerism had not taken over. Outside of working hours we found our own amusement, most of which was free. On Saturday nights a group of us paid regular visits to the Piper's Club in Thomas Street. It was the favourite haunt of traditional musicians and we gradually got to know the various pipers, fiddle players and flute players who were playing in Dublin at that time. The club was a hive of rich traditional music played by very talented musicians, all with their own particular interpretations.

Tommy Potts was from Dublin and his semi-classical style of fiddle playing was in complete contrast to John Kelly's very traditional Clare style. The close fingering technique of Tommy Reck playing on the uilleann pipes was totally different to the way Leo Rowsome practised his open style of playing. Flute players such as a very young Michael Tubridy and a much older John Egan had contrasting styles of playing the same reels and jigs, and the Dublin player of the button accordion, Sonnie Brogan, never ceased to amaze us with the number of tunes he could remember and his clever arrangements of the most simple pieces of music. The piper Johnny Doran, a member of the well-known traveller family and whose father was also a piper, wandered in on a night when Diarmuid Breathnach and a couple of us were at the club. As he sat down and strapped on the pipes, he muttered, 'Give us the butt of an auld cigarette and I'll play ye the Grey Goose!' Johnny was a great performer and he had his own particular style of piping. He used to camp on the side of a lane, a short distance up the road from where I lived.

Those of us interested in learning songs as well as dance music would attend Seán Óg Ó Tuama's Claisceadal classes on Saturday afternoons. These were held in the Royal Irish Academy of Music in Westland Row. Claisceadal is the Irish word for choral singing, but we were not really a choir, just a regular, dedicated group of people who were keen to add to our repertoire of songs. Seán Óg Ó Tuama (1912–1980) was born in Cork, where the family grew up speaking Irish. He had a science degree from University College Cork and taught mathematics and science in Dublin. His mother was a native speaker and she had a large collection of songs.

Seán Óg was a wonderful teacher and had a simple way of presenting his large collection of songs. On arriving at the class, we would all be supplied with sheets of foolscap paper on which a selection of these songs were typed in Celtic script. He would then have us all sing each line, emphasising where the pauses and the ornamentation should occur. This was repeated again and again until finally everyone would have the song completely off by heart. Seán's sister-in-law, Róisín Ní Sheaghdha, accompanied the singing on her harp.

People who would not normally have the patience to listen to the intricacies of traditional singing seemed to have no problem with the way Ó Tuama presented the songs. He was sympathetic, his diction was very clear and he was easy to understand. Seán's smiling face seemed to attract people to sing along with him. Those Claisceadal classes often resulted in members developing a high regard for Irish culture and encouraged participants to take an interest in the more complicated Gaeltacht style of traditional singing. Seán Óg Ó Tuama contributed enormously to popularising songs in Irish during the second half of the twentieth century.

Getting on to the dance floor

Saturday night, in the country and in the city, was for many young people a night for dancing. The Arcadia Dance Hall in Bray was well known to Dubliners, and dances were held there on Saturdays and

Sundays. The resident dance band in the Arcadia was under the direction of Billy Carter. Billy wore a white jacket, as was the fashion with band leaders at the time. His hair was well greased and he sported a black moustache. The rest of the band wore black dress suits. Billy played the violin as well as conducting the band and was referred to, probably unfairly, as 'Billy Carter the cat-gut king'!

Admission to the Arcadia was expensive and even if one succeeded in climbing over the high wall, which was studded with pieces of broken glass, the large gardens surrounding the hall were patrolled by what were known as 'chucker-outs' – today they are called bouncers. They were ordinary Bray locals hired for the night to be on the look-out for anyone attempting to gain admittance without paying.

My main interest in going to the Arcadia was because there was a slight chance of persuading the drummer to allow me play the drums at the interval, when the band members left the stand for their break. The problem was that there were usually three or four other regular 'hopefuls' hanging around, waiting for the same opportunity, and one or other of them usually reached the bandstand before I did.

My brother Ruairí was quite an expert at modern dancing, which was why he loved the Arcadia, and he was also what one might term a 'natty dresser'. It was the era of wide lapels on jackets and a time when every man's tie was tied with a very large Windsor knot. Ruairí and I were always short of money, Ruairí usually having even less than I had, which was probably why he felt that getting into the Arcadia without paying was worth all kinds of risks.

One particularly wet night, Ruairí decided to gamble all and sundry for the sake of a dance at the Arcadia. There was no sign of the 'chucker-outs' and as the coast was clear he threw his coat along a section of the ten-foot wall in order to cover the rows of sharp, jagged pieces of glass. It was a stiff climb but Ruairí managed it without much trouble by first standing on the saddle of a bicycle that happened to be nearby. He reached the top, and, as he hung by his fingertips, there still seemed to be no sign of the enemy. Deciding that he had not been spotted, Ruairí let go and landed safely in a flower bed.

As he hid in the shadow of the high garden wall, he could hear voices coming from the far end of the lawn. The grounds of the International

Hotel were at the rear of the Arcadia and guests from the hotel could enter the dance hall from the gardens. Workmen had been busy in the grounds all that week and the long trenches they had dug in preparation for pipe-laying ran straight across the garden. There was also a wooden hut, where tools were stored and tea-breaks enjoyed during the week. Ruairí could hardly believe his luck. The night was so wet that the men responsible for patrolling the entrance to the hall had taken shelter in the wooden hut and were enjoying a smoke and a chat. Ruairí saw it as an opportunity of a lifetime and one he was not going to miss. He crept up silently along one of the trenches towards the hut, praying that the men inside would continue chatting until he had reached his destination. As soon as he arrived at the hut he banged the door shut, slipped the bolt across and locked in the 'chucker-outs'! The shouts, screams and curses of the men ringing in his ears were soon drowned out by the music of Billy Carter's band as Ruairí innocently wandered into the Arcadia through the now unguarded garden entrance.

Meeting Lailli's parents

I felt somewhat nervous when Lailli invited me to travel with her to the west to meet her parents for the first time. I kept wondering if they might think I was just a friend or if they knew I was really serious about their daughter. Her father, the artist Charles Lamb, was a shy but friendly man and, being from Portadown, had a good Northern sense of humour. As he was interested in trout fishing and spent his spare time angling on the local lake, Loch an Mhuilinn, we had no difficulty in finding common ground for discussion.

Lailli's mother, Katharine, was a wonderfully enthusiastic woman with a very strong personality. She was originally from Kent in England and was the daughter of the writer Ford Madox Ford. She came to Ireland as a young girl to study. Katharine was extremely interested in the welfare of the local community and she was very musical. She knew of my interest in music and we chatted about the music group she had organised for some of the local children.

At a later stage when I got to know her better, she told me that, in common with many other young women in Britain, she had worked on the land during the First World War, when the majority of young men had gone to the front to fight. When the war was over Katharine decided to become a veterinary surgeon. She applied to the College of Veterinary Surgeons in London but her application was refused on the grounds that she was a woman. However, her mind was made up and when she enquired as to what she might do to follow in that profession, she was advised to 'try Ireland as they are mad enough for anything over there!' She did apply to Ireland and her application was accepted. She attended the College of Veterinary Surgeons at Ballsbridge in Dublin where she qualified successfully and became the first female veterinary surgeon in either Ireland or Britain.

Moran's Fishing Tackle

Moran's Fishing Tackle was in Upper Abbey Street in Dublin. It was one of the newer shops in the trade and although it did not carry an extensive range of goods, it was popular with the casual angler and beginners – people who would not be spending large amounts of money on their fishing tackle. Upstairs, it had a repairs workshop of sorts and the business was managed by Joe Moorkens, a young man whom I had known for a number of years. I remembered his father, a Belgian who always wore a black beret and who came regularly to buy tackle at Garnetts & Keegan's. Joe told me that he was leaving Moran's and that if I was interested in the job, he would put in a good word for me.

The shop was owned by Séamus Sweeney, a solicitor from Galway, whose practice was further up Abbey Street, close to O'Connell Street. He asked me to come to his office for the interview. I doubt if there were any other applicants for the job. The interview did not take long and by the time the talking was over I was informed that I could begin whenever I wished.

Séamus Sweeney was a well-built, good-looking man. His Clarke Gable type moustache matched his swept-back crop of black hair. He had the appearance of a man who was not short of money and I got the distinct impression that he was a shrewd businessman. He could appear in the shop at any time but often a week went by before he came in. On a day when a local Dublin lad was in the act of purchasing some hooks

Captain de Buitléar as aide de camp *to President Hyde (left) with Judge Wylie and Harry Franks*

My father and mother on their wedding day

In our Sunday best with my father at Hillsbrook. I'm on the left; Rúairí and Deaglán are on the right

My sisters, Ailbhe, Deirbhile and Colma, on the front steps at Hillsbrook in 1947

The three ages of man! With my prize-winning guinea pig about 1940;
a sandwich tern on Tern Island in Wexford in 1960, and a robin in 2000

With Laillí on our engagement (top) and after our marriage at our first home, Bruach an tSrutha, in the Dargle Valley

Men at work and play: with Gerrit Van Gelderen filming on the Liffey and accepting a Jacob's Award in 1967

Fishing, shooting – and selling – in Hely's of Dame Street, about 1960

Nyoka with Simba, who grew to be the largest lion in captivity and earned a place in The Guinness Book of Records

In a bird hide with Neil Stronach in the Wicklow Mountains (top) and at work with David Bellamy on a midland bog

Seán Óg Ó Tuama with our
daughter Doireann in 1978

With Ceoltóirí
Laighean in France

from me, Séamus Sweeney swept into the shop and walked to the back where the cash register was located. He was dressed as usual in his belted fawn-coloured camel-hair overcoat and suede shoes. My customer glanced over his shoulder at Mr Sweeney, who by now had opened the register and was counting out some money. 'Who's yer man?' the local whispered. 'He's the boss,' I replied. 'He's a real killer isn't he, bleedin' skin shoes an' all, but!' was the lad's immediate response. I took a quick look at Séamus Sweeney and I had to agree that he did appear a bit flashy for a shop like Moran's.

Cheap rods for a quick turnover was Sweeney's business plan and the steel spinning rods we made sold by the hundreds. He had discovered a source in the UK for ex-American army, World War Two tank aerials made of hollow steel. The aerials were in two sections and could be screwed into each other. With the addition of a cork handle, a coat of cellulose paint and a few chromium rings, the aerials could be converted into fishing rods. The rods were assembled by Jack King in a rickety upstairs workshop.

Jack's grimy hands were always covered in traces of cellulose and glue, the result of painting hundreds of steel aerials and sticking ten times as many cork bungs on to them to form the handles. There was no machinery of any kind in the workshop and all the work was done by hand. He was paid per finished rod, which he turned out in large numbers. It was a mystery to me how Jack did not choke from cork dust, created by all the sandpapering of the corks, or how he didn't collapse from the cellulose fumes coming from the gallons of paint he must have used!

A business of my own

Patsy Keenan was a local who came regularly to buy some sea-fishing tackle. Patsy was from the country but had settled in Dublin where he had a small shoe manufacturing business in Parnell Street, a few blocks away from Moran's. As I had been working in Moran's for two years or so, I was becoming restless again. The shop was not being run as a proper fishing tackle business. Séamus Sweeney was not an angler, so the shop did not have the kind of angling atmosphere that either Garnetts & Keegan's or Hely's had. I felt that I could do something in the fishing

59

tackle trade myself, if I were given the opportunity and had premises of some kind.

Patsy Keenan's small factory was at the back of an empty shop. The premises had been closed and unused for some time and Patsy offered it to me at a very reasonable rent. The fact that the building was condemned by Dublin Corporation did not much concern me. As well as the shop, Patsy offered me the use of two ramshackle rooms at the top of a dilapidated stairs. 'They might prove useful as a store, if ever there was anything that you might want to keep in there,' he told me. Whatever that might be, I had no idea at that stage! The next step was to arrange for some capital to purchase initial stock, so I borrowed eighty pounds from a friend and I was in business.

In the early 1950s, the quantity of fishing tackle one could purchase for eighty pounds was minimal, even at a wholesale price. The plan, however, was to concentrate on rod repairs, which I was well able to do and which would not require the spending of large amounts of money. Meanwhile, the gaps on the shelves were filled up with empty fishing reel boxes and anything else I could find or borrow that would give the impression of a well-stocked shop. Fortunately there was a wholesale fishing tackle warehouse a short distance away and if a particular item of fishing gear was not in stock in my place, a customer could always be delayed for a few moments. The usual excuse was that it was in the stockroom and that I would have it down in a matter of minutes. As this was a very regular occurrence, I was kept quite fit, nipping around the corner to purchase the required item.

On the day I opened the shop, I received a telephone call from a Mr Thompson, the managing director of Hely's of Dame Street, asking me if I was interested in a permanent position in the fishing tackle and gun department of Hely's. I thanked him for his kind offer and informed him that I had only just started my own business. He suggested that I might let him know if I changed my mind.

The summer season went well and anglers kept bringing their rods in for repairs, although the amount of cash flow was small. The worry was that when September arrived, the fishing season would almost be at an end and the cash flow would then become a mere trickle. Drastic action and some imagination would be required if I was to survive until the following February. Whatever plan I came up with would have to take into consideration a very small budget.

Finally I hit on an idea. I bought a couple of canaries and put them in a cage with a price tag. Then I placed them on show in the window. They sold the next day and I decided to buy more. After I had off-loaded the second lot of canaries, the next item to be added to the list of livestock purchases were some budgerigars. They sold even more quickly than the canaries and suddenly I found that the business was beginning to go in a very different direction. What was left of the meagre stock of fishing tackle began to gradually move out of sight and make way for various items associated with pet animals and birds. The shop window began to look so different, it led to some confusion for people outside in the street. One particular old gentleman, who some time previously had left an item at the shop for repair, stood at the entrance holding the door-handle and looking around with an air of bewilderment. He was about to go in but hesitated and then muttered, 'Oh, wrong shop!' and off he went on his way, no doubt wondering if he was in another street or if the shop had disappeared into thin air.

My fishing tackle shop had by now very definitely become a pet shop and a new phase in my education was about to begin. I have often heard it said that money can be lost very easily when buying a horse or dealing with people who sell dogs. I have no doubt now that the same applies to trading in cage birds. There is quite a price difference in canaries. The cock sings and the hen does not, so the cost of a male bird can be more than twice that of the female. A hen canary sold at fifteen shillings, whereas a cock would be twenty-five or thirty shillings, with some breeds such as Roller or Norwich canaries costing even more.

When I purchased my first lot of canaries from a Dublin breeder, I was a soft target. 'They're all cocks and great singers!' he announced as he placed the box of canaries on the counter before me. 'They're lovely,' I replied, peering in at the dozen or so brightly coloured yellow birds. 'Are they all cocks?' I asked. 'Every one of them. Wouldn't ye know by the look of them?' he answered. I didn't want to admit that I wouldn't have a clue. Two of the fifteen canaries were singing when I arrived at the shop the following morning and although I waited a week for the others to follow suit, their refusal to perform confirmed that of the fifteen canaries

I had bought, thirteen were hens and non-singers. In other words, I had paid twice the price for thirteen of the birds and I had been done!

It was an early lesson and all future transactions were on the basis that if I was buying male canaries, the birds would be paid for on the following morning, provided the cocks had sung their hearts out. But my education was far from complete and there were other areas where I fell into a similar trap. On reading an advertisement in a daily newspaper, which offered for sale in Co. Tipperary a litter of beautiful Abyssinian poms, I immediately wrote to say that I was interested in taking the whole litter. The owner delivered them in a matter of days, promising that he would forward their pedigrees by return of post. The puppies were gorgeous furry bundles and they all sold within a matter of two days. Nine months later a customer called into the shop and enquired if I remembered the Abyssinian poms. Just as I was about to reply that indeed I remembered them well, a dog the size of a retriever placed his jowls on the counter. 'This is one of those so-called poms,' announced the customer, 'and this is what he has grown into!'

The change-over from fishing tackle to pets coincided with a budgie craze. I had not been aware of the obsession until I began to sell them and, for whatever reason, people suddenly decided that they should buy a budgerigar and teach it how to talk. It was good for business, although I'm sure the success rate in having the birds eventually imitate the human voice must have been pretty low. Those customers who had been successful informed me that they worked with a very young bird and that it required a great deal of patience and dedication to get the budgie to say its first word. Also, they considered it essential to have only one budgerigar; otherwise they would just chatter in budgie-talk to one another.

The shop was located directly opposite Dominick Street, and Moore Street was only a few yards around the corner. Quite a number of the Moore Street ladies, whose stalls lined both sides of that famous street, were regular customers and were forever investing in new pets for sons or daughters, nephews or nieces. At Christmas time a deposit was often made towards a cage and budgie plus all the little extras that might be added to the cage in case the bird might become bored.

As the demand for budgies grew and more people had visions of being the proud owner of a miniature talking parrot, people began breeding budgies to supply the market. The breeders were even arranging their breeding programmes in order to have a supply of young birds ready for the Christmas pet market. Young budgies were not difficult to sell as these were the potential talkers. I bought them by the half-dozen or dozen, depending on expected sales and what birds were available at the time.

Each week I made a point of having something new and exotic in the window and as a result the pet shop became well known. I might feature a snake one week or a monkey the next. Saturday was a popular time for families to visit and during the week when I put a pair of marmosets in the window with a notice indicating that they were the tiniest monkeys in the world, quite a number of people came into the shop. That afternoon when the shop was busy with a number of customers purchasing various bits and pieces, a shabbily dressed local fellow suddenly shoved his head around the door, shouting 'Heh, Mister! How much is de apes?!'

A Dutchman who came occasionally to buy birdseed informed me that he was an illustrator, that he had come to Ireland in response to an advertisement and that he was employed by a Dublin commercial firm. There was no great tradition of commercial art in Ireland and some of the European countries were way ahead of us in that field. As a result there was a growing demand in commercial circles in Ireland for Dutch illustrators and artists, and Irish firms regularly placed advertisements in the newspapers in Holland. My customer's name was Gerrit Van Gelderen and I was soon to discover that apart from his commercial work he was passionate about wildlife. He loved sketching the animals, birds and plants of the countryside and he was also an accomplished photographer. He showed me some of his quick sketches which he had just completed and which I found particularly attractive.

The person who first introduced me to snakes was Nyoka, which is actually the Swahili word for snake. Nyoka was a thick-set man with a tanned swarthy appearance and long, black, wavy hair. He was not tall and this had the effect of making his long arms look even longer. He had a cockney accent and wore a rawhide leather jacket complete with tassels, of the type one would associate with Buffalo Bill. I did not quite understand what he said the first time he came into the shop when he asked me in his cockney accent if I wanted any 'snykes' and I had to ask him more than once to repeat what he had said.

Nyoka spent much of his life in circuses, where he worked with lions, but not in the usual way in which a lion tamer would have five or six snarling lions in a cage and where a whip is used to control the animals. Nyoka never used a whip. He would have only one lion in the circus ring at a time and he would play around with it as if it was an overgrown cat, which in fact it was! His male lion Simba was in the *Guinness Book of Records* and held the record as the biggest lion in the world.

Nyoka asked me if I would like to borrow a boa constrictor and place it in the window for a few days as a special attraction. He arrived the following morning with the snake in a sack. I bolted the shop door before he took it out of the bag just in case some unwary customer might suffer a heart attack on seeing what would surely be perceived as a monster. Both pythons and boas have a very pleasing colour pattern and this one, which looked absolutely huge, was no exception. The longest reported length of a boa constrictor is fourteen feet but they rarely exceed ten feet.

Nyoka's four-foot snake looked huge in my tiny shop. It had a thick body and while resting in its normal coiled position it was difficult to tell its actual length. I made out a display notice for the window: 'Boa Constrictor – 8ft long'. I had added four feet to the snake's actual length on the basis that, as the snake was not for sale, nobody was going to be at a financial loss by being given the impression that it was four feet longer than it actually was! One customer came in to argue about the length but when I handed him a ruler and began to open the window so that he might measure the snake, his immediate reaction was, 'Oh for jaysus sake, leave him where he is! Please! I believe ye!' A week or two after Nyoka had collected his snake, a little old lady gingerly peered in through the door and whispered, 'Is he gone?' 'Is who gone?' I asked, rather puzzled by her query. 'Oh, that monster you had in the window,' she answered. 'I didn't come to buy seed from you for weeks. I was terrified of him!'

The engagement ring

I was now meeting Laillí as often as I could and as she was living in Dublin I would arrange to meet her in town in the evenings, whenever she was free. Her job in the Royal Hibernian Hotel in Dawson Street meant that only some weekends were free. It was on one of her Sundays off that my mother said I could invite her out to lunch at Hillsbrook. Apart from asking her if she would like to come out, I did not tell her what I had in mind except to suggest that she should take the bus to Enniskerry instead of travelling the usual route to Bray.

We met in the village and walked up a quarter of a mile past the Powerscourt Estate, to a picturesque wooded area that slopes down into the valley. It was springtime and as we sat on the grass we could see the Dargle River away below us through the trees. I knew the area well from my days spent fishing and I felt that it was quite a romantic place. There and then I presented her with an engagement ring. There was little time to be over-sentimental on that occasion, however, as it was already midday and my mother was a real stickler for time. The only certainty now was that we would be late as there was a matter of a bus to catch down in the village. When we eventually reached Hillsbrook we were congratulated, that is after I made my excuses, and then Laillí was of course welcomed into the family!

Commercial competition in the pet shop business

The pet shop was doing well at the time and I now had a whole list of contacts where I could order pet rabbits, mice, guinea pigs and budgerigars at short notice. Spratts were the well-known local wholesalers and from them I bought cages as well as quantities of seed. As long as none of the pets remained too long in the shop, eating themselves out of house and home, there was a small profit to be made. At the beginning there was little or no competition, but gradually people began to notice that perhaps there might be an opening in this line of business for them too.

Dublin's main pet shop was The Dublin Pet Store, better known as King's of Capel Street, which had been in the business for a very long time. During the war years there had been a big demand for rabbit meat, and King's pet shop ran regular notices in the newspapers advertising ferrets for sale to hunters. They were the specialists in that field and old Johnny King was very knowledgeable about the various types of ferrets required by hunters. Some were used for bolting rabbits out of the burrows into purse nets; others were attached to a long line before being released into the warren, while others were kept for breeding.

When the infectious viral disease myxomatosis affected the rabbit population, people would not buy rabbit meat anymore and the demand for ferrets came to an end. When old Johnny King died the family kept the business going, but they began specialising in pet equipment and fancy fish rather than ferrets. Pets in general were becoming more popular and there was a growing interest in exotic varieties of goldfish and tropical fish. One or two shops developed their business exclusively to cater for customers who wished to specialise in that area. Uncle George's pet shop opened in Marlborough Street, just off O'Connell Street. Judging by the amount of stock and the variety of pets offered for sale, money did not seem to be a problem. As Uncle George could import birdseed by the ton rather than having to buy it locally by the stone, I knew that the days of stiff competition were not too far off.

6

The World of Music
1950s

Wedding bells

Laillí and I decided to get married at the end of October 1957. My uncle Turlough, a Holy Ghost priest, agreed to marry us in Conamara. Turlough's knowledge of Irish was limited, so we decided to have the ceremony in English, although it was unusual not to have it in Irish in that particular church. We were to be married on a Monday and I arranged that the shop would be closed on that day. Robert, the young lad who worked in the shop, agreed to come in at the weekend and feed the pets, and my sister Ailbhe kindly offered to look after the shop while we were on our honeymoon. Local accommodation was arranged for the guests in Conamara. I had often stayed with the Ó Loideáin family on my weekend trips to An Cheathrú Rua, even before I met Laillí, and they were delighted that I chose to book in with them on the night before the wedding. They seemed to enjoy having a direct connection with the event and were quite excited by the hustle and bustle. Ruairí was in Canada and Déaglán was in England, so I asked Lochlann to be my best man. Apart from the lashing rain it was a wonderful day!

There was a cottage on our land at Hillsbrook, which my mother had said we could have for a nominal rent. It was an offer we could hardly refuse as we could not afford to invest in a house. As a dwelling it was pretty basic and quite similar in appearance and structure to hundreds of other cottages around the country. There was no running water and the nearest we had to a bathroom was a clear brook outside the back door and Broderick's Well a few hundred yards down the road. As I had never lived away from my parents' home, residing in our very own abode was a new experience and one that I very much enjoyed. Even if it was a bit primitive, by the time Lailí and I had cleaned up the place and white-washed the outside of the cottage, it looked very attractive.

Lailí had no great desire to return to hotel work after we married and it never occurred to either of us that she should look for another job. It was accepted as the norm at the time that as far as women were concerned marriage meant retirement from working outside the home. Managing the pet shop was therefore somewhat easier, as Lailí was only too glad to oblige if I needed any extra help. Some of our customers, including Nyoka and Gerrit Van Gelderen, came out from town and visited us at the cottage. During the winter when the circus was off the road, Nyoka moved to Bray. He had to think of ways of earning some money in the off-season, so he rented a shed on the seafront in order to hold a miniature exhibition of live snakes. Included in the show was a small lion cub, which to most people was far more of an attraction than the snakes. But Bray seafront is not the most friendly of places during winter gales and the number of customers coming to visit was rather small.

It was almost a year after we were married that the birth of our first baby was expected. Everything seemed to be fine with Lailí in the months and weeks leading up to the time when she was to be admitted into Holles Street Hospital. She had gone her full term but there seemed to have been complications during the actual delivery. There was no question of my being present during the birth. When I arrived at the hospital I was given the devastating news that the baby boy had died during delivery. It was impossible to find out what had actually gone wrong and it was some time later that a nurse mentioned to me that she had heard that the doctor in charge of the delivery was less than sober and that it was he who was to blame. It was really the saddest day of our lives and the sight of Lailí sitting up in bed putting the finishing touches to a woollen jacket she was knitting only added to the anguish.

The children

Our first daughter Aoife was born on 29 January 1960. Having a daughter was delightful, but the most important thing was that both Lailí and the baby were healthy and that this time there were no complications. The next to arrive was Éanna, a boy, and the space between him and Aoife was only a year. For some unknown reason we kept rotating the children, with the arrival of each of the boys alternating with the girls. Éanna was two years of age when Róisín arrived and having a sister for Aoife to dote over seemed very appropriate. But then Aoife mothered them all, regardless of whether they were boys or girls. The first child, especially when it is a girl, seems to take on the responsibility of her younger siblings and life can be quite a burden on her, the eldest of a family. It is also a time when inexperienced parents are very much at the experimental stage in rearing their offspring and this doesn't help matters.

It was snowing on 10 March 1967 when Laillí went into labour for the fourth time. I immediately called a friend, Pat Egan, who had asked me to contact him if there was an emergency. Pat prayed all the way into the hospital, although his appeal to the Almighty was not for Laillí. The petrol tank of his car was almost empty and Pat was not at all sure if it would last the journey into Dublin. I am glad to say that it did and a baby boy, Cian, arrived safely on that snowy night, and Pat naturally became his godfather. It was eight years later when our last little one arrived and she just missed Patrick's Day by being born on 18 March. No, we did not call her Patricia, we christened her Doireann and she had an over-supply of willing nurses. And why wouldn't she? Wasn't Doireann, according to Irish mythology, the daughter of the fairy-king, Midir?

Gerrit Van Gelderen lived with his wife Lies, in a garden flat of an old house on Conyngham Road, next to the Phoenix Park and overlooking the River Liffey. There were lots of birds flying in and out of the garden and Gerrit never tired of experimenting and taking imaginative photographs of them with his stills cameras. In the evening, inside the house, he would set up the camera complete with flash, close to where a mouse was raiding food on a kitchen shelf. While Gerrit slept soundly in his bed, the mouse would take its own picture by tipping a thread and activating the camera.

The pet mice we sold in the shop were bought from amateur breeders and we bred some ourselves at home. Small pets were in steady demand by children, who sometimes purchased the mice without their parents knowing anything about the arrangement. The animals we bred had to travel to Dublin by public transport, which meant that I had to bring them on the bus. Depending on what livestock I was carrying, a careful choice had to be made as to what seat I should choose on the bus. A cardboard shoe-box containing a dozen or so pet mice might not be very noticeable, but if the occupants began shuffling and scratching now and again it could be quite worrying as the box seemed to amplify the sound.

In those days each bus had a driver and a conductor. The same crew would operate on the same route from year to year and as a result we came to know most of them. There was 'Mutt' the driver, who looked like the cartoon character from Mutt and Jeff. There was 'Tight Skin', who earned his name because of his very wrinkled face, and then of course there was the 'Mumbler', so called because of his habit of mumbling his words.

One morning I was travelling in from Bray with my cardboard box of mice. The conductor on the No. 45 bus that day was 'Mumbler'. I had made way for a passenger who got off at the previous stop and had just sat down again, holding the box on my lap. The lid on the box seemed to have partly slipped off, however, and several of the mice took this opportunity to make their escape. There was pandemonium on the bus, with screams from some of the women and an impossible attempt by one of them to exit through a window. I don't know if I caught all the escapees, but I had no sooner secured the box and the situation had almost returned to normal than 'Mumbler' approached me and mumbled, 'Ye better get yer mouses outta here!'

Music in the city

Music was never very far from my mind and it was something to enjoy after work and at weekends. I became friends with young musicians and often met up with them in Dublin. They included Seán Potts, Paddy Moloney and Paidí Bán Ó Broin. Paidí Bán not only played music but was also an accomplished step-dancer and was the first person I heard playing jigs and reels on a harmonica. Paddy Moloney had been playing the tin whistle since he was a schoolboy and had graduated to playing the uilleann pipes. He had taken lessons from Leo Rowsome, who held classes in the Piper's Club. Seán Potts was also a whistle player, who came from a Wexford family, some of whose members were noted pipers. He had a marvellous feel for the slow airs.

Branches of the Gaelic League were located in a number of the large houses around Parnell Square, including Craobh Móibhí, the Árd Chraobh and Craobh an Chéitinnigh, where evenings of music and singing were held regularly at weekends. Some of us would contribute to these occasions by playing a few tunes or singing a song. Paidí Bán Ó Broin was years ahead of Riverdance in the humorous performances he gave along with his dancing companion Harry O'Reilly. Diarmuid Breathnach had a store of songs and a good voice, and Niall Tóibín caused many a good laugh by his clever impressions of particular characters involved in the Gaelic movement of the time.

Seán Bracken, a fiddle player, invited Paddy Moloney and myself to join a céilí band he was about to form. The Loch Gamhna Céilí Band became quite successful and won prizes at the Oireachtas Céilí Competition, which was held every year at the Mansion House. The band also played on Radio Éireann's *Céilí House* programme and we played occasionally for céilís at our old haunt, Barry's Hotel. Although we received a small fee for playing on radio, we did it for fun, not as professional musicians. We would have been happy to do it for nothing – not that any of us had money to spare, but enjoying the music was actually more important to us than monetary gain. Anyway, at the time, few people paid money to listen to Irish music.

The travails of the business world

Whatever about making money from playing music, it became obvious to Laillí and myself that I was not going to make a fortune in my current business. A few of my regular customers had by now established their own pet shops in various parts of the city. These were mostly small shops and not too much of a worry as far as competition was concerned, but when government import duty was introduced to cover furniture, including bird cages, the situation became more serious. Pressure began to mount in various ways and by now the budgie craze had gone well past its peak. My bank manager was beginning to notice the drop in cash flow and began to query the account. The financial situation was becoming so serious that a decision had to be made as to what steps I should take before matters became worse. I recalled that three years previously, Charlie Thompson, the managing director of Hely's, had telephoned offering me a position in the fishing and shooting department. I got in touch with him now to see if the offer still stood, and he asked me to come and see him the following morning. I was more than delighted when he informed me that I could have the job and that I could begin work as soon as it was convenient for me to do so. It was a relief to both Laillí and myself to know that a guaranteed sum of money would be coming in every week from now on.

There were a number of departments in Hely's, including an office furniture section, a stationery counter and, on the second floor, the largest toy department in the country. Every toy a child could wish for was for sale at Hely's, including Hornby electric trains, Dinky cars, talking dolls, board games, model soldiers and whatever else was the current craze in toys or games during a particular season. The fishing and shooting department was next door to the main shop and quite separate from the other sections. Sheila Norton was in charge of the fishing department and had Mrs Beatty as her assistant, a slightly older woman in her late fifties. Members of the staff tended to address Sheila Norton by her first name, but seemed to know her assistant only as Mrs Beatty. The women had contrasting personalities. Sheila, who had been working in Hely's since she left school, was a very conservative and religious woman and utterly dedicated to Hely's. Mrs Beatty, who was only a year or two in the job, was carefree and always prepared to have a bit of fun. Sheila was popular with the customers but she would rarely joke with them. Mrs Beatty, on the other hand, went out of her way to do some 'leg-pulling' with them. Although both women knew the name of every artificial lure in an angler's fly-box, neither of them would have ever gone fishing.

Our young family

The steady income made it possible for Laillí and myself to think about moving out of the cottage and buying a more substantial house. We did not have to travel very far: a bungalow located only a few hundred yards up the road from where we lived came on the market just at the opportune time.

Radio programmes

One of my fishing customers in Hely's was Fachtna Ó hAnnracháin, Director of Music in what was then Radio Éireann. The studios were located in Henry Street, above the GPO. Fachtna regularly came to the shop to buy a selection of flies before setting off to fish at the weekend. He knew of my interest in music and on one occasion when he was selecting some flies, he asked me if I would like to submit a sample script in Irish for a series of radio programmes on traditional music. He suggested that I might use recordings made on old seventy-eight discs, to illustrate the music of various traditional musicians. He informed me that if the script was successful I would also have to do a microphone test.

I was delighted to be given such an opportunity but I didn't mention that I possessed only two of the discs on which I was to base the proposed series. With the introduction of long-playing records – LPs as they were called – the breakable wax discs were going out of fashion. Over the following weeks, I spent my lunch-hours in various record shops around the city, poking around and searching for any seventy-eight discs I might find hidden among the more modern recordings on the shelves. By the time word came through from Radio Éireann that my script had been accepted, the few discs in my possession had grown to quite a sizeable collection.

The title of that first series of programmes was *Ridirí an Cheoil* (The Knights of Music). There were many more programmes to follow and all of them featured traditional music. I had become friendly with Sonnie Brogan, the Dublin accordion player, and with John Kelly, the well-known fiddle player from Clare. They were of great assistance whenever I needed extra information about particular pieces of music, or indeed the history of a particular musician.

Sonnie had a wonderful memory for tunes and he could tell the origins of many of the titles. It surprised me to learn that so many of them had become confused with the titles of other tunes. When I mentioned a tune called the 'Longford Collector', Sonnie informed me that the famous fiddle-player Michael Coleman used to call it the 'Longford Beggar

Woman' but that the people of Longford didn't approve of that title! Another tune played by Coleman was 'Tell Her I Am', which, according to Sonnie, was known by many musicians as 'A Tailor I Am'. A title that I always regarded as a little strange is the reel known as 'Roarin' Mary'. When I asked Sonnie how the tune deserved such a name, his reply was, 'The correct title of that tune was "Forlorn Mary", but the country fellas either couldn't remember or didn't understand the word *forlorn* and they used the word *roarin'* instead!'

Names given to tunes on the old recordings made in America by Irish musicians also caused confusion. 'O'Rourke's Reel' and 'The Wild Irishman' were recorded by Michael Coleman but as the tunes were listed in the wrong order on the disc, the names are now in reverse to what the original names were, according to Sonnie; for example the reel called 'The Fowling Piece', recorded by the Ballinakill Céilí Band, is a very old reel known as 'The Temple House'.

During the 1950s Irish traditional music did not enjoy the popularity that it does today. It was unusual to hear a jig or a reel on radio prog- rammes apart from those devoted entirely to traditional music. At times it seemed that anything coming from outside the country was better than what we ourselves owned. I felt that if children could be encouraged to listen to Irish music they would soon learn to appreciate it. I was particularly keen that they would hear the music of the tin whistle and the uilleann pipes. With this in mind, I invented a character called Lúidín Mac Lú Leipreachán whose companion was a little mouse called Luichín. I wrote the characters into a series of radio programmes where Luichín was forever getting into tricky situations and he would call on Lúidín to rescue him. Lúidín would suddenly appear and play his magic tune on his whistle and all Luichín's problems suddenly disappeared. There was music at various points throughout the programme, to emphasise the action and to add to the excitement of the story. The person I chose for the series had to be able to play both whistle and pipes in an imaginative way and I knew that the best musician for the purpose was Paddy Moloney.

Paddy worked in the Dublin hardware merchants Baxendales in Capel Street. Each week, on the day of the broadcast, Paddy made the ten-minute walk across from Capel Street to Dame Street at lunch hour and left his pipes with me at Hely's. At a quarter to five on the same day, he would find some excuse to be away from Baxendales for half an hour or so. I didn't have that problem and they seemed to be happy enough at Hely's that I had the opportunity to do a broadcast. Paddy would make his way up to Radio Éireann where I had brought his pipes and we would do a quick rehearsal. The programme would then go out live on air, just after news headlines at five o'clock. The children seemed to enjoy the adventures of Lúidín and Luichín and we enjoyed choosing the music to suit the stories. My father was of great assistance in coming up with witty ideas and original material, which he regularly typed up for me.

A trip to Alnwick

Not having a shop full of animals to look after gave me more time to think of other activities when a normal day's work was over, and these included playing music. But there was still a lot to do in Hely's during the day and lots of customers' requirements to think about. Being the main agents for the world-famous Hardy's fishing rods gave the shop a certain status. Tackle in stock in Hely's was unavailable elsewhere.

When Mr Thompson informed me one morning that he would like me to travel to Northumberland to visit Hardy's rod-making factory at Alnwick, I was only too delighted to accept his offer. Walking into Hardy's extensive workshop at Alnwick (pronounced annik), was my first experience of seeing a large number of craftsmen all working together. There were twenty of them, and as most of them wore tweed caps, the sight looked even more extraordinary! Everything was crafted by hand and the expertise of these men was wonderful to observe. It was said that no good workman ever left Hardy's, and the majority of those I met had over thirty years' experience with the firm. According to Hardy's, the tools and systems in common use by them were unknown to the general trade. They had commenced business in 1872 as engineers, fishing rod and tackle makers, and gunsmiths. Down through the years they had won many awards for the excellence of their products.

Back at Hely's, the experience I gained from having seen how the rods were made added even more material to the long conversations I had with anglers who regularly came in, mostly for a chat but sometimes with genuine queries.

Meeting Seán Ó Riada

A customer who was to have a major influence on my life walked into the shop one day, enquiring about a shotgun for game-shooting. He was a dapper-looking individual of average height and slight build and he sported a small moustache. He wore a fine brown tweed suit and his trilby hat sat at a slight angle on top of his head. He did not seem to be familiar with the various makes of guns but, with a little advice, he eventually chose a twelve-bore shotgun made by the well-known English firm of Webley and Scott. As the gun cost a lot more than he had planned to spend on the day, he asked me to arrange a hire purchase agreement for him. When I presented him with the necessary form, he signed his name *Seán Ó Riada*. He smiled when I asked him if he was the same person I had heard that very morning on radio, playing a very tasteful arrangement of a set dance. As we continued our conversation I rather naïvely mentioned that I had some ideas about music, to which he replied, 'I have some ideas too!'

Seán Ó Riada came regularly to the shop after that first visit and when he mentioned that he had an interest in fishing, I invited him out to try his hand at trout fishing on the River Dargle. He wasn't very skilled at it and in order not to embarrass him, I pretended not to notice whenever he happened to get his line tangled high up in the trees! Apart from that, he was wonderful company and I enjoyed his sense of confidence, his wit and his endless store of funny stories. A former teacher of Seán's, Fr Tadhg Ó Murchadha, had built a summer school in An Ghráig in West Kerry and he invited the Ó Riadas to use it until the summer Irish courses for children began. Seán's fluency in Irish improved rapidly after those holidays in West Kerry. It was there that he made friends with Gaeltacht musicians and singers including Jerry Flaherty and Seán de Hóra, Ballyferriter's best-known traditional singers.

Seán, his wife Ruth and their children lived in an area between Dublin and Bray known as Galloping Green. He was musical director of a small orchestra in the Abbey Theatre and his salary was eleven pounds a week. He informed Ruth that he was receiving only ten pounds – he needed the extra pound for some drink and cigars! During those years the Abbey was located in the Queen's Theatre in Pearse Street, as its original home in Abbey Street had been destroyed by a fire.

On one of his many visits to Hely's, Seán told me he wished to form a group of traditional musicians and asked me to recommend some musicians. I proposed Paddy Moloney and Seán Potts. I also suggested that Sonnie Brogan and John Kelly be invited to join, as I believed that the younger musicians would have a lot to gain from playing along with these older, experienced traditionalists. When I asked John Kelly if he would be interested in joining the group his reply was, 'Arra, Sonnie and meself are too auld for that kinda' thing. Ask some young fellas!' When I persisted and asked him to try it out, he agreed to come 'just to see what it was like!' In later years he was to become one of Seán Ó Riada's most ardent supporters.

I arranged with the musicians to meet at Galloping Green on a Sunday afternoon. We played music until late that night and it was a good opportunity for Ó Riada to familiarise himself with many traditional dance tunes and settings of tunes that he had not previously heard. We began rehearsing in the house on a regular basis and the exciting atmosphere generated there resulted in no small measure from the intensity of the music. Ó Riada directed and accompanied the musicians on his well-seasoned bodhrán, adding real punch to the wildness of the performances. In his poem 'Galloping Green', May 1962, Thomas Kinsella caught the essence of Ó Riada at those early sessions:

> He clutched the shallow drum
> and crouched forward, thin
> as a beast of prey. The shirt
> stretched at his waist. He stared
> to one side, toward the others
> and struck the skin cruelly
> with his nails. Sharp
> as the answering arid bark
> his head quivered, counting.

It was during this time that the Kerry playwright Bryan MacMahon was about to have one of his works produced at the Abbey Theatre. It was a mysterious play about a young man living in a lonely valley who, in a daft effort to develop his neighbours' imagination, endeavoured to convince them that they were a colony of ants. The Listowel Drama Group, from MacMahon's own village, had already won a major award with the play at the Athlone Drama Festival. It had been produced by them under the title *The Golden Folk* and Bryan had since made some changes and re-named it *The Song of the Anvil*. Ria Mooney was the producer of the play at the Abbey and Tomás Mac Anna was responsible for designing the stage set.

As the rehearsals progressed it became obvious that music should feature prominently in the overall production. Bryan MacMahon dis-cussed the matter with Seán Ó Riada, in the latter's role as director of the Abbey orchestra. The members of the orchestra wore formal dress, and MacMahon was of the opinion that this would not be appropriate for the theme of his play. He was also doubtful about the kind of music the orchestra could deliver. 'I'll talk to you again about it!' was Seán's response as he went off about his business.

A memorable night

One evening, some time later, we were assembled in the house at Galloping Green, when Bryan MacMahon arrived. It was to be a very his-toric occasion, although none of us realised it at the time. The large room at the front of the house had a bare, unpainted wooden floor. An old piano stood in the corner close to one of the windows and a variety of wooden chairs as well as a large trestle were placed around the edge of the room. On each side of the Georgian fireplace were rows of wooden shelves packed with books on every subject imaginable. There were hundreds of paperbacks in many languages, books on Irish history, others in Greek and Latin. In between books on filmmaking and science-fiction were fishing and shooting manuals, and a variety of books related to music. The bare wooden floor had a hole in the centre big enough to trap a woman's high heel and was in complete contrast to the elegant period fireplace. Now and again, whenever the ash on Seán's cheroot became a little long, he wandered over and casually tipped the ash into the hole with unerring accuracy, without ever interrupting his conversation!

'Are you satisfied?' asked Seán, glancing in Bryan MacMahon's direction after we had finished playing. But there was no need to ask – the look on

Bryan's face was sufficient. According to Bryan himself, he had been waiting for years to hear music like this. 'If you are satisfied,' added Seán, 'ask those in authority at the Abbey if we can replace the resident orchestra with these musicians for the duration of your play.' Bryan MacMahon had no problem having that permission granted. Meanwhile he continued on with the stage rehearsals. Special straw outfits, which included a particular type of head dress, were ordered and made in Dingle. These were for a scene where the 'straw boys' were to dance in the blacksmith's forge. When the outfits arrived they were regarded by the insurance company as a fire hazard because of all the straw. Dissolved asbestos had to be mixed with the straw in order to comply with insurance regulations. The real danger to health from inhaling asbestos dust was obviously not common knowledge at the time!

Although the musicians had been decided upon, one performer who was vital for the dance scene was missing. 'Where will we find a bones player?' asked Seán. There were very few people using the bones, especially around Dublin. Earnán de Blaghad, the director of the Abbey, suggested asking the actors as, according to him, 'they know everything!' The stage manager, Bert Carroll, gathered the actors and helpers together. Bryan MacMahon showed them a pair of sheep's rib bones and explained how they were played. He had an immediate volunteer in stage-hand Ronnie McShane, who asked to be allowed borrow the bones for a couple of nights. Ronnie was able to master the technique in less than a week and Ó Riada invited him to become a member of the group.

'I have them christened!' exclaimed Seán to Bryan MacMahon some time later. 'I'm calling the group Ceoltóirí Chualann. It relates to the district where we have our practices.' He had combined *Ceoltóirí*, the Irish word for musicians, with *Cuala*, the name of the district between Dublin and Bray, where the Ó Riadas lived. Ó Riada decided to take a completely new approach to the way the music would be used in *The Song of the Anvil*. He arranged with the producer that the musicians would play in the orchestra pit throughout the whole performance. We were to have straw tied around our legs and we were all to wear peak caps. Having a group of musicians perform for the duration of a play at the Abbey had never been done before, and to us the whole idea sounded imaginative and exciting.

Sunday nights at Galloping Green became something of a ritual that we all looked forward to and very much enjoyed. The musicians that Seán had formed into a group for *The Song of the Anvil* would arrive an hour or so earlier than the rest of the guests. This was to enable us to rehearse the music that Seán had arranged for the play. The members of the group chosen to perform at the Abbey were Paddy Moloney (pipes and whistle), Seán Potts (whistle), Vincent Broderick (flute), John Kelly and Martin Fay (fiddles), Sonnie Brogan and myself on button accordions and Ronnie McShane (bones).

Quite a cross-section of musicians, poets and writers would appear at those parties and they took great delight in the music and fun. Well-known musicians such as pipers Séamus Ennis and his father old Jim Ennis, Tommy Reck and Clare piper Willie Clancy were there on occasions. Seán Mac Réamoinn and Ciarán Mac Mathúna and his wife Dolly McMahon were colleagues of Ó Riada since his days in Radio Éireann, as were John Skehan and his wife Winnie Butler. Poets Tom Kinsella, Seamus Heaney and John Montague were particular friends of Seán's, and Garech de Brún, a member of the Guinness family, was also regularly in his company. For formal occasions Garech dressed in a well-tailored tweed suit. For other occasions he would appear in a colourful Aran *geansaí* and tweed trousers, complete with a hand-woven Aran *crios* or belt. In a bygone age it was fashionable for the nobility to have their own personal harp players. Garech didn't have his own harper but he did have his own personal fiddle player. It's not known how good Máirtín Byrnes was at horticulture but he was a good traditional musician, which is perhaps how he got the job as Garech's head gardener on the Luggala estate. Money being a lot less plentiful than in these modern times, Garech was nevertheless following in the tradition of supporting a traditional musician. He had Máirtín earning part of his keep by playing music and the balance was made up by having him gardening on the estate.

Although the button accordion was my usual instrument, Seán Ó Riada asked me to play the bodhrán for *The Song of the Anvil*. Not having had any experience of playing a bodhrán, I was naturally quite nervous about using the instrument for what was to be such an important run of performances at the National Theatre. There was a particular section in the play where the rhythm I was expected to beat out on the bodhrán ran counter to the music, and that had me really worried. Seán assured me that I would have no problem in keeping to the beat as he would write it out for me. He was well aware that most members of the group were not proficient at reading music but this did not seem to worry him. When he jotted down my music for the bodhrán on a sheet of paper, it was far from what I had expected and read as follows: *Ham Butter and Eggs, Ham Butter and Eggs, Ham Butter and Rashers and Sausages, Ham Butter and Eggs.* It worked perfectly! I often wondered what members of the Abbey audience thought while returning to their seats after the interval, if they happened to pass close to the orchestra and looked over my shoulder to see a breakfast menu on my music stand!

Meanwhile, Seán was also hard at work in the Damer Hall on Stephen's Green, where he was directing the music for his own play on Eoghan Rua Ó Súilleabháin. It was a ballad opera in which sections of folklore were interwoven with poetry and song as well as dances choreographed by Pádraig Mac Léid. To all of this Ó Riada had added his own musical arrangements. Seán named the play S*pailpín a Rúin nó Eoghan Rua agus an Ceannaí Glic* (My Darling Labouring Man or Eoghan Rua and the Crafty Dealer). He had great admiration for Eoghan Rua Ó Súilleabháin, Munster's popular poet and raconteur (1748–1784). Some would even say that he partly modelled himself on Ó Súilleabháin. In a review of the play which appeared in *The Times* of London, it was noted: 'The significance of this work lies in the fact that it is the first appearance in Irish dramatic literature of an earthy tradition which lasted in Ireland from the Middle Ages until the eighteenth century. To find its equivalent we must go back to Rabelais or Villon.'

Seán Ó Riada was a complex character and he did not easily reveal his true self. Writing about him in the *The Irish Times*, his friend the film-maker Louis Marcus said of him, 'There were too many of him to be contained in one frame, however wiry. One day he would insist on speaking French, another only Irish. Sometimes he would be a Montenotte Corkman, other times a Viennese academic and yet others a West Cork peasant. But there was more to this than masks and mimicry, for he was contained in all of these elements.'

It was obvious to many of us that nothing mattered to Ó Riada as much as his music, and I found it was through music that one could learn much about his character. The love song 'Aisling Gheal' was a piece of music that he would play over and over again after he discovered it in A. Marten Freeman's collection of 1914. Freeman had recorded the song from a traditional singer from Baile Mhúirne in Co. Cork, Peig Ní Dhonnchadha. Ó Riada recognised the sophistication of the music and the ability of the unaccompanied singer to vary the notes so that each verse was different to the previous one. He mourned the fact that so many of our great songs were not being listened to and that they had been replaced by what he regarded as inferior music. When I first heard him playing 'Marbhna Luimní' (The Lament for Limerick), one could see that he was deeply affected by that period of Ireland's tragic history and he often spoke of the loss we suffered at the changing of the old order during those times. There are similar examples in relation to more recent periods of history, illustrated in *Mise Éire* and *An Tine Bheo*, and one cannot but be moved by his imaginative use of our great songs in the music of these historic films.

7

Ceoltóirí Chualann
1960s

*Launching Ceoltóirí Chualann – The Horseshoe – Entertaining the film
directors – Fleá Cheoil an Raidió – The critics – Ceol na nUasal*

Launching Ceoltóirí Chualann

After *The Song of the Anvil* had completed its run at the Abbey Theatre
and Ó Riada's play on Eoghan Rua Ó Súilleabháin had finished in the
Damer Hall, Seán began working more seriously with his group of
traditional musicians. What he planned was a complete change from the
traditional céilí band style of Irish dance music. He wanted to get away
from the customary style of playing a number of jigs or reels, one after
the other, twice or three times, with no variation. This particular fashion
dated from 1926 when the céilí band was invented by Séamus Clandillon,
Radio Éireann's Director of Music, in order to have dance music for his
studio-based programmes.

Seán Ó Riada experimented in many different ways with Ceoltóirí
Chualann. The members who had played at the Abbey remained, with
one exception. The young Clare flute player Michael Tubridy, who had
been playing music for Seán's play in the Damer, was brought into the
group to replace Vincent Broderick. Seán seemed to have particularly
liked Michael's Clare style of playing and his fluent Irish. The only
change with regard to musical instruments was that I gave back Seán's
bodhrán, which I had used for the play, and concentrated on playing my
button accordion.

Some of Seán's arrangements were simple and varied, while others were
more complicated. In the straightforward pieces individual musicians
might, for example, play solo parts throughout. Other compositions

83

would have the group split in two, with some of the musicians playing counterpoint. Some compositions were given to the musicians on sheet music, and those of us who could not read music had to learn off the whole arrangement by ear. Seán had a particular interest in having the musicians play slow airs. With this in mind, he borrowed my accordion one night and brought it home with him. Having worked out its limitations and possibilities, he made a series of arrangements for slow airs where only the bass notes of the accordion were to be used, while the rest of the musicians played the melody. It was very effective with songs such as 'Mo Chailín Bán', 'Cill Mhuire', 'Carraig Dhonn' and 'An Raibh Tú ag an gCarraig?' He also had Martin Fay play slow airs on the fiddle. Martin played with Ó Riada in the orchestra at the Abbey and he was also a member of the then Radio Éireann Light Orchestra. As he had been trained in classical music, he had the advantage of being able to interpret whatever musical notations Ó Riada might place before him.

Seán's plan was to launch Ceoltóirí Chualann at the Dublin Theatre Festival on 10 September 1961. As one would expect when Seán Ó Riada happened to be involved, this was not going to be any ordinary affair! A concert of this kind might not be unusual today, even in a venue such as the Shelbourne Hotel, but in 1961 it was unheard of, especially when it involved a group of Irish traditional musicians playing in a new and revolutionary fashion. Presenting Ceoltóirí Chualann to the public, however, was only part of Ó Riada's plan. The concert would give him an opportunity to stage a night of genuine traditional music, song and poetry.

A few weeks before the Dublin Theatre Festival was to begin, Seán asked me to write personal invitations to all members of the government and to President de Valera, inviting them to *Reacaireacht an Riadaigh* (Ó Riada's Recital). Dress was to be formal for the guests and the musicians were to be in their Sunday best. We had a lot of work to do in preparation for the concert. One piece of music in the programme was most unusual, at least for traditional musicians, but we enjoyed trying to master its complicated arrangement. None of us had played anything like it before, and as far as Ó Riada was concerned, the intention was probably as much to confuse the critics as it was to include the totally unexpected. Anyone reading the review of it the following morning was in no doubt that it confounded at least one prominent newspaper critic! The arrangement was an Ó Riada version of a shortened *Seventh Symphony* by Beethoven, which he named *Beethoven's Fancy*. Ó Riada was of the firm belief that people were listening far too much to composers such as Beethoven, to the exclusion of some of the great composers of music from other parts of the world, including India and China. He once stated on radio that Beethoven must be revolving in his grave as a result of his compositions being played over and over again. Whatever his reason for choosing this piece of music, who would ever have thought that two elder traditional musicians like John Kelly and Sonnie Brogan, who could not even read music, would be playing Beethoven in one of Dublin's principal hotels, at a time when a traditional musician would hardly be allowed inside its doors.

Reacaireacht an Riadaigh was a memorable evening. Included in the programme were traditional singers Áine Ní Ghallchóir and Darach Ó Catháin, uilleann piper Tommy Reck and poets Máire Mhac An t-Saoi and Máirtín Ó Direáin. Also included in the programme were the writer Seán Ó Riordáin and the poet and writer Seán Ó Tuama. President de Valera and most members of the Cabinet attended and the contributions and performances from the various artists were received with warm enthusiasm. Seán Ó Riada's new folk orchestra, Ceoltóiri Chualann, had been launched in style!

The concert was a one-night only performance but it was far from being the end of the affair. On 1 March 1961, Seán Ó Riada recorded the first of a series of radio programmes for which he retained the name *Reacaireacht an Riadaigh*. It included music played by Ceoltóirí Chualann and literary readings by Niall Tóibín. Niall took part in the earlier editions of the series but eventually Seán Ó Riada was sufficiently confident in his standard of Irish to do the readings himself. Listening to those recordings of Ó Riada's voice, one can clearly hear the influence that his holidays in the Kerry Gaeltacht were having on his Irish at that time – he developed a great fluency and knowledge of the language in a relatively short space of time. The only singer in the series was Darach Ó Catháin, for whom Ó Riada had the greatest admiration. Darach was from the Co. Meath Gaeltacht of Ráth Cairn but his people were originally from Conamara and both his music and dialect were in the traditional Conamara style.

In a strange way *Reacaireacht* nearly caused the total disbandment of Ceoltóirí Chualann. Seán, being short of money as usual, suggested to Gael Linn that they use some of the *Reacaireacht* tapes to make a long-playing record. The musicians heard of the LP only when it went on sale in the record shops. They were so annoyed at not being paid for what they regarded as a commercial recording that they threatened to resign. It was a real crisis and Ó Riada was quite upset at their reaction. He decided to have nothing more to do with Ceoltóirí Chualann. When I realised how serious the situation was, I went looking for Ó Riada, and, after searching several of his usual haunts, I eventually found him at the Pearl Bar in Henry Street, just across from Radio Éireann. I argued with him for a while and tried to impress on him the importance of the group. Eventually I persuaded him to find enough cash, as soon as possible, to pay the older musicians, John Kelly and Sonnie Brogan, whom he did not know very well. I suggested that it would be easier to deal with the younger musicians and I volunteered to speak to them if he could promise to pay them at some future date. It had all been a simple mistake on Ó Riada's part but it was ironed out in the end and Ceoltóirí Chualann were once more on an even keel. No more surprise recordings were ever again to appear on the market!

The Horseshoe

Whenever we were to have a radio recording of *Reacaireacht an Riadaigh*, Darach Ó Catháin travelled to Dublin by train and Seán Ó Riada would arrange to pick him up at Heuston Station. One particularly cold morning in mid-winter, Seán, having collected Darach, suggested that they call into John Kelly on their way to Radio Éireann. John had a shop at the top end of Capel Street, next door to the Four Seasons pub. The shop was called The Horseshoe and looked as if it had been transported from John's own county of Clare and dropped right into the middle of Dublin. It was a very small shop and if five customers happened to arrive there at the one time, the last person would probably form the beginning of a queue outside the door. There were two tiny counters at an angle to one another with hinges on one which allowed it to be lifted so that John could go in behind the counter, or for that matter come out. A two-foot by three-foot glass case sat astride both counters, where John was hidden from view whenever he wished to play a tune to himself.

You could buy almost anything in The Horseshoe, from a wooden chair or fiddle hanging out of the ceiling, to a bicycle repair kit from the glass case or an evening newspaper off the counter. I asked John for an *Irish Times* once but he told me that he didn't sell Protestant papers. On the grey winter morning that Seán Ó Riada and Darach arrived at the shop, they were almost blue with the cold. 'Good God, lads, but ye look frozen!' remarked John, as they stepped inside the door. Seán said, 'It's that east wind coming up the River Liffey. It would cut you in two. They don't have that kind of a wind in Cork.' 'I have the cure for ye here,' said John. 'Wipe the dust from those three glasses – they've been on the shelf for a while.' Placing the three small glasses on the counter and bending down almost out of sight, John pulled an old-style delft hot water bottle from its hiding place beneath the counter. Screwing off the cap, he carefully poured out a transparent colourless liquid into each glass until all three were full to the brim. 'That'll knock the frosht off ye like nottin' else will. It's the best poitín in Co. Clare!' he joked, raising his glass towards the low, tobacco-stained ceiling. 'Sláinte!' the three chorused as if with one voice.

The Horseshoe was a well-known stop for traditional musicians, especially those coming up to Dublin from the country or passing through on their way to or from England or the United States. John was a great source of information and was known the length and breadth of the country. He knew where most traditional musicians were located, even those living overseas, and if he didn't know, he would put you in contact with somebody who did. John and his friend Joe Ryan, also a fiddle player, were to be seen regularly in the Four Seasons pub next door, especially on Friday and Saturday evenings and on Sunday mornings, and people came regularly to hear their duets. Other musicians often joined in with John and Joe on these occasions, exchanging tunes and stories.

The long soft seat under the large window was the usual perch for the two fiddle players, and there was room for just one extra player on this seat. Other musicians sat on chairs surrounding the small round table in front of John, on which there was an array of pint glasses standing shoulder to shoulder and holding various levels of stout or beer. One Sunday morning John and Joe were on their own and the spare place beside John was occupied by a pale, slightly built individual in a striped blue suit who showed no sign of participating in the lively music. It wasn't until the two fiddle players had started into another set of reels that he slipped his hand into the inside pocket of his jacket and produced two dessert spoons. John, out of the corner of his eye, saw what his blue-suited neighbour had in his hand and as he glanced at Joe both musicians turned their eyes in despair towards heaven. Generally speaking, traditional musicians will put up with bodhrán players as long as they are not drowned out by them. But a spoons player to John Kelly and Joe Ryan was the worst possible kind of nightmare. In their experience, the sense of rhythm displayed by the spoons player more often than not went completely astray. Sonnie Brogan once said to me, 'The day they call them things an instrument, I'm goin' to throw me box in the Liffey!'

The spoons player, having plucked up sufficient courage to produce his shiny implements, was now enjoying himself to the full. The spoons were held in his right hand back to back and, in order to make the necessary clicking sound, were being run down continuously along the four fingers of his open left palm. As an added variation, occasional flurries with the spoons were also made down along his left sleeve and even down along the left leg of his trousers. Eventually the music came to a stop and it was John's turn to call for a drink. 'Mick, whenever you're ready!' John shouted across the floor to the barman behind the counter. 'What is it to be this time, John?' asked Mick. 'A pint of beer for Joe here, a pint of Guinness for me, and eh....' John hesitated for a moment and then, jerking his thumb at the spoons player, he added, '... And a bowl of soup for yer man here!'

Ceoltóirí Chualann's first LP recording was with a young singer from Cork, Seán Ó Sé. He had been singing regularly with the Blarney Céilí Band, and Ó Riada felt that Ó Sé's voice would suit a particular song that he wished to record on disc. The song, 'An Poc ar Buille', was written by the West Cork Gaeltacht poet Dónall Ó Mulláin. The poet describes how, on his way to help his workmates, he meets a mad Billy goat. He goes on to tell about the animal's crazy antics rampaging around the countryside, chasing both a policeman and a parish priest! The song became an almost instant hit. Seán Ó Sé was thereafter invited to join Ceoltóirí Chualann and subsequently made many more recordings with the group.

Entertaining the film directors

It was in 1962 that Ó Riada mentioned there was a possibility that he might be commissioned to provide the score for a film of Synge's play *The Playboy of the Western World*. He was not sure at that stage what the outcome might be, but the directors were flying in from London and meeting with him to discuss the project. Rather than a very formal meeting at some rather obvious location such as the Shelbourne Hotel, Seán decided on a plan. There was a spacious basement in the house at Galloping Green and some days before the meeting was to take place, Ronnie McShane, who could turn his hand to almost anything, was invited out to the house. He was instructed to clean out the basement and give it an ample coating of whitewash to make it look like a country kitchen one would expect to see in Conamara or Co. Kerry. A load of hand-cut turf was ordered for the open fireplace to make the atmosphere more realistic.

When the film directors arrived they were whisked straight from the airport to Galloping Green, almost before they knew where they were. We were all gathered together in the rather smoky basement along with our instruments, having been given strict instructions that as soon as we heard the knock on the front door we were to play 'like bats out of Hell', which is what we did. The directors were just given a quick peek at us for a moment before they were ushered upstairs for a substantial feast prepared by Ruth. Not a morsel of it was to come in our direction. Our instructions were to keep on with the music, play whatever we liked, and whenever the meal was over and the guests were on their way down to the basement, we were once again to make it sound really wild!

One might be of the opinion that there was something of the country squire about Seán Ó Riada, and indeed there were times when he seemed to enjoy that image. His purchase of an expensive shotgun from me in Hely's when he knew little about the sport of game-shooting would help to reinforce that impression, as would his suggestion to a Scandinavian filmmaker that he be interviewed while he stood in mid-stream complete with fly-rod in the Sullane River in West Cork, even though he wasn't much of an angler. The atmosphere he created around the brace of pheasants that Ruth had prepared for the film directors' lavish meal was another example of his enjoyment of that role. Seán had propped up his shotgun in a prominent position beside the fireplace, in full view of his guests. To complete the picture, an open box of cartridges with some of its contents loosely spilled on the mantelpiece gave the distinct impression that the pheasants were the result of a morning shoot by the man of the house. There is no knowing what exciting tales Seán told them at the table that day about large catches of fresh-run salmon and his early morning adventures hunting wildfowl. The film directors were most impressed, totally unaware that their host had probably never shot a pheasant in his life and that the birds had been purchased by Ruth in a poultry shop the previous day!

The meal was scarcely over when Seán slipped in to tell us that he had clinched the deal and was being given the contract for the music. The directors eventually arrived down to where we were in the basement, and the scene must have looked and sounded quite extraordinary to them. The sound of wild music being played on unfamiliar instruments, the heavy smell of turf smoke, the dimly lit, cavernous space, must surely have given them the feeling that they were in a very different world, and so indeed they were!

Preparing a score for *The Playboy* was a particular challenge for Ó Riada. In a ninety-minute film covering many different scenes and moods, he had to rely on an amateur group of traditional musicians to provide all the music. The result was a considerable achievement and the musical arrangements succeeded in capturing the spirit of the play. Siobhán McKenna, who played the part of Pegeen Mike, came to hear us at the recording in the Phoenix Hall in Dame Lane and was extremely enthusiastic about the music. Her whoops and cries, added to by Ronnie McShane's, can be heard in the recording of the wild dance scenes. During one of the arrangements, the recording had to be stopped several times as John Kelly could be heard tapping his foot in time to the music. After two or three attempts to silence John's foot, Seán suggested that he remove his shoe. When we resumed playing again, John's stockinged foot could still be heard tapping away, almost as loudly as it had been before he removed his shoe. 'What's wrong, John?' called Ó Riada from behind the glass panel. 'He has a hammer toe!' shouted Sonnie Brogan, before John had a chance to reply. The problem was eventually solved when a cushion was placed under John Kelly's foot.

Whatever about the merits of the actual film *The Playboy of the Western World* – and there were questions about the choice of actors – the time chosen to launch the film was most unfortunate. It was the week that President John F. Kennedy was assassinated. Whether *The Playboy* would have done well or not we will never know, but the film never got a fraction of the extensive publicity the directors had hoped for when they launched it in the US.

Fleá Cheoil an Raidió

In 1963 Seán Ó Riada was invited to take part in a new weekly radio series, *Fleá Cheoil an Raidió*, which featured Ceoltóirí Chualann and Seán Ó Sé as well the actor Éamon Keane doing story and poetry readings. Eoin Ó Súilleabháin, son of Muiris Ó Súilleabháin, who wrote the classic *Fiche Bliain ag Fás* (Twenty Years a' Growing), acted as *Fear a' Tí* in the early days of the series, a role that was later taken over by Seán Ó Síocháin. Subsequent programmes included Éamon Kelly, who replaced Éamon Keane as the *seanachaí* (storyteller). Éamon Kelly immediately fitted into the series and every programme from then on included one of his highly descriptive and humorous stories. Although his only aids were an old battered hat, a coloured scarf and the chair on which he sat, Éamon had the rare gift of being able to build up the atmosphere of the traditional storyteller of past ages.

During the series, two programmes would be recorded on a Saturday evening and two on a Sunday. We played either in a studio at Portobello Bridge or in one opposite the Parnell Monument in O'Connell Street. The harpsichord had been introduced into the group at this stage and was hired for each performance. Apart from giving the group a new sound, this instrument gave Ó Riada far more scope in the arrangements, especially of songs. He had a great interest in the harp but there were no traditional harp players that he could call upon at that time to join his group. During some of the sessions at Galloping Green, he would insert brass drawing pins into the hammers of his piano, giving it a metallic sound that perhaps reminded him of the missing wire-strung harp. The harpsichord now satisfied this interest. The range of traditional music used in the series was quite extensive, with light-hearted songs such as 'The Galbally Farmer' contrasting with 'An Buachaill Caol Dubh'.

There was always a great sense of fun whenever Seán Ó Riada was in charge and he was well able to bring the audience with him when we performed any of the more light-hearted songs. Ronnie McShane had his own mischievous sense of humour and made a point of explaining in detail to anyone who was prepared to listen, that the bones he was playing were those of his poor grandfather. During one of the recordings of *Fleá Cheoil an Raidió*, while we were playing a slow air as an accompaniment to Seán Ó Sé's singing, Ó Riada was at an angle to the audience, conducting the musicians by nodding his head as he played the harpsichord. Ronnie was out front, closest to the audience. Although the song was not a humorous one – in fact it was a sad love song – the audience began to titter. Ó Riada, not wishing to be distracted from his conducting by turning towards the audience, threw a querying glance in my direction, but I couldn't enlighten him as to what was going on. Later we discovered that Ronnie, thinking that the audience might become somewhat bored with Seán Ó Sé's love song, was holding up his foot; the audience could see plainly written in chalk on the sole of his shoe: *second last verse*!

A competition for solo traditional musicians was included in the series. In each programme a competitor was invited to perform his or her piece. The recordings were listened to at the end of the series and a judgement made as to who should be the overall winner of the competition. At the end of one particular series, Seán Keane, a good-looking, fair-haired fiddle player, was judged to be the winner. He was an extremely talented player and shortly afterwards was invited to join Ceoltóirí Chualann. In describing the latest member to join his group, Seán Ó Riada announced to some friends that he now had 'a young musician who looks like a Greek god and plays like an angel!'

The critics

Seán Ó Riada and Ceoltóirí Chualann had their critics, both inside and outside of traditional music circles. John Kelly told Seán that while he was at the Pipers' Club the previous night, the well-known flute player John Egan had been 'giving out' about Ceoltóirí Chualann. 'He was givin' out about all this shtoppin' and shtartin' the musicians were doin' with the music!' complained John. 'Ask him if he would like to join the group!' was Seán's immediate reply. We never heard any more comments coming from the Pipers' Club after that.

In the 1963 summer edition of *CEOL – A Journal of Irish Music*, an article appeared severely criticising the group on their performance while on radio:

> In one of the *Fleá Cheoil* programmes, one of the accordion players played a slip jig known as 'The Whinny Hills of Leitrim'. He is followed by the flute player who also plays another slip jig of the same name. Both then play together, each his own air and the whole group joins in this free-for-all, but which side the other players took in this musical duel we are at a loss to say. Such treatment of music can hardly be regarded as a serious effort towards developing a new music art form.

However, the writer did admit that 'Ceoltóirí Chualann numbers among its members some of the best players in the country.' The editor of *CEOL* was Breandán Breathnach, who in the early days of Ceoltóirí Chualann was one of its severest critics. In later years he was to find far less fault with the group. Breandán Breathnach (1912–1985) is regarded by many as the most important individual in traditional Irish music circles during the last century. His work on behalf of Irish music and culture cannot be overestimated. He collected a huge volume of dance music and invented an ingenious method of identifying particular tunes by a code system. Today, the Irish Traditional Music Archives uses this system on a regular basis.

Breandán Breathnach worked as a civil servant in the Department of Agriculture but as the importance of his work was gradually recognised, he was fortunately transferred to the Department of Education, where he devoted his time to what had originally begun as a hobby. In 1968 he was very involved, with others, in forming Na Píobairí Uilleann, and the organisation now has its own fine headquarters at Henrietta Street in Dublin. I met Breandán on many occasions both in the Pipers' Club and in the company of Sonnie Brogan and John Kelly, whose particular versions of tunes are included in his published collection of dance music, *Ceol Rince na hÉireann*. He could play the pipes, although he rarely seemed to have done so in public and I saw him perform only once and to a very small group.

Ceol na nUasal

In 1963, a year after resigning from the Abbey Theatre and moving to the West Cork Gaeltacht, Seán Ó Riada was appointed Assistant Lecturer of Music at University College Cork. He continued to travel to Dublin at weekends to take part in recordings of the radio programmes *Reacaireacht an Riadaigh* and *Fleá Cheoil an Raidió*. I had instructions to arrange rehearsals in one of the rooms in Radio Éireann during the week, while Seán would post to me the tape of the music that we were to use in the programmes, which he had recorded on his rather ancient piano. He had bought a large old house in Cúil Aodha which had belonged to the poet and school teacher Domhnall Ó Ceocháin. Domhnall's daughter Máire had won the Oireachtas traditional singing competition in Dublin on several occasions, with a style of singing that was quite unique. Her version of particular songs were often used by Seán Óg Ó Tuama in his Claisceadal classes, one of the favourites being 'An Cuaichín' (The Little Cuckoo).

Some members of Ceoltóirí Chualann were earning a few extra pounds playing at various venues in the evenings. Paddy Moloney, Seán Potts and Martin Fay played regularly in the Chariot Inn in Ranelagh, long before it was fashionable to have a traditional group performing in such a location. Garech Browne offered them the opportunity of making a recording for his company, Claddagh Records, if they would form a group. Michael Tubridy (concert flute) and David Fallon (bodhrán, and the only non-member of Ceoltóirí Chualann) joined and the new group was given the name The Chieftains. Garech asked Seán Ó Riada if he would have any objection to his musicians being recorded in this way and although Seán agreed to allow Garech to go ahead with his project, he was not very pleased about it. He stipulated that the record sleeve should mention that the musicians were members of Ceoltóirí Chualann. The name did appear on the sleeve of the first disc but there was no mention of Ceoltóirí Chualann on any further recordings. When the first recording was released, Seán Ó Riada was generous in his *Hibernia* review: 'What a pleasure it is to say at the outset that this new Claddagh record is splendid. The music on it has been arranged and directed by Paddy Moloney, who is one of the most gifted pipers in Ireland today ...'

Although Seán Ó Riada had begun to revolutionise the way in which

Irish traditional music was being played by groups of musicians, he wanted to take it a step further by raising it on to a higher level and thereby gaining more respect for Irish culture in general. He had begun to take a great interest in the music of the harpers, and the tapes he kept on posting to me for the rehearsals included more and more of their beautiful compositions. Traditional musicians had never fully accepted the harpers' music, which they regarded as not being authentically traditional. The possible exception to this was 'Carolan's Concerto', and there had been only one contemporary recording of this fine tune – a Gael Linn record played by the Dublin piper Tommy Reck. It is difficult to understand why ancient harp music had not been regarded as authentically Irish. The harp had been played in Ireland for hundreds of years. However, the harpers were paid by the nobility, composed music in their honour and regularly played in the big houses. So there may have been a reaction to all this by a downtrodden people who would have perceived it as belonging to the landed gentry. This was music that was best forgotten about in an emerging, independent Ireland.

Ó Riada had a very different point of view and saw his latest production, *Ceol na nUasal* (The Music of the Nobles) as he liked to call it, as an opportunity to help the community appreciate a part of our culture that had been long neglected. Much of the music chosen by Seán was by the blind harper Turlough O'Carolan (1670–1738). Bryan McMahon, describing the revival of O'Carolan's music by Ó Riada, said to me once: *'Bhí anam Traolach Uí Chearhbálláin ag imeacht ar fud na hÉireann ar seachrán ar feadh na céadta bliain go dtí sa deire thiar thall, ghlac sé seilbh i gcolainn an Riadaigh'* (Turlough O'Carolan's spirit had been wandering around Ireland for centuries until eventually it took up its abode in Seán Ó Riada's body).

Music of other famous harpers that Seán arranged for Ceoltóirí Chualann included 'Marbhna Luimní' (Limerick's Lamentation), 'Tiarna Mhaigh Eo' (Lord Mayo) and 'Tabhair Dom Do Lámh' (Give Me Your Hand) by Ruadhrí Dall Ó Catháin. Ruadhrí Dall was so celebrated in his own day as a harper that he was invited to Scotland to play his compositions at the Court of King James VI.

'Tiarna Mhaigh Eo' is a tune that was played over two hundred years ago, but it was not really accepted as part of the Irish traditional musician's repertoire. It was included in the *Neal Collection*, published in the

95

eighteenth century, and was referred to by Nicholas Carolan, director of the Irish Traditional Music Archive, in his notes accompanying a facsimile edition of that collection:

> *Ye lord Mayo's delight.* Attributed to the harper Thady Keenan by his acquaintance Charles O'Conor of Belnagare ... and by Bunting ... but also by Bunting ... to the bard David Murphy, a poor dependant of Lord Mayo. Murphy wrote the words of the associated praise-poem, according to O'Conor ... to regain his master's favour after offending him. The subject, according to O'Sullivan ... was Theobald Burke, Sixth Viscount Mayo (1681–1741). O'Sullivan can hardly be right in identifying David Murphy with Murphy the famous eighteenth-century harper. The words of the praise-poem survive.

In November 1967 Ceoltóirí Chualann gave a very successful concert in Dublin under the title *Ceol na nUasal*, which included the above-mentioned tunes. A press release by Gael Linn, which coincided with the release of a record under the same title, stated:

> Seán Ó Riada last night presented a concert in the Provost's House at Trinity College, Dublin, with Seán Ó Sé, tenor, and Ceoltóirí Chualann. Any apparent incongruity in a performance by a folk group in such a setting is explained when we realise that they were playing not merry, rollicking folk music as we think of it nowadays but the gracious, highly formalised music of seventeenth-century Ireland. This is the music played before the highly sophisticated and musically appreciative members of the great households when the patronage system was still in operation and a nobleman's standing was judged as much by the quality of the musicians and poets whom he could attract around him as by the vastness of his estates.

The following week Ceoltóirí Chualann played in the Whitla Hall, Belfast, and Seán Ó Riada was chosen as Composer of the Year by the organisers of Festival 1967. Seán Ó Riada's classical compositions and arrangements, including his latest work for orchestra, Nomos No.1 *Ferrariae Dux Hercules*, were also performed and took place on six different evenings during the Festival.

8

Television
1960s

Amuigh Faoin Spéir – A wedding interlude – Partnership
with Gerrit – The Wexford Slobs – A trip to the Azores

Amuigh Faoin Spéir

I was still working in Hely's and playing with Ceoltóirí Chualann when
Telefís Éireann first came on air. It was only natural that, having experienced broadcasting on radio, television might be the next step. A magazine
programme called *Broadsheet*, under the editorship of Frank Hall, was
transmitted each evening during the week. I was asked to contribute a
brief weekly piece on wildlife. One evening, on my way out of the studio,
I met Síle Carden, who worked as a production assistant for the executive
producer and author James Plunkett. She asked me if I would be interested in submitting a proposal for a series on traditional music. I didn't
give an immediate answer but promised her that I would give it some
serious thought.

After leaving the studios at RTÉ, I contacted Gerrit Van Gelderen and
told him about the offer. 'Tell them you'll do a wildlife series. *We'll* do a
wildlife series!' exclaimed Gerrit, hardly able to contain himself. 'I'll
make you the best-known wildlife person in Ireland, Éamon. Tell them
we'll do a really good wildlife series!' (He was to regret 'the best-known
wildlife person in Ireland' bit in later life.)

We arranged to meet the following day and talk through our plans.
Gerrit's gift of being able to make quick sketches was to be an attractive
part of the programme. He expressed his ideas graphically and while we
spoke he drew, with a thick black marker, a big letter S on a large sheet
of paper that lay between us. His suggestion was that we would base the

pilot programme on the mute swan, Ireland's largest wild bird. The mysterious beginning to the first programme would be the appearance of the S on the television screen, which would gradually develop into a drawing of a complete swan. The programme was to be studio-based but that did not worry us much, as Gerrit said he could produce a real live swan on the day of the recording! As the programme was to be in the Irish language, I asked my father if he could think of a suitable name. It didn't take him long to come up with the title *Amuigh Faoin Spéir* (Out Under the Sky). Our submission was accepted and Ireland's first home-produced wildlife series for television was born.

Gerrit had promised to produce a live swan for that first programme and, true to his word, he set out in his currach in the dead of night up along the River Liffey, where he managed to creep up on an unsuspecting mute swan. The carpentry shop at RTÉ had received instructions from us to have a wooden, straw-filled pen prepared for the bewildered bird. As presenter of the programme, I sat on a table facing the camera and talked in general about Ireland's largest bird. At a given signal, Gerrit jumped into the pen, grabbed the struggling swan, brought it over to where I was and 'plonked' it on my lap. I cannot for the life of me remember how the script went, nor have I any wish to, but I suppose I explained to the viewers that the struggling bird I held in my arms was actually a swan. In spite of how ridiculous that sequence must have looked, the series became, in Gerrit's words, 'A howling success!'

Various birds and other animals were brought into the studio for different programmes but none was as big or as awkward as our first feathered guest. The first producer of the series, Louis Lentin, was not very sympathetic to wildlife, nor indeed did he seem to have any under-standing of animals. He certainly did not welcome advice from what he regarded as two amateurs and he always let everyone know that he alone was in charge of the production.

On one occasion I borrowed a pet red squirrel for a programme on small mammals. The squirrel was in a cage that I had placed on a table in the studio. When Louis came on to the floor to check out the format we were to follow, he peered disapprovingly at the little animal and remarked: 'I want that cage opened as soon as we begin recording.' 'But the squirrel will escape!' was my reply. 'I said the cage is to be opened!'

he retorted. I knew there was little point in protesting any further. Louis had made up his mind as always and he wasn't going to take advice from anyone, especially an inexperienced beginner!

As the countdown began in studio, I was perched as usual on the table facing the camera. The floor manager was to my left, out of shot, waiting for the signal from the producer to open the little cage door … five, four, three, two, one, and on the word 'Action!' the floor manager gave the signal and I introduced the programme on the subject of the squirrel. I described the animal and Gerrit's drawing began to take shape on the screen. As I mentioned how quickly a squirrel could move in the tree-tops, I thought I caught a glimpse of what looked very like a squirrel flying across the studio floor. Glancing towards the far end of the set, I could now plainly see that it was indeed a squirrel. There were heavy dark-blue drape curtains surrounding the whole studio, reaching almost up to the ceiling, and acting as a sound barrier. The squirrel didn't hesitate when it reached the edge of the floor but flew straight up the drape as if it were a pine tree. Meanwhile, the studio cameramen did their best at wheeling the old-style heavy cameras in its direction, bending backwards and attempting to keep the squirrel in shot as it flew around the tops of the curtains. I cannot remember how my commentary went as it was not in my prepared script but I probably tried to act as if a squirrel doing a 'wall of death act', in the style of motorcyclists in a circus, was an activity that occurred in the studio every day!

When the programme was over it took some time to capture the squirrel and return it to its cage. Louis Lentin eventually appeared on the studio floor, as was the custom after a broadcast or a recording, to thank the crew and the participants. On this occasion, however, no attention was paid to either Gerrit or myself and we seemed to have been purposely excluded from all these traditional niceties. As the producer made his way towards the exit, he came abreast of the squirrel's cage where he paused for a moment and peered in at the little animal. The squirrel was by now sitting inside its cage and quite innocently gnawing a hazelnut. The sight of this bespectacled mortal glaring in at it prompted the little creature to suddenly stop chewing, thinking perhaps that it was about to have another taste of freedom. Both stared at each other for a moment, the squirrel remaining absolutely motionless. 'You little f----r!' remarked Louis as he turned on his heel and strode out of the studio.

As a title for a nature series, *Amuigh Faoin Spéir* was fine but it was in some ways a contradiction. Although we were using real live animals and birds, everything that appeared on the screen was coming from a studio. What we really needed was to have the wildlife filmed in its natural habitat. I did not have a camera nor had I ever used one. Gerrit Van Gelderen had taken some film as a hobby and he owned a 16 mm Bolex camera. However, the camera was in the pawn shop. I had no experience of pawn shops, but whenever Gerrit needed to borrow money, he seemed to use those establishments. Perhaps it was a Dutch custom! Now, because there was a small but steady cash flow as a result of the TV series, it was possible for Gerrit to retrieve the camera.

Obtaining a few small tins of film from RTÉ was easy enough, and shooting a couple of short wildlife sequences did not cause Gerrit any great problems. The difficulties began when some of the cameramen in the newsroom objected to a 'pair of independent rookies' supplying programme material on film to RTÉ. One cameraman, Billy St Leger, said that *he* was quite capable of supplying any required sequences of wildlife on film. We had planned a programme about birds in the city for the following week and so we asked Billy to supply some footage of house sparrows. He had no experience of filming birds of any species or any other forms of wildlife but he set off as confident as if he were going to film a quick sequence for a news story. Later we were informed that a person was seen crawling under the seats in St Stephen's Green, throwing crumbs at sparrows that he was trying to attract close to his lens! Billy returned empty-handed, and happily we were left in peace in that regard from then on.

Being assigned a new producer who had a good deal of imagination, and who showed a real interest in what we were attempting to achieve, added excitement to the programmes. Bob Quinn allowed us to use some of the footage that Gerrit had filmed with his Bolex camera, and our hope was that we would keep increasing the amount of film sequences as we progressed. Television is such a part of everyday life now that it is impossible for younger people to imagine how it was during those early days of RTÉ. There was only one station to watch, in black-and-white, and it came on during the evenings only. It was like having a captive audience. In schools of the 1960s, nature classes or nature tables were rare. Because of this, *Amuigh Faoin Spéir* generated a great deal of interest among school teachers and children alike, and the queries we received by post were endless. The programme became so popular that people would often hum the signature tune at us in the street. Even today people tell me that when they were young, watching *Amuigh Faoin Spéir* was a ritual practised weekly in their home. Sometimes I am approached by people telling me that their interest in wildlife was as a result of watching the programme.

The contract for the early series of *Amuigh Faoin Spéir* was between RTÉ and myself but, rather than play the part of paymaster to Gerrit each week, I asked for the contract to be split evenly so that we would receive our cheques independently. In retrospect, it may not have been the best way to do business and an accountant would probably have advised against such a move, but then both of us were far from being high-flying professional businessmen. The Controller of Programmes at that time was a Scandinavian, Gunnar Rugheimer, who liked our series and saw its potential. As a result we never had a problem in being commissioned to supply more of the same. Rugheimer's word was law and he left no one in doubt as to who was in charge at RTÉ. Apart from Gerrit and myself, there were no other programme-makers operating on a completely independent basis at that time and although the recordings for the series in the early days were done at RTÉ, we were never members of the RTÉ staff. Working as independents had one disadvantage – there was no guarantee that we would be given another contract when a series came to an end.

Making a weekly TV programme and working in Hely's at the same time was becoming more difficult for me. The job was fine but the hours were from 9 am to 5.30 pm Monday to Friday, with a half-day on Saturday, and this was tying me down too much. Playing music with Ceoltóirí Chualann was mostly at weekends, which was easy enough to manage, but I knew that sooner or later I would have to make up my mind about the future. Gerrit had even said to me on one occasion, in his very pronounced Rotterdam accent, 'Éamon, when are you going to give up selling fish-hooks to Britishers?' referring, no doubt, to that long list of Anglo-Irish gentlemen who regularly favoured Hely's with their custom.

A wedding interlude

The various radio programmes I scripted and presented were enjoyable, especially ones such as *Have You This One?* and *There and Back*, where I chose traditional tunes that had been carried by emigrants to America and Canada and demonstrated how they had changed in the process. I used live musicians in the series, including Paddy Moloney, Seán Potts and Michael Tubridy. Paddy was about to take a big step in life. He had fallen in love with Rita, who worked with him in Baxendales Hardware Stores in Capel Street. Ronnie McShane, the bones player in Ceoltóirí Chualann, who was always willing to help a damsel in distress or indeed anyone else who needed assistance, had promised to arrange for a car to collect Rita on the morning of her wedding. He was at Ardmore Studios, doing some work on the set of the film *Shake Hands With the Devil*. The actor James Cagney was one of the principals in the film and a spectacular car had been imported from the US to be used by Cagney in the film. It was a very long, large, yellow-coloured Dodge automobile with a fold-back hood. Somehow or other, Ronnie managed to procure the car, complete with a driver in uniform, and arranged for it to be at Rita's parents' house on the day and at the appropriate time.

Rita, dressed in her finery, was waiting to be collected when the chauffeur drew the long yellow automobile up to the gate. Never having seen a car like it in her life, she could hardly believe her eyes. 'I'm not getting into that!' she protested. 'I want a black car. I'm not getting into it. I'm not going, that's all!' And she sat down in disgust. The driver was by this time inside the house and wondering what the fuss was about. Rita's father was, to say the least, a little confused as to what he should do next. He could hardly take off to the wedding in the yellow automobile minus his daughter. Not quite knowing what to do, he offered the driver a drink, but in attempting to open the bottle of stout, he accidentally broke it. The second attempt was equally unsuccessful and he made smithereens of another bottle. Spilt stout was now flowing all over the floor and Rita's father decided that enough was enough. Standing at the table and banging it hard with the palm of his hand, as was his fashion whenever he became upset, he called angrily, 'Madam, get into that car and go up to where that poor little bollicks is waitin' for you in the church!' Rita's father was not a man given to cursing in public but obviously he felt that there was dire need for it on that occasion.

The photographer for the wedding was also 'compliments of Ronnie McShane', and he was in complete contrast to the flashy American automobile that Ronnie had procured. Jimmy Meehan, complete with camera, arrived on a motorbike that he parked at the side of the church. As he marched up to the altar it was clearly visible to all in the congregation that the seat of the photographer's trousers was missing. Apart from all that and Rita having to call on the services of her brother because of the failure of the best man to turn up, the rest of the wedding went quite well! A group photograph taken by Jimmy Meehan at the wedding included Paddy Moloney, Rita and a few chosen friends. The photograph appears in a recent publication called *The Chieftains* and all the individuals in the picture are named, with one exception. The person entitled 'unknown' is me!

Partnership with Gerrit

Television during the 1960s was exciting and the atmosphere in RTÉ was a completely new experience for most of the people working there. Some of the talent was brought in from overseas, including a number of Irish people who had worked in television in other countries. There were plenty of opportunities for making mistakes and most of us learned from these blunders and gained valuable experience. The Director of Music in Radio Éireann, Fachtna Ó Hannracháin, who had given me my first opportunity at broadcasting, had advised me at the time to try and work from outside the station. I felt that this advice made a lot of sense and as a result it never occurred to me to apply for a full-time position at RTÉ.

When I told Laillí that I was thinking of giving up my job in Hely's she responded anxiously, 'But you can't. No, you can't leave Hely's!' Our conversation was in Irish, as always. *'Tá brón orm, Laillí, ach d'fhág mé Hely's trí lá ó shoin!'* (I'm sorry, Laillí, but I left Hely's three days ago!) I said. The situation must have sounded rather worse to Laillí than it actually was, but I knew that if my plans to concentrate on making TV programmes did not work out, I wouldn't have a problem getting back into the fishing tackle trade. I believe that at various stages during one's lifetime, opportunities arise when we are given a choice to go in either one direction or the other and the decision taken then can alter one's world forever. Here, staring me in the face, was a chance to make a complete change and it was too good to miss. Hely's were quite considerate when I said that I intended to leave the firm. Mr Brewster, one of the directors, asked me if I would consider working a shorter week. I tried it for a while but it only complicated matters. The girls in the pet department didn't approve of my decision to leave and one of them told me that I was mad to give up a pensionable job. 'What is Laillí going to do?' she asked. I was quite confident that Laillí and our children were not going to starve and that my mind was made up.

Entering into a partnership with somebody who was born and bred in another country was a completely new experience for me and quite beneficial in that I could now observe life in Ireland from a Dutchman's perspective. Gerrit Van Gelderen had been brought up in Rotterdam where his father was employed by the city's Parks Department. The family lived in an area where a variety of wildfowl could be seen. As happened to many Dutch people during the Second World War, Gerrit had been taken prisoner by the German occupying army and forced to work in a munitions factory. He was only a boy at the time and the experience was to affect him in later life in a variety of ways, most notably in his dislike of Germans. When we were awarded the Jacob's Award for *Amuigh Faoin Spéir*, I suggested that we should share the trophy by displaying it in each other's homes for a certain period and that he should have first go. After a few days he returned it to me saying that I could keep it. He had noticed that the St Brigid's cross, incorporated into the design of the trophy, threw a shadow on his wall that was a perfect representation of a Nazi swastika and he could not bear to look at it.

Gerrit Van Gelderen was a dedicated naturalist and he had worked as an illustrator in a natural history museum in Holland. He quickly became very knowledgeable about much of Ireland's wildlife. Like all naturalists, he was curious and it didn't take him long to discover most of the best areas in Ireland in which wildlife could be observed. His quirky cartoons, in which he highlighted Ireland's negligence of its wildlife and environment, were both effective and amusing. He had a loose style of sketching and painting which was eminently suited to illustrating the many aspects of wildlife he wished to portray on television. When we began adding our own film sequences into the *Amuigh Faoin Spéir* programmes, I would spend most of the day in Gerrit's rented garden flat at Conyngham Road on the banks of the River Liffey, near the Phoenix Park. There were times when the work would not be completed until the early hours of the morning.

Van Gelderen was by no means an easy person to work with. He had a short fuse and was likely to blow his top if anyone persisted in disagreeing with him. His reaction to another person's point of view could at times be quite funny and unconsciously witty. When RTÉ began transmitting religious programmes, material was supplied by a newly formed team known as *Radharc*, supported by the Catholic Church. It included a few priests under the direction of Fr Joe Dunn, a fine man, totally dedicated to filmmaking. Discussing various projects, Joe told me that he loved the work so much that he would continue to make films even if RTÉ didn't pay him anything. Gerrit and myself were in a different situation and we were constantly arguing with RTÉ about the amount being paid to us in fees. In one of our many meetings in the office of RTÉ's 'financial wizard', John Barragwaneth, we tried to impress on him the fact that the fee he was offering us was too little. Barragwaneth, whom Gerrit insisted on referring to as 'Barracuda', then suggested that the *Radharc* team were supplying programmes for a similar fee. This suggestion was of course only adding insult to injury, as far as Gerrit was concerned. 'What!' he barked at Barragwaneth. 'That's all very well but *Radharc* have a vow of poverty, and we don't!'

On another occasion when we were again discussing contracts and the miserable fee being offered, Barragwaneth handed Gerrit the contract form showing the proposed budget for each of the programmes. Gerrit looked at the sheet of paper in disbelief and then roared at John Barragwaneth: 'What you fecking think we eat, fecking grass?!!'

During that period and for a long time after that, RTÉ had this rather crazy approach where they costed their own in-house programmes without including the salaries being paid to the crew or the cost of equipment or travel. They would then compare this under-cost budget with the overall budget for a programme being submitted by us. It took many years of argument before they began to change this method of accounting.

105

Along with all the preparations involved in producing *Amuigh Faoin Spéir*, I had also to supply short topical pieces for *Newsbeat*. This involved coming up with an idea several times a week and having it illustrated with cartoon drawings. Working into the small hours at Van Gelderen's place was often the result of his taking a break in the middle of work and falling asleep in a chair by the fire. There was no arguing with an artist who was waiting for inspiration to come his way! I would sit in hope that Gerrit would soon wake up and that he would feel sufficiently inspired to put pencil or brush to paper. When eventually he did awaken, it did not necessarily mean that inspiration suddenly manifested itself. A strict routine did not really suit him, which is probably one of the reasons why he was prepared to head off at short notice to some other location here or overseas.

Eventually the Van Gelderen kitchen became too cramped for our post-production activities and it was with a sense of relief on my part that we were able to rent a basement from a Dutch artist friend of Gerrit's in Monkstown. The new location was about halfway between Dublin and Bray and not alone did it give us more space, it meant that after work Gerrit would now be just as anxious to get home as I was and hopefully we could in the future both look forward to finishing at a more reasonable hour.

Gerrit's influence in the area of conservation was considerable, and the high standard he set for aspiring wildlife artists should not be under-estimated. During that period RTÉ presented programmes that used the illustrations of another artist. The pictures were not unlike the humour represented in British seaside postcards. Van Gelderen knew that young people would copy those illustrations and he hated seeing this kind of standard being set. One young boy who used to watch *Amuigh Faoin Spéir* religiously was Killian Mullarney, now one of the best bird artists in Europe. The recent *Collins Bird Guide,* which features hundreds of Killian's paintings, won the British Trust for Ornithology's award for the 'Best Bird Guide Ever'. When Killian was a schoolboy he wrote to Gerrit telling him that he liked to draw birds but that at times he found great difficulty in drawing their feet. In his reply to Killian, Gerrit wrote, 'When I have trouble drawing birds' feet, I draw them standing in grass!'

The Wexford Slobs

If there were an award for the best bird county in Ireland, it would surely go to Wexford. The Royal Society for the Protection of Birds in Britain described the Wexford coastline as 'packed with important bird areas, a jewel for Ireland to take pride in and protect'. And according to the British Trust for Ornithology, 'The South Wexford Coast is studded with magnificent sites – not just for the Irish but in the European context.' Over 240 species of birds have been recorded in the county and some enthusiastic birdwatchers have seen and recorded as many as 100 species in a single day. Not only is the county famous for its birds, it also has very special plant species and communities. One such plant is cottonweed, which grows nowhere else in Ireland or Britain.

Wexford was our favourite county in which to film birds. There we had a choice of observing breeding bird populations in spring and summer and photographing winter migrants during autumn and winter. During the 1960s no provision had been made to safeguard the many thousands of wildfowl wintering in the Wexford area known as the North Slob, and we fought a battle royal on their behalf by regularly highlighting the problem on *Amuigh Faoin Spéir*. There was plenty of support to be had from interested birdwatchers, including that wonderful old gentleman Major Robin Ruttledge, Ireland's best-known ornithologist.

The white-fronted goose that is seen in Ireland was once thought to have been the same species as that which winters in Britain. The ornithologist, painter and broadcaster, the late Peter Scott, who was a devoted wildfowler before becoming a committed conservationist, used to shoot birds on the Wexford coast. In 1948 he and his companion C.T. Dalgety first recognised that the white-front wintering in Ireland was of the Greenland race, and not the European race, which is the goose commonly seen in Britain and which breeds in north-eastern Europe and northern Siberia. It was an important discovery, as the Greenland white-fronted goose population began to go into a steep decline during the early 1960s.

Thanks to Major Ruttledge and others, the Greenland white-fronted goose was given protection, and the Wexford Wildfowl Reserve is now flourishing, complete with a centre and high tower that caters for visitors from many parts of the world. During the winter months, the height of the season, between nine and ten thousand geese, along with many thousands of wild ducks and waders, can be observed on the Wexford Sloblands. It is also a good place to see the Irish hare; the entire area of the North Slob is the only statutory hare reserve in the country.

The attraction that Wexford held for me in the early days of wildlife filmmaking were those large flocks of white-fronted geese wintering on the Sloblands and the masses of terns nesting in spring and summer on Tern Island. The island, which disappeared in the winter storms of the mid-1970s, was located between Raven Point and Rosslare Point. It was an attractive sandy island where very large numbers of geese and waders would roost at night in safety, from autumn to early spring. Gerrit and I used to travel out to Tern Island in Peter Bent's flat-bottomed wooden boat, commonly known as a cot. Although the cot is really a river craft, it was commonly used by wildfowlers in the sheltered bay of that coastal area of Co. Wexford. Peter was a wildfowler and one of the last to use the old-fashioned punt-gun. He and his uncle Andy, a wildfowler of renown, lived along the shoreline in the area known as the Burrow. They knew every inch of the bay and, regardless of the time of year, Andy left his bedroom window open so that he could hear the calls of the wildfowl. We would leave the car near Andy's gate and sail out to the island with Peter. The flat-bottomed cot was ideally suited to the shallow sandy sea floor, clearly visible under the boat. An ordinary rowing boat has a keel and would become stuck on the sandbars in those inshore waters around Rosslare Strand.

By the end of April the wildfowl left on their journey to the far North and the island would then be taken over by about 2,500 terns arriving from Africa. All five species found in Ireland nested on Tern Island but by far the greatest number of those were roseate terns. Terns are often called 'sea swallows' because of their forked tails. They are graceful birds, with long pointed wings, pale grey mantle, white underparts and a black cap – an artist's dream and an ideal subject for the photographer and the painter.

Amuigh Faoin Spéir and a bank strike were to change one young ornithologist's direction in life forever. Oscar Merne was employed in the Bank of Ireland and came to work with us during their first strike. When the dispute came to an end, he had no wish to return to the world of high finance. Oscar was more knowledgeable about birds than either Gerrit or myself and he continued working with us for a number of years. He accompanied Gerrit on a trip to Iceland, which was an experience in itself. At one stage during the trip Oscar reprimanded Gerrit for disturbing a pair of nesting falcons and for being careless in the way in which he was attempting to film them. Gerrit blew his top and informed Oscar in no uncertain terms that he was 'fired'. Gerrit then sped off in his jeep, leaving Oscar wandering around in the Icelandic tundra, miles from anywhere or anyone! After several hours the jeep returned and Gerrit reinstated his erring young ornithologist. Filming then continued more or less as if nothing had happened. When Oscar was assisting us with the programmes featuring the North Slob, little did we think that one day he would be appointed as warden on the Wexford Wildfowl Reserve (1968–77) and that he would eventually become a Wildlife Research Officer with the National Parks and Wildlife Service.

A trip to the Azores

During the period that Gerrit Van Gelderen travelled to Iceland, my first overseas safari was to the Atlantic islands of the Azores. At Gerrit's suggestion we had begun to work more independently of each other by this time. He was never one to hide his feelings and he had recently said to me in general conversation, 'Éamon, I would make much better films if you were not involved in them!' I had already been told by Gerrit's wife that I was 'sponging on Gerrit's artistic ability'. Van Gelderen himself confirmed this opinion when I quoted to him what his wife had said: 'Well, aren't you?' I had no wish to part company with Gerrit. I felt that, whatever his shortcomings might be, the success of *Amuigh Faoin Spéir* was as a result of pooling our different talents and personalities. But now, whatever about sentiment, there were clear signals that Gerrit was becoming restless and would prefer to work on his own. On his suggestion we both began filming and editing our own programmes in the series, although I continued for a time to do the commentaries on both my and Gerrit's programmes. My sister-in-law Nóra, a talented artist, joined me as production assistant, and in the beginning I operated in a front room of my home. Gerrit and I eventually went our different ways and began making nature programmes under various titles.

In planning for the first overseas safari, I asked a soundman with whom we had done some work in the dubbing department at RTÉ if he would like to come on the Azores trip. He was quite prepared to come and was looking forward to it but his wife didn't fancy the idea and he had to turn down my offer. Pat Hayes, who also worked in the sound department, asked if he could come. I knew Pat as a shy lad who spoke mostly in short sentences; in fact he was so quiet that he was hardly noticed among the other soundmen. Apart from that, I knew that he was efficient. He seemed enthusiastic when I mentioned that I planned to record some good sound on the trip and I was happy to have him accompany me. I was also hoping that with a proper soundman we could also record some local music. When I asked Pat how he began in the sound recording business he gave me his usual short answer, 'I was the door in *The Kennedys of Castleross*!' *The Kennedys* was a long-running radio series, broadcast every day at lunch-hour. Various bits and pieces in the studio were used for sound effects in the series. One important item that was constantly in use was a small wooden door, barely big enough for a leipreachán to fit through. Whenever a character in the play entered or left the room, Pat's job was to open or close this little door, to create the proper effect. That famous door in *The Kennedys of Castleross* was Pat's entry into the fascinating world of sound.

As we prepared for our trip, we were constantly asked where we were going. Most people were puzzled at the mention of the Azores and did not seem to have the remotest idea as to where this was; others thought it had some connection with anticyclones. One person whom I didn't expect to be familiar with that part of the world was Paddy, the big, burly, ex-army man who acted as security on the main gate at RTÉ. Shortly after my return from our trip he spotted me as I came into the RTÉ building. 'Ah, there ye are, Éamon,' he greeted me. 'Haven't seen ye for a long time. Where were ye?' 'In the Azores, Paddy,' I replied. Paddy tilted back his head, looked skywards and closed his eyes, 'The Azores, the Azores...' He paused for a moment, opened his eyes and looked at me. 'Eight hundred miles west of Portugal, to whom they belong. Isn't that it?' 'You're dead right, Paddy,' I exclaimed, marvelling at both his accuracy and his ability to remember back to what was obviously a well-drilled geography lesson, written into his school copybook no doubt, way back when he was probably only ten or eleven years of age.

There are nine islands in the Azores Archipelago; the largest is São Miguel (288 sq. miles) and the smallest is Corvo (7 sq. miles). To be absolutely accurate, the nearest point on the coast of Portugal to the Azores island of São Miguel is 780 miles, so Paddy was only twenty miles out! The islands, which are volcanic, are well populated and enjoy a mild, temperate climate. Owing to the influence of the sea, the seasons begin about a month later than on the continental mainland. February is the coldest month and August is the warmest. High humidity during the warm season can be a little uncomfortable and there were some days during our trip when we would have loved to feel an Irish wind on our faces. We flew from Lisbon to the main island of São Miguel, and we had a considerable amount of trouble with both customs and security at the airport in Ponta Delgada. At that time Portugal and the Azores were under the fascist dictatorship of Antonio de Oliveira Salazar. The islands were agriculturally based, with the heavy work being shared between men and women. The farmers did not own the land. They were mostly tenants, paying rent to absentee landlords as well as to the government in Lisbon. The islanders were not allowed to leave or travel from one island to another without a government permit. I couldn't help but wonder what it would be like if our own Aran Islanders had to have a special permit before they were allowed leave their home to visit Galway!

It is all very different now, of course, in the Azores, since the bloodless revolution in Portugal put an end to the dictatorship. Today, the people of the Azores can come and go as they please. But we were two days trying to get through security and not having much success. To make matters worse, at no time was it made clear to us what the problem was. Eventually I got so fed up I said that I wished to talk to Antonio de Oliveira Salazar and to please get him for me on the phone. I didn't think there was the slightest chance that Salazar would be available but the security people looked at me in a strange kind of a way and then, without any explanation, decided to allow us through!

The best-known naturalist in the Azores was Colonel José Agostinho, with whom I had been in correspondence in preparation for the trip and who was of great assistance in advising us when and where we should visit. The colonel had a special interest in birds and made several important discoveries regarding the birds of the Azores, especially on the Island of Terceira, where he lived. He advised us to first visit Sete Cidades on São Miguel, as we would be flying from Portugal directly to the island. Sete Cidades was pretty remote during the 1960s, and the journey on untarred dirt tracks leading up to the plateau and then down to a crater lake was rather bumpy. The lake was our destination. This was set in a beautiful area surrounded by mountains covered in trees. Japanese red cedar and acacia grew on the plateau, and on the lower slopes there were masses of shrubs such as myrtle and pittosporum. These provided plenty of cover for small nesting birds.

On arrival at the lake we saw women in black shawls kneeling on rocks at the edge of the lake, scrubbing large white sheets. A number of sheets that were already washed lay drying on grassy areas along the shoreline. The women who had finished the work were making their way back home, barefooted, each one carrying a huge white bundle on her head. Now and again a farmer carrying a long stick would arrive, driving his herd of cattle to the water. There was a mad tussle whenever bulls from two different herds happened to meet, head-butting one another in the water, their bellowing and snorting adding to the shouts of the herdsmen. Eventually they would be separated and the latest arrivals were left in peace to enjoy their fill of badly needed fresh lakewater.

The wooden house we were given under the trees at the edge of the lake in Sete Cidades was an ideal location from which to observe the various activities around the water's edge. Soon after the women had gone home and the men had driven away their cattle, the air became still and the atmosphere changed. It all seemed to be in preparation for the evening performance of the lake's own natural orchestra. The introduction of a very different set of sounds was gradual at first, as if in an overture, with one or two members of the orchestra making their own distinct musical contributions. The second movement was by the flute section and was completely taken over by the birds, as dozens of canaries performed from the seclusion of the trees. It was our first time to see wild canaries and, unlike most of the pet canaries we had seen back home in aviaries or in cages, the wild ones are green. The famous British ornithologist W.R. Oglivie-Grant visited the Azores on behalf of the London Museum and in describing the canaries in his report wrote:

> They are bright, lively birds, always on the move, the males constantly chasing one another or their mates, and singing their delightful varied song both when at rest and on the wing. With greatly distended throat and measured emphatic beats of the wings they pass like larks slowly overhead, singing with all their might, and so puffed up with self-importance that they appear twice their normal size.

Following on from the overture, the rest of the arrangement went a little astray as the whole valley began to echo to a crescendo from some of the less musical members of the orchestra. Hundreds of croaking edible frogs had raised their heads from below the surface of the lake and joined forces to almost drown out the voices of their avian neighbours. Pat Hayes of course was in his element, recording many minutes of their mating calls, as the male frogs fought with their companions in their attempt to win female attention. Having ears and eyes for sound only, Pat was very happy with the whole performance! The edible frog is bigger and greener than our own common frog and the plump hind legs are the edible part; these I'm sure are quite tasty, but neither of us was interested in considering them as part of some future menu.

Of the nine islands in the Archipelago, we were fortunate in being able to land on seven. Having flown from São Miguel to Terceira, we travelled by boat to the other islands. The island of Faial with its population of 15,000 people is known as the Blue Island because of its numerous fields being divided with colourful hydrangea bushes. We took a launch out of Faial to film the whaling activity. The whales were hunted by men in open boats, using hand harpoons. It was a very dramatic and highly dangerous business, with fishermen in small boats hanging on for hours to a huge marine animal at the end of a rope. In its fight for life, the monstrous sperm whale would set off at speed, dragging with it the boat and its excited crew. Its prolonged struggles to reach greater depths in the safety of the ocean were usually in vain. I am glad to say that all forms of killing whales are now prohibited in the Azores. The whales are attracting visitors to the islands who are far more interested in observing and photographing those wonderful creatures than seeing them being killed. The local tourist board has been quick to realise that this is benefiting the local economy, as has happened in many other areas of wildlife around the world.

When we eventually landed on Terceira we met our adviser, Colonel José Agostinho, and he arranged that we be brought into the mountains where they were rounding up the wild bulls. Although television in Ireland was still transmitting in black and white, I had brought some extra rolls of 16 mm Kodak 16 ASA colour film with me in hopes that programmes in colour were soon to be a reality. It was in the mountains of Terceira that we were able to capture our first colour sequences. The bull-herds, who wore wide-brimmed black hats, were superb horsemen and looked quite dramatic. As they spent long hours in the saddle, these riders favoured a long stirrup. The part of the stirrup that held the horseman's sandled foot was made of wood and was box-like to protect the rider from having his limbs crushed as he rode between the animals.

There has been a very long relationship in the Azores between the islanders and their wild cattle. They have a form of bullfighting, but, unlike the bullfights in Spain, the animals are not killed. The bull's horns are padded and it is then let loose in the streets. 'Bullfighting on a Rope', or *Mascardos da Corda* (Masked Men of the Rope), as it used to be called, is an exciting but crazy occupation. The bull, held on a rope by a group of men, can hardly be described as being under control as it chases who-ever happens to be unlucky enough to be in its path. If the bull happens to turn, which it is quite likely to do, the men let go of the rope and jump over the nearest wall. Padded horns are no protection against serious injury and casualties are not unusual. Some bravadoes practise a game called 'Parasol Luck' which consists of putting up an umbrella in front of the bull and attempting to avoid its horns in the subsequent charge.

Terceira's position on the main trade route to South America meant that invasion from many quarters was common. The island's coastline with its many natural harbours resulted in its being very difficult to defend. The struggles against the Spanish occupation between 1581 and 1583 were catastrophic, especially for Angra do Heroismo, the capital of Terceira. The town was sacked by Spanish soldiers and many of its leading citizens executed. After their raid on Angra at the beginning of

July in 1581, a Spanish fleet of ten ships sailed around the coast and anchored in Salga Bay on 25 July in the same year. They bombarded the coast with their artillery, creating a very difficult situation for the defenders. Friar Pedro, an Augustinian who was involved in the fighting, thought of driving wild cattle against the Spanish troops in order to scatter them. Word was sent out to the men to round up the animals as quickly as possible. Over a thousand head of wild cattle were herded and driven down the mountainsides, amid shouts and musket shots, scattering the terrified Spaniards who fell back to the shoreline. Those who didn't lose their lives in the stampede and the fighting were drowned as they tried to reach their ships. We were several hundred years too late to photograph the battle but we did succeed in capturing sequences on film of the colourful herdsmen rounding up the wild bulls as they careered down the mountainside!

Choosing the Azores for my first safari trip was a good choice and it would be over thirty years before I had the opportunity to return with a film crew to film on the Island of Terceira.

9

Recording Our Heritage
1960s

Conamara again – Salvaging the Galway Hooker – At home
in Conamara – The Blaskets – Herons at Russborough House –
Exploring the ocean floor – Ó Riada, the film director

Conamara again

By now I had invested in a Volkswagen minibus for carrying around my
film equipment. Sid Neff, a friend from my early angling days, now
employed in the graphics department of RTÉ, designed an impressive
Amuigh Faoin Spéir logo. I was ready for off! Travelling to Conamara in
the minibus was a change from those hitch-hiking days, when Diarmuid
Breathnach and I would set off on long weekends, first catching a bus to
Lucan and waiting there for some kind driver to pick us up. Apart from
the filming, Conamara was also an ideal place to bring the children on
holidays. There was a choice of safe beaches, and the language spoken by
our children at home was much the same as the dialect of the local
children in the village; there were no communication problems at any
stage. Half a century later and the children still love to visit that same
area and bring their own children with them.

Away back in the 1950s, I had been attracted to Conamara by the
music, the song and of course the people, but I did not know that I would
be returning a decade later to film a way of life that was fast disappearing.
I spent a lot of time in areas such as Caorán Beag, just outside the village
of An Cheathrú Rua, where corn and hay were grown in small fields surrounded by miles of loose stone walls, so typical of much of Conamara.
At the end of summer, the crops were cut by hand with a *corrán* or hand-
sickle. *Súgán* ropes were fashioned out of handfuls of hay. One person

would turn the hay rope with a *corrán* while another kept adding more material to it from the pile of hay at his feet. Meanwhile, as the man with the *corrán* kept walking backwards, the length of the rope increased. The song 'Casadh an tSúgáin' is related to this craft. In the song, the old woman gets the young man proposing to her daughter out of the house by having him hold the *corrán* and walk backwards until he walks out the door and she locks it behind him!

As one wandered along the Conamara shoreline, canvas-covered, canoe-like craft known as currachs were to be seen in every bay. They were coated in black tar and some were lying bottom-up against the stone walls, waiting to be launched. They reminded me of long, shiny, over-sized beetles. The Irish word *curach* means 'unsteady', which is how the craft might seem to the inexperienced, but in the hands of oarsmen in Conamara or Aran, they can be manoeuvred with incredible skill. For those western people, the currach was the most useful and versatile of all the various craft used around the Conamara coast. It could be carried on the shoulders of a three-man crew at short notice, to or from the water's edge. Not alone was the currach used for laying lobster pots and fishing, it was also useful for transporting a cart-load of turf or seaweed. If you lived on one of the many offshore islands and you wanted to buy a box of matches or a pound of sugar, the currach was your only means of getting over to the mainland.

The first time I went to film the locals in Caorán Beag, they were quite hesitant about having their pictures taken as they were not sure how I might portray them, but after they had seen themselves on screen, they could not do enough for me. Pádraic Ó Cualáin, or Pat as he was better known, was the local man with whom I became most friendly. He was prepared to take part in any film sequence I wished to arrange. This might involve the launching of a currach in order to go out and cut seaweed with a long-handled sickle, or beating a sheaf of oats with a flail, to show how they did it before the threshing engine arrived in that part of the country. Stiofán Jackie, a relative of Pat's, lived in the cottage next door. Stiofán didn't speak English but he had beautiful Irish and he always looked forward to taking part in any activity I wished to include in a film. When I asked him if he had enjoyed any of the programmes, he said that he had never seen a film of any kind, not even the ones in which

117

he himself had taken part but that he liked nothing better than to be 'out taking pictures'!

In those days the traditional working boats, known as Galway hookers, were making daily runs to the Aran Islands with their loads of turf or peat. Up to and during the 1940s, everything that was available for purchase in Conamara had been transported around the coast by those dramatic-looking craft. There was no proper road system and the general supplies for the traders were carried by the hookers. The men who sailed them depended completely on wind and sails to get them to and from their destination, and they had to know the coastline like the back of their hands. Turf was the most widely used fuel in Conamara for centuries and the hookers were used to transport it across the bay to places where it wasn't available – limestone areas such as the Aran Islands, Ballyvaughan in Co. Clare and Kinvara in Co. Galway. The first boat to arrive at a pier could usually command the best price and as a result, competition was intense, with the hookers regularly racing each other across the bay. When the boats were pulled up at the pier during times of low tide, some of the boatmen would apply butter to the hull of their craft in order to make the boats travel faster. Johnny Bailey told me about a particular day when they were bringing turf to Aran: 'One day when I was a lad, my father and I were in the mouth of Casla Bay. It was a calm day; we had put butter on the boat and she was loaded up. I looked under the rudder and I saw this huge thing licking the butter off the boat. I had never seen a basking shark before. My father was under the deck getting a cup of tea and I ran and told him a big fish was eating his boat!'

During the 1950s other fuel supplies were introduced to the different areas and the demand for turf began to wane. Bottled Kosangas was brought by the larger ferries to Aran, where it became known locally as 'cosy gas'! These new fuels eventually led to turf becoming redundant altogether.

Watching the last of those Galway hookers operating out of An Cheathrú Rua, one could sense the end of yet another chapter in our history. The best known of those boats was Mike O'Brien's *Tónaí*, which carried turf from Sruthán pier; and another was Johnny Jimmy Phaitín MacDonnacha's *An Mhaighdean Mhara*, which worked out of Caladh Thaidhg. Johnny Bailey's famous hooker *An Capall* stopped trading out of Rosaveal in 1959. Although they were among the last of the boats carrying turf, the remains of many more in various stages of decay were to be seen abandoned in different locations along the shoreline. Some of the hookers were bought and refurbished by interested people living in other parts of the country, but sadly most of the old boats were left to sink into oblivion where they lay close to the shoreline. The scene I was filming during the 1960s was the beginning of the end of the Galway hookers' turf trade. By 1972, the working life of the Galway hooker and all that went with those activities was over, or so it seemed.

Salvaging the Galway hooker

An old boat that had been lying on the shoreline in Greatman's Bay in Conamara was bought during the 1960s by Denis Aylmer and brought to Dublin. The boat was subsequently sold and then left lying for five years in the Board of Works yard in Dún Laoghaire. A Dublin man, Johnny Healion, who had spent his holidays camping in Conamara when he was a young lad, had often gone sailing with the hookermen and had grown to love their boats. Johnny was deeply impressed by the sailing skills of Johnny Jimmy Phaitín and Mike O'Brien. He had never forgotten the sight of those large, dark sailing boats coming across the bay towards Caladh Thaidhg or Sruthán: 'The hooker would race in at high speed towards the harbour. As it approached the pier, it would miraculously glide into the landing, so smoothly, the skipper could literally stop her by just pushing his finger against the pier wall.' Many years later, Johnny Healion wanted to buy a hooker but couldn't find one anywhere in Conamara. In 1975, he discovered *The Morning Star*, lying apparently abandoned in the yard of the now Office of Public Works. Having made some enquiries, and finding that the boat was for sale, he bought her. She was in poor shape and it took him many months of work to refurbish the boat. Unlike some of the old hookers that were brought from the west and converted into yachts, Johnny kept to the original traditional shape of her quarter deck and open hull. By the time he had completed the work, *The Morning Star* was glistening in several coats of paint, complete with new rig and tan-coloured terylene sails. She looked like a brand new traditional Galway hooker. The hooker was brought by road to Carna in

Conamara the following year, to take part in the Festival of Naomh Mac Dara, an annual event to honour the local saint and in which traditional boats took part. There was huge interest by the local people in the return of the beautifully restored *Morning Star*, which incidentally won the main race at the Festival that year.

And so commenced the revival of the traditional West of Ireland boats. Johnny Healion had set an example that others were to follow and the movement then spread to Dublin. The bare hull of the 31-foot hooker *St John* was brought back from Strangford Loch by Johnny Healion's brother-in-law, Mick Hunt. The *St John* was also beautifully refurbished. The founding of The Galway Hooker Association in 1978 resulted in a restoration programme being put in place. This was followed the next year by several regattas being held around the Conamara coast. More refurbished boats appeared, including *The American Mór* and *An Mhaighdean Mhara*. A little fellow who came sailing with me during the 1960s, on what I was sure would be the last of the old boats, now has his own Galway hooker. It is *The Star of the West*, and was newly built by Johnny Healion in 1994 for our youngest son Cian!

The revival of the West of Ireland work-boats is a perfect example of keeping an old tradition alive and bringing it into the present century. But there was far more to it than refurbishing the boats. A whole vocabulary of sailing terminology in the Irish language was also kept alive. It is all part of our history in an ever-changing Ireland.

A reminder of Conamara's rich maritime tradition can be seen across from the village of An Cheathrú Rua. Standing alone at the entrance to Cuan Casla and overlooking the bay are the remains of a well-preserved coastal battery. The history of seafaring Conamara is really the history of Conamara itself, and the battery dates from a period when the English, fearful of a French landing on the coast during the nineteenth century, used the experienced Conamara seamen as guides to build a whole series of coastal batteries. The structures were also used to keep an eye on the coastal smuggler families trading out of a whole series of sheltered harbours on the south Conamara coast. They included the O'Malleys from An Cheathrú Rua, the Comerfords from Leitir Mealáin, the McDonaghs from Roundstone and the O'Malleys from Cleggan. Those families traded with France and imported sherry from Cadiz. The building of the batteries gradually put an end to the coastal traffic and the rich trade that had previously brought wealth and prosperity to the South Conamara coast.

At home in Conamara

Long before I had ever visited the west, Lailli's father Charles Lamb had been recording those boats in his paintings. During his student years, Lamb mixed in a group that included the writer Pádraic Ó Conaire. Ó Conaire encouraged him to go and observe the people of Conamara and to experience the wonderful light and scenery in that part of the country. Lamb took Ó Conaire's advice and paid a visit to Conamara. Shortly after that he went to live there and settled in Conamara for the rest of his life. His many paintings of Galway hookers include scenes of some of the boats being loaded with turf at a pier and others under sail. His work is a very important historical record of Conamara and its people from the 1920s to the 1950s.

Lailli's mother, Katherine, looked forward to seeing her children and their families and she was always happy to see our lot arriving for the summer holidays. Being on her own in the west must have been extremely lonely for Katherine, especially since the death of her husband in 1964. She had met Charles Lamb at an exhibition of his paintings at St Stephen's Green in Dublin, where she had been introduced to him by a friend. They married and Katherine went with him to the Conamara Gaeltacht. She practised as a veterinary surgeon in An Cheathrú Rua until she started a family. Katherine learned to speak Irish when she was forty and insisted on speaking it to her Gaeltacht neighbours. Charles and Katharine Lamb had five children, John, Peadar, Mary, Lailli and her twin sister Tina, who died when she was twelve years of age. All the children spoke Irish fluently.

Charles Lamb RHA was one of the first twelve academicians of the new Ulster Academy of Arts. The National Gallery, recognising his importance, featured one of the Lamb paintings on the front cover of their recent book *Discover Irish Art*. Also, he was the only painter to settle in Conamara during the 1930s and 1940s, where he documented in his paintings much of the social history of the countryside.

The black-and-white film sequences I took in the west during the 1960s were usually captured during the holidays. Lailí and the children would sometimes join me and we would all sail for a day or two to the Aran Islands on one of the Galway hookers. This was the only method of travelling straight across from Conamara, although one could take the much longer route by travelling on the passenger ferry from Galway. The one disadvantage of sailing in these boats was that if the wind dropped, it could take forever to reach your destination as the boat did not have an engine. This happened only on a few occasions, when we were suddenly becalmed on our way back from Aran. On those never-to-be-forgotten trips, we didn't succeed in reaching the shore until the early hours of the following morning.

The Blaskets

Other islands around the coast were also featured in our programmes. One of the great adventures of the early *Amuigh Faoin Spéir* series that I filmed happened on the Great Blasket, just off the Kerry coast. We had gone to cover the final week of a month-long sea-safari named *Operation Seafarer*, which involved a group of British and Irish ornithologists joining together to count the birds on the various islands off the Kerry coast. We had just taken five British ornithologists off the lighthouse rock known as the Tíreacht. They had been on the island for a number of days and, as they were almost completely out of supplies, had hoped to go shopping on the mainland the next day. The boatman said it was a bit late in the day and decided instead to land the group on the Great Blasket where they could camp for the night. He promised that we would all be picked up the following morning.

After an uneventful night on the island, we dismantled our tents at daybreak, packed up our equipment and waited for the boatman to come back from Portmagee, which is further around the coast. There was no sign of the boat and on day two we were still on the island waiting to be collected. One of the birdmen was Oscar Merne, who had previously worked with us, and he had brought along his wife Margaret and baby for a day-trip. They were expecting to spend just one night on an island and then return to the mainland. The baby had been born in March and

Ceoltóirí Laighean in 1972 at the launch of The Crooked Road *and at a concert outside Cologne Cathedral in 1976*

Ceoltóirí Chualann in the group's very last appearance. It was the Carolan Tercentenary Concert at the City Hall, Cork, on 28 June 1970. Ronnie McShane is not included as he was in London. Sonnie Brogan is also missing as he died in 1965.

A photo I took myself of Seán Ó Riada at one of Ceoltóirí Chualann's rehearsals

Our son, Cian, with Ned Maguire on the Dargle

Dick Harris on White Lake, Co. Meath, in the 1970s

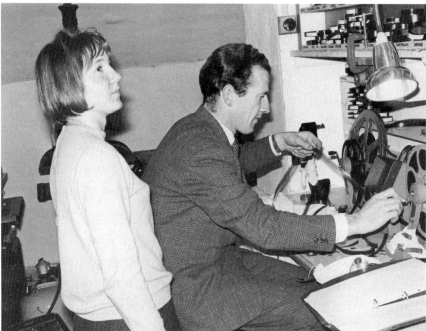

Outdoor and indoors. Filming hen harriers in Wicklow (above) and with Susan Brewster in the Amuigh Faoin Spéir *cutting room*

With Pat Hayes on the coral beach at An Cheathrú Rua

Ned Maguire fishing the River Suir

Sid Neff with Ned Maguire

Filming on the Dargle for Amuigh Faoin Spéir,
with Nóra de Buitléar and Pat Hayes

At work overseas: filming children for our series, high in the mountains of Lesotho (above) and in the Sinai for a programme on the Red Sea

this was July, so the little fellow was quite small. Luckily Oscar's wife was breast-feeding her baby and he was actually fed better than the rest of us. If she hadn't been feeding him in this way, things could have been very serious indeed. Oscar ended up opening a couple of tins of baby food to supplement the meagre remains of their own food box. Although we had plenty of food to last us for a few weeks, we shared it with the English birdmen who had run very short of supplies. The group had hoped to check out the Great Blasket Island for Manx shearwater and storm petrels and then go back to the mainland and stock up with supplies and move on to one of the other Blasket Islands, where they had planned to do a detailed survey.

On the day we landed on the Great Blasket, the artist Maria Simmonds-Gooding was working at her paintings and had been on the island for a number of days. Maria was a regular visitor to the Blaskets, including Inis Icealáin and Inis Tuaisceart. The fact that the islands were uninhabited did not seem to worry Maria, who had even persuaded some of the Dún Chaoin men to teach her how to snare rabbits so that she would not go short of food whenever she went camping. They knew Maria, as she lived over in Dún Chaoin, but they could never get used to this tall, slender, faired-haired woman spending days alone on the island with only her dachshund for company. Everyone knew that the fairy people inhabited those islands and that the ghost of a strange calf had been seen several times on Inis Icealáin. Maria swears to have seen this calf herself on one occasion!

Maria had arranged for a *naomhóg* (the local name for currach) to pick her up the following day. The Dún Chaoin men, being highly dependable, would arrive without fail unless there was a fog and would be at the island's little pier at the pre-arranged time. Day three was a Saturday and Maria and her dog had already gone off in the *naomhóg*, and as there was still no sign of our boat arriving everyone was becoming anxious. It is so convenient now with mobile phones, but we had to do with lighting fires on the high point of the island, hoping that somebody would realise that the smoke was a distress signal. We shook napkins and waved coats at anything that went up or down the Sound. Nobody paid the slightest attention to our efforts. They seemed to think that we were just enjoying ourselves. On the fifth day a *naomhóg* carrying two passengers came across the Sound in the direction of the island and landed at the pier just below us. An English doctor and his wife who often visited the Blaskets had come to spend a camping holiday on the island. We looked hungrily at their food supplies and they offered us loaves of bread and cheese. Just before they landed, a small Shell tanker happened to pass up the Sound and again we waved and shouted and to our surprise it blew its horn. We had no way of knowing if the ship's response was another 'Nice Sunday morning, boys!' or 'Message received!' Meanwhile soundman Pat Hayes offered to go back with the *naomhóg* men after the doctor and his wife had come ashore, to see if he could organise some other boat to take the birdmen, ourselves and the equipment off the island.

The tanker's skipper had in fact alerted the Valentia Lifeboat after realising that we must have been in some kind of trouble. The *naomhóg* in which Pat had gone off was only halfway across the Sound when we saw the lifeboat steaming towards us. Pat hailed them before they reached us and the lifeboat made a temporary stop as he was taken aboard. By now the wind was beginning to freshen and as soon as the lifeboat reached the pier, the lifeboatmen got us off the island as quickly as possible. Once on board, a feed of meat and hot soup did wonders for us. We were barely on our way when the boat that had originally left us on the Great Blasket the previous Tuesday could now be seen heading at speed in our direction. They had heard the call to Valentia and decided, in their own interest, that they had better collect us. Our adventure naturally received some publicity and the boat that had left us marooned on the Blaskets lost its licence shortly after that episode. An amusing headline appeared in one of the newspapers the following day. It said: 'Man rescued at sea after drifting in a currach for five days.' This was in reference, no doubt, to Pat Hayes, who had not been long enough in the *naomhóg* to have even reached the other side of the Blasket Sound!

Filming around the countryside for the various programmes was only part of the work. When all the material was eventually brought home it was processed and then shot-listed before being edited. A commentary script was written and recorded for each programme, and all the necessary sound effects added. I was beginning to run out of space as there were other projects that would not be possible to develop without having some extra room. I had arranged with a firm in Shannon who built good quality cedar houses to erect one at the bottom of my garden, which I could convert into a studio. The cedar building was originally designed to include three rooms, but I told the suppliers not to include the rooms as I needed to have a generous amount of open area available. By now, Pat Hayes had left RTÉ and had come to work for me full-time. There was no limit to his ideas as to how we might set up a sound-desk in the new building. Hayes had recently got married to Rosemary, who informed me that a large percentage of their overseas honeymoon had been spent by Pat sitting on a bar stool, complete with pencil and sketch-pad, designing a sound-desk for my studio!

The character I had created for radio in 1961, Lúidín Mac Lú Leipreachán, was about to become a television star. My sister-in-law Nóra designed a whole series of drawings of the various characters, which were to be used as cut-outs. Pat built a simple animation table and fixed up a Bolex camera in an overhead position to film the actions of the characters, frame by frame. Animation work is painstaking and a minute of a character's movements can take a whole day. By modern standards, it was a very simple set-up and having some of the characters minus their legs saved us filming a lot of extra movements! There was quite an amount of experimentation and I took on the task of imitating the voices of the different animals. Paddy Moloney played whistles and pipes for each of the programmes, but in comparison to what we had done on radio, there was a great improvement in the quality of the arrangements. Pat could now mix sections of whistle music with the sound of the pipes by back-tracking and we used Paddy's talents to far greater advantage. We could not have done this when we were on radio, as the programmes at that time were going out live. Some of the pieces of music we recorded were in later years to form the basis for arrangements that Paddy prepared for his own group The Chieftains.

Herons at Russborough House

Life was fairly hectic as a result of the busy schedule but it was really enjoyable spending so much time in the countryside surrounded by wildlife. I had discovered a colony of nesting herons at Russborough House near Blessington in Co. Wicklow. I had seen the stork-like birds from the road the previous year and decided to go in before the nesting season and ask for permission to film them. The estate was owned by Sir Alfred Beit and he was very interested to hear that someone was at the front door seeking permission to film his herons. He came down with me to the small lake where the birds had their nests about twenty-five feet up in the topmost branches of the trees. It was an unusual choice of location for the herons as they normally go for the highest trees they can find, and there were plenty of those a short distance from the lake. There was very little disturbance at Russborough House in the late 1960s and the herons felt quite safe in their present location close to their fishing grounds. I explained to Sir Alfred that in order to get on a level with the nests, we would have to construct a platform on some scaffolding and thus erect a proper hide in preparation for the coming season. He thought it a great idea and seemed quite excited about the project.

My friend Peadar Mercier was working in Cramptons, the builders' providers at Ballsbridge in Dublin, and he was able to organise a lorry-load of scaffolding for the bird-hide. Pat and myself spent a day assembling our miniature skyscraper in a position where we would have a good over-view of the colony. The season moved on and the herons began building by adding to the previous year's untidy nests of branches and sticks, which they then lined with twigs and bits of dead grass. The males were carrying most if not all of the deliveries, while the females remained building at the nest. They had become quite accustomed to the unusual structure close-by, which was my reason for putting it up so far in advance of the nesting season.

Whenever I approached the hide I made sure that Pat accompanied me. It was important that we would be in view of the birds and that they would see us approaching and climbing right up to the hide. The adult birds would take off as we came across the field and would then watch us from a distance. When I was safely inside the hide and had the camera equipment properly set up, Pat would then climb down and leave the location. Luckily birds cannot count, and the herons, seeing that the intruder had gone off, and forgetting about the one inside the hide, observed that it was now safe for them to return! By following this pro-cedure every time and remaining absolutely quiet once I was inside the hide, there was little danger that the birds would be disturbed.

We did not wish to run the risk of disturbing the birds while they were at the egg stage, as they would be far more likely to desert the nest before the chicks arrived. We therefore decided to allow the herons to get on with the work of incubation, which would take about twenty-five days. It would be another fifty days or so before the young herons would be ready to fly.

We returned after a few weeks, mainly to see how the birds were progressing but also with the hope that we might be able to capture a sequence of the adults feeding the chicks. Before making our approach to the heronry, I looked through my binoculars to see how much activity there might be, but I could see none. I said to Pat that it was unlikely all the birds would be absent at the same time. When we got closer to the nesting area it was clear that disaster had struck! There was no sign of any herons or chicks in the colony. All the nests were empty! While trying to figure out what had gone wrong, I glanced towards the high beeches on a hillock a short distance from the lake. On the very tops of the trees I could see the silhouettes of five or six herons against the sky. They had obviously been frightened by something or someone and had decided to move residence. There were signs that some of the herons had already made an attempt at building new nests, in what they obviously regarded as a safer location. The birds would only act in this way if they had been disturbed, but what had alarmed them so much that they had all deserted their traditional nesting site?

It took me a while to discover the cause of their panic. After some discreet enquiries, the trail led me to none other than the 'Lord of the Manor' himself. It seemed that Sir Alfred liked to surprise his friends by showing them something extra special whenever they came on a visit. What could be more exciting than a peek at the colony of herons? Sir Alfred's friends were encouraged to go climbing up into the hide to see what they could see! Being obviously inexperienced in field-craft and having no idea of how to approach nesting herons in the wild, their careless curiosity had eventually caused the birds to abandon their nests. And put an end to my heron safari at Russborough!

Exploring the ocean floor

The small budgets given to us made it absolutely impossible to make the kind of wildlife programmes that were being seen on British channels.

One way in which we tried to match that excitement was by finding unusual places in which to film. The ocean floor was one such place, surrounded by mystery and legends where exotic creatures lived in deep and dangerous waters! The waters around Ireland's coast provide habitats for a whole range of interesting wildlife. Yet they had remained almost forgotten.

Advances in diving equipment meant that we could soon start thinking about exploring this strange world of otters, dolphins and seals and hopefully capture on film some of the exciting habitats in which these animals lived. I knew that if we were to have any success in filming marine life we would require plenty of experience. In the 1960s, Dr Brendan Keegan of University College Galway was one of a small band of divers studying marine life on the sea floor. We were fortunate in being able to spend a lot of time with the UCG team, testing the equipment and refining our skills.

Every day we went out, we were going out somewhere that seemingly nobody had been before. We had a little bit of local lore, perhaps a small piece of information from a local fisherman, but only from the point of view of looking at the sea floor as it was and the things that were on and in it. Every day was a great adventure and at the end of three or four years we had amassed an amazing amount of information, and people are still using that information today. Nobody had formally surveyed the west coast of Ireland in the Galway Bay area; and in Cill Chiaráin in particular, with its inlets and sub-bays, it produced a wealth of information.

Ó Riada, the film director

During the 1960s Ceoltóirí Chualann also made their appearance on television in glorious black and white. The title of the series was *Aililiú* and it showed Seán Ó Riada and the musicians playing on stage, as well as various activities in the countryside. Ó Riada had bought himself a small Bell & Howell 16 mm mute film camera, and when he negotiated with Teilifís Éireann to make a series that was to feature Ceoltóirí Chualann, he insisted that only his film footage should be used in the programmes. This was irrespective of the fact that he had no experience of filmmaking! A day or two after one of the programmes was transmitted, a letter appeared in the *Evening Herald*, headed 'Pig chase' and it went as follows:

Sir, All those who viewed *Aililiú* on Teilifís Éireann at 7.15 p.m. on the 4th inst., must have been revolted at the disgusting scene of juvenile barbarity depicted, to the loud accompaniment of a band vigorously playing Irish airs. We were shown a boy of about ten years of age chasing a young pig round a field to the point of exhaustion, brutally kicking it whenever he comes within range. When he catches the little pig, after the latter is tired out, he proceeds to swing out of his ears and tail and in other ways persecute it with a savagery amazing on the part of so young a boy.

As an example of youthful sadism it is a brutal success, but what is the purpose of it? Is it a demonstration to foreigners of the 'kindly relationship' of the Irish child to 'the gintleman who pays the rint'? Eventually the boy falls down himself, exhausted after his 'blood-letting' at the pig's expense and a dog comes on the scene but acts more like a Christian than the youthful human. Exhausted also by now, the band also collapses and the curtain falls. What cultural entertainment, to be sure! – Yours, etc.

The part of the programme that seemed to have upset the letter-writer so much was a sequence of Alastair, Seán Ó Riada's young son, playing with his pet pig and chasing it around his back garden. Alastair ran after the little pig and gave it a kick in the backside whenever he caught up with it! The sequence was to the accompaniment of a jig called 'The Gander at the Pratie-Hole', a tune that has a very definite beat and probably helped to emphasise the kicks. We were seen on stage playing the tune in the studio, before and after that particular episode. It was not very well filmed and 'the kicking of the pig' piece probably looked a lot worse than it was in reality. While understanding the letter-writer's annoyance, I doubt if Alastair's pet pig suffered very much, if at all.

I can honestly say that the only time I ever felt Seán Ó Riada was not happy to see me was when I arrived in Cúil Aodha on an afternoon when he was in the process of shooting a film. I had called to his house and was directed to where I was told he was on a neighbour's land, '*ag scannánaíocht'* (filming). I drove down a short distance and pulled up on the roadway beside a field where he was shooting a number of scenes. Having got out of the car I received a fairly lukewarm greeting, and I could see that Seán was in no mood to welcome me. I would not have intruded had I known he was filming, but in any case, as I had brought both my mother and my father along and we had driven a long way, I had no wish to delay.

The whole setting that day was dreamlike as well as amusing. Ó Riada was in the middle of a small field, dressed in his best suit and wearing a pair of sunglasses. The atmosphere he was creating was quite glamorous and Ó Riada seemed to be almost imagining himself as a Hollywood director. As I got back into my car I could hear him call out 'Roll the camera'. This must have been a command to himself, as he was also sup-posed to be the cameraman! A young Kerry lad who was acting as an assistant immediately shouted 'Shot five, take one!' and clapped a board. This would be the normal procedure when sound and pictures are being synchronised, but the camera was mute and incapable of taking any sound and there was no recording machine or soundman in sight. I don't think anyone ever saw the finished film and therefore I cannot comment on the quality of the final product, but Seán Ó Riada's approach to the activities in Cúil Aodha that day certainly added a real touch of class to the whole operation!

Ó Riada had read a lot about Hollywood and his intention was to make spectacular films in Cúil Aodha at some time in the future. As one who never believed in starting at the bottom, Seán had already procured a high chair where he could be bodily elevated above whatever scene he might wish to shoot. It was an iron chair made for him by a local black-smith. On the back of the seat he had inscribed *Director*. Apart from the various black-and-white filmed inserts used in the *Aililiú* TV series, I did not see any other films that Seán may have made, although there were days when I knew he was 'on location' in and around Cúil Aodha. He did seriously consider the film business for a while and even invited Ronnie McShane, the bones player, to go and live in Cúil Aodha and assist him in setting up a studio. A company was formed which was named Draighean (Irish for blackthorn) Films, and there were plans at the time for a war film where Ó Riada would use archival footage of scenes from the Battle of the Somme and intersperse them with film footage taken by himself in the West Cork countryside. He used Ronnie as one of the actors and also invited another member of Ceoltóirí Chualann, Martin Fay, to take part. The location for the battlefield was across the road from the Ó Riada residence, where Seán sought permission from his neighbour to dig out a ditch. Uniforms, helmets and rifles were borrowed from the local unit of the FCA, the voluntary defence force. In one of the scenes, Ronnie McShane was instructed to sit out in the middle of the field by a campfire, and fry some sausages. The one and only member of the attacking forces, Martin Fay, was given orders by Ó Riada to crawl up along the ditch and fire at Ronnie. The scene was quite hilarious, with Ronnie dropping the frying pan in the fire and promptly taking off across the fields! There was no budget available for hiring garments and therefore the only difference in the uniforms being worn by the members of the opposing armies, namely Fay and McShane, was that they wore different hats!

That was probably the only time that the high chair was used by Seán, after which the unwieldy piece of equipment was abandoned and could be seen lying unused in the Ó Riada garden. He eventually gave up the idea of making films on his own. Some years later Seán presented me with a script he had written for a short film, which he called *Caisleán an Mhúraigh*. He planned that we would work together on it, but unfortunately he died before we had the opportunity to do anything with it.

A film in which Ceoltóirí Chualann was involved was directed by an independent producer on behalf of the BBC, and it was made in Cúil Aodha during the 1960s. It included Pádraig Ó Tuama, or Peaití Thaidhg Pheig as he was better known, and many other singers and poets from the area. Part of the programme was filmed in the Ó Riada kitchen and that was where Ceoltóirí Chualann performed. The film was edited and completed in London but it was seemingly never transmitted. A copy of the film was sent to Cork Airport, where it remained for some time awaiting collection by Seán Ó Riada. Nobody seems to know what happened to it after that. Years later, after Ó Riada died, Seán Ó Mórdha made a film called *The Blue Note* in which he illustrated, in part, the history of Ceoltóirí Chualann. It was his intention to use archival material from the BBC documentary in his production and although he made several attempts at that time to trace the missing film, he was not successful.

10

Ceoltóirí Laighean
1970s

The death of Ó Riada – Ending and beginning – The musicians –
The recordings – The events – A choice to be made

The death of Ó Riada

On 30 March 1969, Seán Ó Riada, Ceoltóirí Chualann and Seán Ó Sé
gave a memorable concert in the Gaiety Theatre to celebrate the bicentenary of the eighteenth-century poet Peadar Ó Doirnín. The concert
was produced by Seán Ó Mórdha. Gael Linn planned to record it but
because the electrical system in the Gaiety interfered with the sound, it
was decided not to go ahead with the recording. I felt strongly that this
historic occasion should be preserved and I discussed the matter with my
own soundman, Pat Hayes. Although Pat was mainly involved in field-
work for my wildlife films, he had a very musical ear and had recorded
Paddy Moloney and other musicians for me on many occasions. He was
a very good technician and he suggested bypassing the electrical system
altogether and using two battery-operated Nagra sound-tape machines.
As there is a limit to the size of tape that can be used on the Nagra, one
machine would be at the ready to take over from the other. This was to
guard against running out of tape before reaching the end of any of the
set pieces of music.

Gael Linn's director, Roibeárd MacGórain, agreed to have us record
the whole concert. Pat brought along his wife Rosemary as assistant and
they sat in the orchestra pit, operating the machines. This was a position
from which they could also observe the activities on stage. The concert
was a complete sell-out, with President Éamon de Valera and other
dignitaries attending. The musicians taking part were: Seán Ó Riada

(harpsichord), Seán Ó Sé (vocal), John Kelly and Martin Fay (fiddles), Paddy Moloney (uilleann pipes and whistle), Seán Potts (whistle), Michael Tubridy (flute and whistle), Éamon de Buitléar (button accordion) and Peadar Mercier (bodhrán).

Each piece of music was introduced by Ó Riada. Niall Tóibín, who read some of Peadar Ó Doirnín's poems, was also Master of Ceremonies. Two of Ó Doirnín's poems for which Ó Riada had especially composed the music were heard as songs for the first time. One was the beautiful air 'Mná na hÉireann' and the other was 'An Spéirbhean Mhilis'. 'Mná na hÉireann' became popular some years later when it was played by The Chieftains as the theme music in the film *Barry Lyndon*. Whether it was by accident or design, the film credit for the music on the film mentioned The Chieftains but omitted to name the composer, Seán Ó Riada.

The recording of the Gaiety concert was issued under the Gael Linn label with the title *Ó Riada sa Gaiety*. It was a milestone in the history of Ceoltóirí Chualann and, after almost forty years, the recording is still in demand.

The Carolan Tercentenary Concert given at the City Hall, Cork, on 28 June 1970, was Ceoltóirí Chualann's last appearance in public. It was fitting that it should end by honouring the harper-poet Turlough O'Carolan, for whom Seán Ó Riada had such admiration. O'Carolan was a most important figure in Irish musical history, linking the old Irish art tradition and the European tradition of his time.

Within a year of Ceoltóirí Chualann's last concert, Seán Ó Riada was taken seriously ill, suffering from cirrhosis of the liver, and was brought to the Bon Secours Hospital in Cork. The situation was so desperate that Garech de Brún arranged to have him flown to London where he would come under the care of a famous consultant at King's Hospital. His wife Ruth hardly moved out of the room during the days and nights that Seán lay in hospital. I went to visit him. He was only forty years of age but he looked like an old man. However, there was a slight improvement in his condition and I made my way back to Ireland, but I was only home a day or so when I had a telephone call from Ruth informing me that Seán's condition had become serious and could I return to London as soon as possible. She said a taxi would be waiting for me at Heathrow. I caught an evening flight to London and although I enquired about the taxi on my arrival, there was no sign of it. Having decided that there must have been some confusion in the arrangements, I then made my own way to the hospital.

The following morning the taximan, who it seems had in fact been waiting at the airport for me the previous night, came to the hospital hoping to collect his fare. I was told by the hospital porter that the taximan asked, 'Is Mr O'Ryeadda's butler around?' Luckily for me, the hospital staff were not aware that the patient from Ireland had been accompanied by any of his household staff! Seán improved a little on the following day. The last I saw of him was when I gave him a shave before he went down again to the operating theatre. I hardly knew what to talk to him about; he was so unlike the vibrant, charismatic character we had come to know over the years. He made a last comment to me as the nurses were preparing to wheel him down to the theatre and he not knowing what was in store for him when he arrived there, 'Bíodh an diabhal acu!' (To blazes with them!). Two days later Seán Ó Riada was dead.

The coffin was flown back to Cork and the cortège began its journey on the road that Ó Riada had travelled countless times. As it passed through Macroom, Ballymackeera and Ballyvourney, people lined the route along the way. Shopkeepers pulled down blinds and closed their premises and children were allowed out of school to say a prayer and wish Seán Ó Riada their last goodbyes. Cúil Aodha had never seen such a crowd of people and on the morning of the funeral the little church could only accommodate a fraction of those who came. Amplifiers had been erected so that those outside could hear the ceremony. The mass was celebrated by Ó Riada's good friend, Fr Donncha Ó Conchúir, the parish priest. Peadar, Seán's eldest son, played the organ and took charge of his father's beloved singers, Cór Chúil Aodha. The Clare piper Willie Clancy played, as did the accordion player Tony McMahon. Ceoltóirí Chualann played as the coffin was carried down the aisle and out of the church. I can safely say that it was the saddest tune we ever played. Once outside the church the music was taken over by a lone piper, Alf Kennedy, who led the lonely procession to St Gobnait's graveyard. It was heartbreaking to watch Ruth at the graveside with Peadar and her little ones gathered around her, all standing in the rain near Seán's parents and his sister Louise.

The loss of Ó Riada was enormous, and his death left a void that could never be filled. In the circumstances, the best we can hope for is that his memory be kept alive. When Ceoltóirí Chualann had made their last public appearance at the Carolan Tercentenary Concert in Cork, Pat Hayes recorded it. After Ó Riada's death I suggested to Roibeárd MacGóráin that we should honour Seán Ó Riada by making some of this music available to the public. In January 1972, Gael Linn issued a long-playing record with the title *Ó Riada*. There were twelve pieces of music on the disc, six tunes from the Gaiety concert that had not been included on Gael Linn's previous LP, *Ó Riada sa Gaiety*, and six tunes from the Cork concert. A colourful image of Seán Ó Riada for the cover of the LP was painted by my sister-in-law Nóra. Seán Mac Réamoinn wrote on the sleeve of the record:

> Since O'Carolan's day, a process of social and geographical fragmentation, ending only partly in our own time, caused an inevitable corresponding fragmentation in our literary and musical tradition and even in the language itself. It was to restore those fragments, and see them once more part of a living organic culture, that Seán Ó Riada devoted, literally, the best years of his life, as an artist and as a man.

In a review of the record in *The Irish Times* on 24 January 1972, Charles Acton wrote:

> Taken all round, this record will sell in enormous numbers – and I hope that royalties will accrue to his family and not only to Gael Linn's coffers. I am glad that there is a good deal of Ó Riada's own speech, his own introductions to various items. He once wrote: 'I am not an amiable man,' but in writing that he defamed himself. The fact is that his own platform personality was amiable, took his audience into full sympathy with him and created that ideal bond between performer and audience. This record is an example of that persuasive, inspiring personality that everybody will want to treasure.

In the 1960s, during the early days of Ceoltóirí Chualann, Seán Potts rather innocently asked Ó Riada if he thought we would ever have a following such as The Beatles were enjoying. Ó Riada's immediate answer was, 'No we won't! We'll have a following of a dedicated crowd of people. My hope would be that other groups would be formed and that they would follow our example.' His wish was realised. Groups of musicians were already beginning to take a lead from what we had been doing and were even playing the same tunes. One of the earliest examples of this was a group called Planxty, with singer Christy Moore and uilleann piper Liam Ó Flynn among its members. The manner in which groups were playing Irish music had changed forever.

Ending and beginning

A few months before Ó Riada's death, Len Clifford of Gael Linn and myself were in Seán's company in the Shelbourne Hotel, on Dublin's Stephen's Green. We discussed Ceoltóirí Chualann and we tried to impress on Ó Riada that it would be a tragedy if the playing days of the group were to be at an end. Although he had mentioned it in a radio interview, Ó Riada had never officially informed the members of Ceoltóirí Chualann that the group was disbanded; we just did not play any more after the Cork concert in 1970. Now Ó Riada surprised us by suddenly announcing he had plans to form a new group that would be even bigger and better than Ceoltóirí Chualann. The group, according to Seán, would have additional instruments and Liam O'Flynn would be invited to join. In the months following our meeting, Ó Riada's health began to deteriorate.

After Seán Ó Riada's death his orchestra was rudderless and could hardly continue without him. Meanwhile, The Chieftains, whose rank-and-file were all members of Ceoltóirí Chualann, had been playing away under their leader Paddy Moloney. They included Seán Potts, Michael Tubridy, Martin Fay, Seán Keane, and Peadar Mercier. John Kelly, Seán Ó Sé, myself and of course Ó Riada, were the only members of Ceoltóirí Chualann who were not with The Chieftains.

Much of the music played by Ceoltóirí Chualann had not been commercially available to the public and I felt it would be a pity if it were to be forgotten. Gathering together a group of young musicians to play some of Ceoltóirí Chualann's music seemed to me to be an ideal way to pay tribute to Seán Ó Riada and at the same time to keep particular tunes alive. It would also give young musicians an opportunity to have a direct link with Ó Riada, even though they had never met him in person, and would develop in them an attachment to the Gaeltacht in Cúil Aodha. The new group, Ceoltóirí Laighean, was launched on Saturday 4 March 1972 at the Rupert Guinness Hall in Dublin.

The musicians

Ceoltóirí Laighean was modelled on Ceoltóirí Chualann in the number of personnel and type of instruments, though I decided not to include a harpsichord. Finding a young harp player was of more interest to me, especially as this was an instrument that Ó Riada had wanted to have in his own group. The first person I invited to join Ceoltóirí Laighean was Mary Bergin, a wonderfully talented musician whose main instrument was the tin whistle but who could also play the concert flute and the fiddle. Locating a harp player was difficult but eventually I discovered a musician who was enthusiastic and young enough to learn the large volume of music I hoped we would play. When I first met Aibhlín McCrann she was preparing for the Leaving Certificate and was studying the harp at the Municipal College of Music in Dublin. Aibhlín was the eldest of five children, whose father had died the same year as Seán Ó Riada – a tragic event which in a strange sort of way made a connection between Aibhlín and Ó Riada. Mona McCrann, Aibhlín's mother, was a very determined woman but she had a good sense of humour, a necessary quality when looking after five school-going children without outside help. One would have to possess a sense of humour to survive the sound – Aibhlín playing the Irish harp in one room, and her youngest sister Maighréad playing classical music on the violin in the room next to her. Maighréad was to become RTÉ's Musician of the Future in 1986, and seven years later, concertmaster of the Austrian Radio Orchestra.

The fiddle player John Kelly had told me that Sonnie Brogan and himself were far too old when in 1960 I had asked them if they would join Ceoltóirí Chualann. John must have suddenly felt younger, because some eleven years later he approached me wearing a worried look and asked me if I was going to invite him to join this new group that I was putting together! I could hardly refuse and welcomed both John and his son

James as members of Ceoltóirí Laighean! James was John's youngest son and whenever Ceoltóirí Chualann were travelling down the country, James was smuggled under his father's overcoat into my minibus. It eventually paid off as James, following in his father's footsteps, had become an exceptionally good fiddle player, who possessed the gift of perfect pitch and a style of playing that belied his age. The poet Tom Kinsella wrote about John Kelly:

> … the Clare fiddler John Kelly who, with his knowledge of traditional tunes and local styles, became Ó Riada's guide into a virtually hidden world. John Kelly has hidden memories of how traditional musicians were regarded up to that time, and as keen a sense of the dignity Ó Riada restored to them. He is now the senior musician in Ceoltóirí Laighean, and has brought his son James into the group.

Paddy Glackin, a little older than James, was an obvious choice for the group. He was making a name for himself as a musician in the Donegal style of fiddle playing. Apart from his expertise in playing the faster tunes, he also had an understanding of traditional songs, which no doubt was assisted by his fluency in the Irish language and the ability to interpret the songs. Paddy's father, Tom Glacken from Donegal, also played the fiddle. He was a sergeant in An Garda Síochána and a popular man up and down the country. Paddy, his brother Séamus and, in later years, his youngest brother Kevin, were very much encouraged by their father, who brought them with him wherever he happened to be playing.

Having three whistle players who regularly played together and who were accustomed to one another's style was a definite advantage when it came to arranging particular pieces of music. Peter Phelan was an uilleann piper and whistle player. Mícheál Ó hAlmhain was accomplished both on the concert flute and the tin whistle, and, with Mary Bergin making it a trio, the sound produced by the whistles was in unison and very sweet. The Offaly button accordion player Paddy O'Brien had over a thousand tunes, which he could play without referring to a single written musical note. He had great energy in his music. His accordion and my own completed the number of instruments. It was easier at times to direct the musicians while playing the bodhrán, and whenever I was not performing on the accordion I kept the rhythm going on the goatskin. Some years later Mel Mercier took over the percussion. Mel was a son of Peadar Mercier, who had played with me in Ceoltóirí Chualann, and he was later to study music more seriously at university, specialising in percussion.

The connection with the West Cork Gaeltacht, where Ó Riada had been living, was very important and I was fortunate in having two singers, Diarmuid Ó Súilleabháin from Cúil Aodha and Seán Ó Liatháin from nearby Baile Mhúirne. Both were members of Ó Riada's Cór Chúil Aodha and they had a very good selection of traditional songs. Diarmuid was one of Seán Ó Riada's favourite singers and Seán Ó Liatháin was a nephew of the great Cúil Aodha singer Pádraig Ó Tuama, or Peaití Thaidhg Pheig, as he was known to most people. Many of Ó Liatháin's songs were learned from his uncle Peaití. Again to quote the poet Tom Kinsella:

> But for Ó Riada the music was as much a means as an end in itself, a means towards cultural integration; language, song, and music fitted into, and fulfilling, a way of life. It is an ideal, requiring a very special community (at times, in Cúil Aodha, it seems close at hand ...) and it is this ideal that brought Ceoltóirí Laighean into being – to realise, in music and song, whatever of it is possible. It is highly appropriate that their members should include two very fine individual Gaeltacht singers, Diarmuid Ó Súilleabháin and Seán Ó Liatháin.

The recordings

In order to keep up the enthusiasm of the musicians, it was essential that we would have some forthcoming event for which the group would have regular rehearsals. Although we received payment for radio and for public appearances, we were strictly speaking not a professional band, as most of us had jobs that we could not afford to be away from for too long. Radio programmes recorded in Dublin were ideal as they suited all the musicians. After our first concert in Dublin, I put together a series of radio programmes called *Rachmas Ceoil* (A Wealth of Music). These were half-hour programmes where the group played a variety of dance tunes as well as Carolan pieces and slow airs, interspersed here and there with readings in Irish by Lailí's brother, the Abbey actor Peadar Lamb.

Ceoltóirí Laighean's first recording on disc was on 19 December 1972, when we were invited by Breandán Ó Buachalla, Professor of Irish at University College Dublin, to perform at a public concert in the university, in aid of Scoil Dún Chaoin, the Gaeltacht school on the Dingle Peninsula in Co. Kerry. The concert was recorded in stereo by Pat Hayes and the disc was named *The Crooked Road*, after the title of the reel we played at the opening of the concert. The disc was released in the spring of 1973. Both Diarmuid Ó Súilleabháin and Seán Ó Liatháin performed with us at the concert and among their songs was included 'Dé Bheatha-sa, A Pheaití', a humorous piece composed by Seán's uncle, Peaití Thaidhg Pheig, and Diarmuid Ó Riordáin. The song was the result of a plan conceived by an Oireachtas committee some thirty years previously, to introduce a competition in which a newly composed conversational piece of words in song would form an exchange between two singers. Peaití and his old friend Diarmuid Ó Riordáin had won first prize at that when they sang it for the first time at the Oireachtas Festival in Dublin. Alternate verses are sung by each singer and then both join together to sing the chorus. In the song Peaití is welcomed back from a period spent on John Bull's Island, from where he has escaped the demands of the taxman. Everyone in Cúil Aodha was of course aware that Peaití had never left Ireland, let alone spent time working in England!

Other pieces on the recording include 'A Ghrá, Luí Láimh Liom' (O Love, Lie Beside Me) played on the harp by Aibhlín McCrann, a piece that Ceoltóirí Chualann played but never recorded. Another harper's piece, 'Murtach Mac Cana', composed by the harper O'Carolan in honour of Morgan Magan who died in 1738, was played by the whole group. 'The Gravel Walks', the second last tune on the disc, is a good example of the energy and ability of the musicians in their playing of traditional dance music. I was fortunate in having my father translate the various songs into English, which he did in verse form, and Séamus Ennis wrote the sleeve notes for me in his own inimitable fashion:

In the sense of the word nowadays, Ceoltóirí Laighean are not a group as such but a company of musicians such as would foregather in neighbourliness to derive pleasure from playing in unison – and a stroke of good fortune comes the way of those who hear their strains.

What they have does not at all flavour of other directed and meticu-
lously rehearsed groups and it is no wonder how they inspired their
audience, who are also present to be heard on this record, or how much
it inspires me when I hear it. I will leave them for no further praising.

As musicians these are of wide versatility: a girl of true tin-whistle
and a girl of cherished harp-playing; a man of uilleann pipes and tin-
whistle; three men of the fiddle – two of West Clare descent and one of
Donegal Rosses' folk; Paddy O'Brien and Éamon of the button accordions (and Éamon and his bodhrán or tambourine); John Kelly, the
most senior of the three fiddle men, fully at ease with his concertina.
Place among them the two songsters of the Muskerry tradition and
you have the select spell of pleasing, amusing authenticity for your
ears. If for ears, you'll find it's for heart and fidgety feet too. Sound
success to them!

One further disc by Ceoltóirí Laighean was recorded in December 1975
and called *The Star of Munster*. Meanwhile, two new members had
joined the group: Michael Gavin, the concert flute-player, and Michael
Crehan, who played both whistle and pipes. The uilleann piper Peter
Phelan had left the group at this stage, so in fact the number of musicians
was only increased by one. The reason for using the name *The Star of
Munster* was that it was one of the best-known reels among older generations of traditional musicians. Daniel Francis O'Neill (1848–1936),
Chief of Police in Chicago, first heard it played in that city in the 1870s
by the Mayo piper Jimmy O'Brien. O'Neill was later to include it in his
own *O'Neill Collection of Irish Music*. The tune was a great favourite with
Seán Ó Riada and Ceoltóirí Chualann, who played 'The Star of Munster'
as a slow air and followed it by playing the tune as a reel. This was the
version that Ceoltóirí Laighean recorded.

Diarmuid Ó Súilleabháin and Seán Ó Liatháin also contributed two
songs to the recording. One of the songs was 'Mo Ghile Mear' (My
Dashing Darling), which Ceoltóirí Chualann had played at Ó Riada's
funeral. The second song, 'An Chruach Tobac' (The Tobacco Heap), was
another humorous exchange by Peaití Thaidhg Pheig and Diarmuid
Ó Riordáin, in which Peaití, according to the song, has returned from his
adventures in a tobacco factory in England. It was all pure imagination as

usual, on the part of both of those two great old characters from Cúil Aodha! We recorded two slow airs that Ó Riada had given to Ceoltóirí Chualann, 'Carraig an Aoibhnis' and 'An Spéic Seoigheach'. Both tunes had been collected by Edward Bunting in 1792 and, although Ceoltóirí Chualann may have played them once, neither tune had been recorded by them.

The events

An invitation from West German television to play at a folk festival in Cologne during the summer of 1976 added an air of excitement to our rehearsals. All the musicians were keen to go, especially as this was to be our first overseas trip. Everything was to be paid for and we would also receive an appearance fee. The only musician who was hesitant about the trip was John Kelly, who kept making excuses as to why he might not be able to travel. Whenever I asked if he was coming or not, he answered, 'I'm not sure that I can leave herself and the shop.' At the rehearsal the following week I explained to John that he would have to tell me definitely if he was travelling with us or not. 'Ah, sure put me name down anyway!' was his reply. 'John, the air-tickets have to be paid for tomorrow, otherwise I will have to cancel your seat,' I explained. 'All right then, I'll go!' It was not his little shop in Capel Street that was actually worrying John Kelly. He had never been outside Ireland in his life and the thought of travelling through the clouds was just a little too much for him!

Our flight was booked from Dublin to London with a connecting flight from there to Cologne. The British Airways flight that morning carried a number of serious-looking business people. John was nervous as he sat beside me on the plane. His first reaction on seeing the ground sinking away from us as we became airborne was to take out his concertina and begin playing. I was not at all sure of the reaction of the passengers, or indeed of the air hostesses, who were in the process of making their flight announcements. John seemed to be oblivious to everything except the tune he was playing and in fact might as well have been on his favourite perch in the Four Seasons pub next door to his little shop, playing a duet alongside his old friend Joe Ryan. He played the two-part reel three or four times and then stopped. At first there was a moment's silence, and then a round of applause broke out as the passengers clapped in appreciation! John was now completely relaxed and as we flew over a thick carpet of clouds he remarked, 'Isn't it marvellous to be flying so low over the sea!'

The concert in Cologne was held on a stage in front of the famous Gothic cathedral. Eight folk groups, all from different parts of Europe, participated in the festival and Ceoltóirí Laighean, being the only Irish group, received a tumultuous reception from the audience. As soon as we commenced playing, dozens of young people climbed on to the stage and danced to our music in their bare feet.

There was another continental trip in April 1978 when we were invited to take part in a concert in Brittany advertised as the *Clec de Caucriauville Grande Fête Populaire*. It wasn't until the performance was over that I discovered we had been playing for the communists! There were of course various appearances by Ceoltóirí Laighean in different parts of Ireland, in locations as far apart as Ballyferriter in Kerry to Gweedore in Donegal, where we were always received with warm enthusiasm. Our concerts in country places were as a rule more enjoyable than those in the city. Perhaps there was less formality about them and more contact with the general public before and after the perfomances. Transporting the musicians to different parts of the country in the *Amuigh Faoin Spéir* minibus meant that I had to act as both driver and chaperone, but at least it ensured that we would all arrive in the same place and at the same time. Thankfully, in all our travels we never had an unpleasant incident, either in relation to the performances or on the journeys to the various locations.

Whenever we had an engagement away from the east coast, I would drive from my home in Co. Wicklow into Dublin and pick up the members on the way. The last stop before heading out of town was The Horseshoe, John Kelly's shop in Capel Street. As I pulled up at the kerb in the street outside with a minibus full of musicians, John would give his wife some last-minute instructions with regard to the running of the shop. His fiddle case and concertina, along with his overcoat and small travel bag, were then heaped onto the back seat of the minibus. That done, John would rush back into the shop and arrive out again with a big Cidona bottle full of holy water. While the blessings of the Almighty were invoked on behalf of all those travelling, the musicians would dive for cover, knowing that John Kelly was about to splatter the contents of the bottle inside the bus, half-drowning us in the process!

One of the more enjoyable concerts was held at Scarriff in Co. Clare. The venue was a very large lounge bar, where various musical evenings were organised. At one end of the lounge there was a large platform, eight or ten inches in height, which was capable of accommodating a reasonably large group of musicians. Performing on such a low stage gave the feeling of having the audience seated among the musicians, which helped build up a very good atmosphere. When the concert came to an end, the musicians just stepped off the stage and began chatting away to members of the audience, some of whom they already knew. Laillí, who had accompanied me on this particular trip, noticed that the various instruments lay scattered around the platform, as if abandoned by their owners. Being seriously concerned that some of them might be damaged or, worse still, disappear altogether, she gathered them up, one by one, and placed them in a spot in the corner of the stage. A local Clare wit who was leaning against one of the pillars close to the stage had been watching Laillí's activities in the confines of the platform, as she lifted each instrument and moved it to a safer place. When she stepped off the stage close to where the Clare man stood, he turned to her and remarked, 'Be God, mam, but you'd make a livin' tied to a stone!'

A choice to be made

As professional artists are well aware, there are only a certain number of times you can stage an act or a concert on an island the size of Ireland. If one is to survive, locations further afield need to be considered. Performing at a concert here and there and not quite knowing when or where we might be playing next, was not very satisfying for the members of Ceoltóirí Laighean. I had been invited to bring the group on a tour of the Continent but as there was no satisfactory agreement and the deal was to be with people I did not know, I declined the offer. At the same time a recording company was interested in offering me a contract to make four commercial discs of the music of Ceoltóirí Laighean. This would be a big commitment, for the musicians as well as for myself.

The point had been reached where I would have to give some very serious thought to future activities. If I were to move into a fully professional field with the group, it would more or less put an end to my film work and the question I had to ask myself was whether I wanted to travel the world with a music group or make more wildlife films. I was not a professional musician and there was a limit to what I could do musically in developing a whole new programme for the group. I had achieved pretty much what I had hoped for with Ceoltóirí Laighean over the years. The young musicians now had Ceoltóirí Chualann's music to add to their own large store of traditional tunes and all of them were already making names for themselves as good solo artists. Paddy Glackin's and James Kelly's talented fiddle-playing was much in demand around the country and Aibhlín McCrann had become an accomplished harp player and had by now taken a degree in music and Irish.

All the musicians were busy enough not to have to worry about the continuation of Ceoltóirí Laighean. Meanwhile, as far as I was concerned there were still many more natural history films to be made, and as the opportunity existed for me to look for more film contracts, I decided that I should devote my time in the future to wildlife filmmaking.

11

Miles and Miles of Music
1970s

Angling issues – Sardinia – A venture into publishing – Séamus Ennis –
A trip to Ethiopia – A Hundred Thousand Wings! – Solidarity and
support – The Killarney safari – In memory of Tommy Kehoe

Angling issues

The arterial drainage scheme of the 1960s and 1970s did much damage
to what were once regarded as the best trout and salmon rivers in
Europe. The consequences for our stocks of salmon and trout as well as
for a whole variety of other aquatic life in the affected rivers was devastating. Almost all our limestone rivers have been severely damaged – the
Kells Blackwater, the Suir, the Maigue, to name just a few. Those rivers
had stocks of wild trout that were the envy of anglers from all over the
world. In many cases, what remained of long stretches of those rivers
were featureless canal-like waterways with dangerously high banks and
little vegetation. Sid Neff, a true conservationist, who had travelled all
the way from the US to fish in Ireland, could not believe what we were
doing to such a valuable national asset. It was even more difficult for him
to understand that it was being done with government approval!
Even when the authorities were having second thoughts about the
scheme and when there were signs that it might come to an end, the
activity continued. The excuse was that because the machinery and
personnel were already in place they had to be used. Serious damage to
the environment never seemed to be an issue.

On his first visit to Ireland, I had introduced Sid to another angler
friend, Ned Maguire. Now Sid had returned to live and work in Ireland,
and both men went on regular fishing trips together. Weekend safaris

were organised wherever there were good trout rivers to be found. Their discussions and arguments about various methods of angling were endless. Ned was a very traditional fisherman and Sid was, in contrast, a modern scientific angler; and this difference gave both of them plenty of scope for long, complicated conversations, Ned tending to pass sarcastic remarks about Sid's 'new-fangled tyings of flies'. A hidden element of competition always existed between the two of them and they never let it be known, therefore, that each secretly admired the other's particular skills. Ned had already featured in *Amuigh Faoin Spéir* and now I was about to have another interesting fishing personality in Sid, who had a very different approach to angling as a sport.

Sid Neff had an admirable conservation policy of returning every fish to the water after catching it. Ned Maguire never grew accustomed to this. For an angler to spend so much time and effort stalking a trout and then battling with it only to return it to the river after landing it, seemed to Ned to be totally unnatural and against all traditional angling instincts.

There was one particularly fine trout with which Sid had to do battle on the Kells Blackwater and which Ned observed with chagrin from the distance. It was a fine still day and the two anglers walked along the riverbank. Sid could hear from several yards away an irregular 'plop' in the water every now and again. Ned's hearing was not as sharp as it used to be and he depended more on his eyesight than on his sense of hearing. A slight disturbance on the surface of the water close to the riverbank was the tell-tale sign that at least one good fish was feeding.

Insects emerged, one by one, out of their nymphal skins, floated downstream like delicate sailing boats and then almost immediately became airborne and flew off to find a mate. Those that delayed their take-off to float a little longer on the surface water were in real danger of being picked off by a hungry fish. For the trout, it was only a matter of hanging in the current and waiting until the tiny morsel floated downstream and appeared in its 'window'. The fish moved gracefully upwards towards its prey and then, barely breaking the surface of the water, opened its mouth and gulped at the fly. It then reversed neatly to its original position, and hung once more in the current waiting for the next floating victim.

The hatch on the river that day included a sedge fly, known as a grey flag, and a small mayfly, which anglers generally referred to as a medium olive. Ned, who was fishing from the bank a short distance away from Sid, began by tempting a rising trout with a medium olive, which he skilfully cast in the direction of the fish. In spite of his efforts, the trout did not seem interested. Meanwhile, Sid had already landed two nice fish on his expertly tied imitation of the grey flag. When he saw that Ned was having no success with the trout he was covering, he called to him. Ned wandered over to the spot where Sid was watching another fish rising a little further upstream. 'Give me that fly,' Sid said gruffly. Ned detached the medium olive from the end of his line and handed it over to his companion. Sid began adding an extra length of a fine nylon point on to the end of Ned's line. He then selected an imitation of a grey flag from his own fly-box and tied it on to the end of the point. 'Now, try that and you might catch something!' he muttered. Ned retreated to his spot and he could see that the fish was still feeding. He cast Sid's imitation of the grey flag in his direction. The fly landed just a little ahead of the fish, there was a swirl and the fly disappeared underwater. Ned's reaction was to quickly raise the tip of his rod and he successfully hooked a fine trout – one pound, fourteen ounces in weight and in prime condition.

It was now time for Sid to concentrate on his own fishing. He had spotted a slight swirling splash created by a rising trout just a little way up from him, and he reckoned that it was a pretty sizeable fish of at least three pounds in weight. As he slid silently down off the bank and into the river, the water came almost halfway up Sid's chest-waders. Moving slowly upstream behind the rising trout, he made a few false casts as he paid out what he judged would be the correct amount of line. He then made the final throw that would land the floating imitation fly upstream and just ahead of the trout. The fly landed beautifully but passed down ever so slightly, a few inches to the right of Sid's intended spot. As the fly continued floating on its way down towards the angler, there was no visible movement from the trout. Sid made no attempt to retrieve the line until it was well clear of the small area where the fish was feeding. To retrieve the fly at too early a stage could create a slight disturbance on the surface, completely scaring the fish off its feeding routine.

Sid cast his line out a second time, and on this occasion it landed about a foot in front of where the feeding trout had recently broken the surface. There were some natural insects also floating downstream and at times it was difficult to distinguish the artificial from the natural ones. Suddenly and without warning the trout moved, barely showing above the water as it gulped at the artificial fly. Sid hesitated for barely a moment, allowing the fish to take the lure and turn downwards. Then, with a sharp flick, Sid raised the tip of rod sharply and tightened the line. The rod shuddered slightly and bent into an arc and with a burst of energy the fish took off and raced downstream, making Sid's reel sing while yards of line, pulled by the panic-stricken fish, zipped through the water. As the trout attempted to seek refuge in clumps of weed in the long stretch of river, it took particular skill on Sid's part to prevent it from causing the line to become snarled in a variety of obstacles. The very fine nylon point at the end of the line did not allow for any rough handling of the fish and Sid had to keep following it as it fought its way downstream.

A little further on and it headed straight for a cattle fence that was stretched across from one bank of the river to the other. A whole series of winter floods had choked the barrier with bits and pieces of driftwood, carried from several miles further up. The trout made straight for the cover of the fence that ran down under the pile of rubbish. Sid could see that there was no way he could get his rod under it to follow the fish on the other side and he quickly snipped the wire with a small sharp pliers hanging from his fishing jacket. The fence and its mass of weed and driftwood swung like a pendulum across the river, leaving the way open for Sid to continue his way downstream and continue his battle with the fish.

The trout fought every inch of water in its bid for freedom and eventually after almost fifty minutes Sid was able to land it. It was a magnificent trout measuring almost twenty-one inches and weighing three pounds, eight ounces. Sid quickly photographed and weighed his quarry before carefully lowering the trout back into the water. Gently working it up and down until it had fully recovered, he then loosened his hold on the fish and allowed it to swim off and enjoy its life in the river.

The art of angling means far more to Sid Neff than just catching a large trout. The whole science of studying the river, watching the aquatic insects and being able to identify them and knowing which particular fly the fish are feeding on at that moment, is what excites Sid. His own imitations of a whole variety of aquatic insects on which the trout feed are so beautifully fashioned that they are without doubt works of art.

149

A few days after Sid Neff's angling experience on the Kells Blackwater, I met Ned Maguire and happened to mention the fine trout that Sid had caught. Ned's only response was: 'By God, but do you know what, I never saw a man or a fish suffer so much!'

Sardinia

The 1970s was a busy period for me. It involved, among other things, a great deal of filmmaking around Ireland as well as in some overseas locations. Pat Hayes and I drove the *Amuigh Faoin Spéir* minibus all the way from Co. Wicklow, across the Alps, down through Italy, and finally on a ferry over to Sardinia. It was the last foreign location that I would film in black and white. Sarda was the local language spoken in Sardinia, although the Italian government did not permit it to be taught in the schools and therefore the official language spoken was Italian. I am not sure what language Hayes had in mind when a local helped us with some very heavy baggage. Pat, in attempting to show both his appreciation and surprise at the man's strength, held his own two arms above his head and, flexing his muscles like some advertisement for Charlie Atlas or some similar weight-lifter, he uttered the never-to-be-forgotten words: '*Multi Homo!*' I don't know what the islander must have thought, but he gave Pat a wide grin and nodded!

Filming the wildlife of the island was my main interest but we also recorded traditional music played on a very ancient instrument known as the launeddass, the triple pipes. The sound produced was similar to our own uilleann pipes but with a more limited musical range. The launeddass seems to have originated with the shepherds, who made them from reeds collected from a nearby marsh while watching over their flocks. Three reeds are used, a long one of about three feet in length known as the basso, which is attached to two finer reeds of half the length and half the thickness. One of these is used as an accompaniment to the basso. The third reed is the canto, which has a very small, thin mouthpiece. Unlike our own pipes there is no bag, and the musician uses his cheeks as sacks for the air. It is a very skilful method and requires a lot of practice. The cheeks are kept inflated by breathing through the nose and then exhaling to create the wind for the pipes. An experienced player can do this for long periods without any break in the music and without showing any apparent signs of stress.

Several of these instruments were featured in a spectacular parade we were fortunate enough to see. *Cavalcata Sarda* is held in Sassari on the Feast of the Ascension every two years. It was at one time reserved for visiting royalty but it eventually became a festival of the people. Groups from all over Sardinia attend and both men and women wear colourful traditional clothes. Some of them ride horses through the streets, and the various districts from all over the island are represented. It wasn't wildlife in the strict sense, but we filmed and recorded it anyway and it made quite a 'colourful' black-and-white programme with plenty of Sardinian music!

A venture into publishing

In between the various filming activities around the country, there were other projects that were indirectly related to those nature programmes. Leo Hallissey, a teacher in a school at East Wall in Dublin, was acting as a part-time editor for the publishers Gill and Macmillan. Leo was extremely enthusiastic about anything he happened to be working at, and, being very much involved with children's projects on nature, he felt that there was a great need for a suitable book on Irish wildlife that could be used in the junior classroom. It was difficult to refuse Leo's request and after some lengthy discussions, I agreed to write a simple nature book that would awaken children's interest in some of the more exciting aspects of wildlife in the Irish countryside. The book was published in 1974 and eventually the project became a series of three books with the title *Out and About*. It was widely welcomed by teachers and used in schools in many parts of the country. The first book was illustrated by the well-known wildlife artist Richard Ward, and the two later editions were done by another artist, who for some unknown reason spelt his second name back-to-front, making it Eldnar instead of Randle! Book one was translated into Irish by my father in 1976. The other two were translated shortly afterwards by the Department of Education. The Irish language series was issued under the title *An Saol Beo* and these were also published by Gill and Macmillan.

151

Séamus Ennis

Nature, music and the Irish language have always been very much interwoven through my life. They have affected what I have done in a whole
variety of ways, from the people I came to know, the girl I married, the
family we reared and even to the place in the Conamara Gaeltacht where
we spent most of our holidays. There was one man in whom I had a
particular interest and who had spent a great deal of time in the various
Gaeltacht areas, including the same part of Conamara with which I was
familiar. It was the folklore collector and uilleann piper Séamus Ennis,
who had travelled all over Ireland, England, Scotland and Wales, collecting music and stories for Radio Éireann, the Irish Folklore Commission
and the BBC. During the 1970s, Ennis's health was deteriorating and I
was anxious to record some of his material on film before it was too late.
I telephoned his doctor, Ivor Browne, who had a genuine interest in
traditional music and especially in the uilleann pipes – this was probably
the reason Ivor had taken such a personal interest in Séamus Ennis's
welfare. He was naturally delighted to hear of my plans and advised me to
make the film as soon as possible. I approached RTÉ with the proposal
and consulted Liam Ó Murchú, who was in charge of Irish music
programming, but his response was that they had no money available for
such a programme. My immediate reaction was to say to him, 'Look,
Liam, Séamus Ennis is not all that well. Supposing I were to come in to
you in the morning and announce that Ennis had died, what would you
say then?' 'O, Jesus!' replied Liam, 'Go and make the film!'

Séamus Ennis's first visit to my studio was on 8 March 1973, when we
began discussing the various sequences we might include in the film. He
was a great talker and it was not long before we were given a big slice of
his family history. According to Séamus, his grandfather, a fiddle player,
was a descendant of a stable boy from Scotland who eloped with his
employer's daughter and her jewellery and subsequently bought a farm
at Naul, in North Co. Dublin. He had a family of thirteen. The second
youngest son, James, was Séamus's father. James decided that farming
was not for him and he got a job as a boy clerk in the Department of
Education in Dublin. He cycled eighteen miles in and out from Naul every
day. He had a great interest in the bagpipes and was a founder of the Naul

Pipe Band. He could also play the flute and entered a competition in London, which, according to Séamus, he won. James bought a second-hand set of uilleann pipes made by Coyne, a pipe-maker in Thomas Street, and John Brogan of Harold's Cross got the pipes into working order for him. He took lessons from the piper Nicholas Markey, whom Séamus described as, 'A curator of a men's lavatory near Mountjoy Square'!

Séamus's parents married in 1916 and went to live in Jamestown, Co. Dublin. After Séamus completed his Leaving Certificate course at Coláiste Mhuire, Colm Ó Lochlainn offered him a job at ten shillings a week at the Sign of the Tree Candles, proofreading and writing manuscripts for *Claisceadal* (choral singing) leaflets. Séamus worked for Ó Lochlainn for four years before securing a job in 1942 with the Irish Folklore Commission as a folk music collector, at a salary of £3 per week. In 1947 he went to Scotland for six months and in August of the same year he joined Radio Éireann as Outside Broadcast Officer. He travelled the country and built up a large archive of material, much of which is still in Radio Éireann.

A man about whom Séamus Ennis spoke a great deal was Colm Ó Caoidheáin, a traditional singer from Conamara. Ennis had collected two hundred and ten songs from Colm and many of those songs would have contained a large number of verses. What is surprising about Colm Ó Caoidheáin's vast store of songs and music is that the man couldn't read or write. As I was most keen to include Colm in the film, we arranged to travel to Carna where he lived and to bring Séamus and himself together for a session.

Séamus told me that the first time he had gone to visit Colm Ó Caoidheáin in search of music, Colm thought he was just another one of those individuals who regularly came to bother him. He decided that he would discourage Séamus by singing for him one of his most difficult tunes. When he began to sing he closed his eyes, as is the fashion with many traditional singers. Séamus immediately began writing down the notes, which he was well accustomed to doing. When Colm finally came to the end of his piece he opened his eyes and exclaimed (in Irish) 'Have you got it?' Séamus replied that he thought he had, and promptly took a tin whistle out of the inside pocket of his jacket. The piece of paper was still on the table where Séamus could read it and he played the tune straight through. Colm stared at him wide-eyed, exclaiming, 'You're a ghost!' After that episode Séamus had no problems and they became good friends. Colm gave Séamus all the music he had and that wonderful collection of Ó Caoidheáin's, beautifully written in Séamus 's neat handwriting, can be seen today in the Department of Folklore at University College Dublin. We included a sequence of Séamus at the university discussing his collection with Seán Ó Súilleabháin, who worked at that time in the Department of Folklore. That trip we took to Carna was the last time that Séamus Ennis and Colm Ó Caoidheáin were to see each other. As work on the film was nearing completion I asked Séamus Ennis if he had thought of a title. His immediate reply was: 'Miles and miles of music', and that is what we eventually called the film.

A trip to Ethiopia

I had never been to Africa and the opportunity came to visit a small part of that great continent when in 1975 I received an offer from Ethiopian Airlines to fly a crew to Addis Ababa, the capital of Ethiopia. The government of Ethiopia wanted to have the richness of their wildlife promoted on television, in order to encourage tourists to their country. The economy was in a poor state and at that time no other African nation had fewer doctors or cars per 1,000 people. I first flew out to Ethiopia at the beginning of January in order to make the necessary arrangements and to take a look at the various locations that I hoped to film. Ethiopia is an ancient African nation with very distinctive cultural traditions, and on my arrival there the very first impression I had was of scenes straight from the pages of the Bible. The sixth of January, the Feast of the Epiphany, is of special significance in Ethiopia and I arrived just as the celebrations were about to begin. Many local people were to be seen carrying a lamb or a kid goat on their shoulders as they made their way to the festivities. Being particularly keen to get to the coast, I travelled to Asmara, through the mountainous area of Eritrea and down to the Red Sea. It was my intention to film the rich underwater life of the coral reefs along the Eritrean coast.

Back home, it took a little time before I had the trip organised but eventually everything was ready in the spring of that same year. I had invited two experienced marine biologists from University College

Galway – Brendan Keegan and John Mercer – to form part of the group. Soundman Pat Hayes came along, as did my sister-in-law Nóra in her role as production assistant. When we arrived in London we were informed that the political situation in Ethiopia had deteriorated and that there was a possibility we would not get to Eritrea. On reaching Addis Ababa we learned that they were prepared to fly us down to the coast but in no way would they agree to bring us back! We were now in a situation where we had two marine biologists with us, a load of diving gear, including underwater photographic equipment, but with no hope whatsoever of ever seeing the ocean. The African bush would not be the favourite habitat of a marine biologist and I could sense Keegan and Mercer already beginning to feel dehydrated in this parched rough desert. To quote Brendan Keegan: 'Having gone to see the coral reef and arriving home with an elephant, it would be hard to justify our two or three weeks away, delightful and all as it might have been!' After a few days both biologists decided that there was really no point in driving around the African desert and so we brought them back to Addis Ababa, from where they began their return journey to Ireland.

Having left all our diving gear in storage, we prepared to film whatever wildlife we could capture in a much drier habitat than what had been in the original plan. The Volkswagen minibus we had been given was a typically tourist-looking vehicle, painted in the black-and-white pattern of a zebra. It was driven by an African driver called Ephrem, who suggested that we should make our way down the Rift Valley to the banks of the River Awash, where the Ethiopian government had begun to set up a wildlife park. We seemed to be the only visitors around so we had the area pretty much to ourselves. There were several species of antelope to be seen in the park, including a herd of oryx, that exotic animal with the very long horns, which was responsible for the many stories surrounding the mythical unicorn.

What I found more fascinating than the antelope were the bush women who now and again appeared out of the scrub. They had Arabic features and were brown-skinned and they wore shoulder-length hair. Clad in a rough leather skirt that was held up with leather thongs across the shoulders, they wore a heavy woven cotton cloak and coloured beads around the neck. They wore roughly made leather sandals and each carried a wooden staff. When I came close to one of them walking on her own, I could see that both her arms were covered in silver bangles. I asked Ephrem to enquire if she would sell any of the bangles. She told him that if she parted with any of them, her husband would kill her! And she meant it, as the silver she wore was a demonstration of her man's wealth. These Ethiopian people were a complete contrast to ourselves in that they could survive day after day in the hot dry desert, whereas if we got lost in the same area we would have been in dire trouble after less than twenty-four hours.

At Lake Abiata we filmed flocks of wild flamingo and a memorable bird known as a black heron. This bird has a clever way of using its wings in order to see its prey. It spreads both wings out over its head as a canopy to reduce flare on the surface of the water. We filmed many other species of wildfowl and wading birds, including the strange-looking saddle-billed stork.

The most exciting part of the Ethiopian trip was our safari from Mui to the banks of the River Omo, which eventually runs into Lake Rudolf across the border in Kenya. We flew down from Addis Ababa in a battered second-hand aeroplane, originally owned by Aer Lingus. Mui is in a very isolated area and we landed amid clouds of dust on an earthen runway, which had at one end a small shed serving as an air terminal. We were met by our guide Karl Forsmark, a Swede who was a big-game hunter turned conservationist. Karl had originally come to service the Ethiopian army's planes and he liked Africa so much that he stayed. As we were driven from the airstrip by Karl, the plane we had arrived on took off for its return trip to Addis and our last link with the outside world disappeared in another cloud of desert dust.

Although we were in a really wild place, Karl Forsmark's camp was pretty well organised. We had not expected to have iced drinks served to us in Mui but Karl and his lovely Dutch wife Anja had even installed a fridge run on bottled gas. Karl informed us that we did not even have to move out of our chairs to see wildlife in his camp. As he pointed out the creators of a mini-riot in the upper branches of the trees, he told us that the Colobus monkeys were the landlords in these woods.

Karl's long experience in tracking the big game of East Africa was invaluable when it came to locating the large herds of buffalo that we hoped to film. Every now and again he would stop the jeep and examine the ground for signs of animal tracks and then climb up onto the roof to get a wider view of the area. Buffalo might not have the same profile as lions and rhinos, but many experienced hunters regard the buffalo as one of Africa's most unpredictable and dangerous animals. We had nothing to fear from zebras, which were in the same location, but we took Karl's advice in not trying to get too close to the buffaloes. Now and again we stopped among a clump of trees, and Karl pointed out a man-made trap prepared by local poachers, which he said could be as dangerous for the inexperienced as the wildlife. In the evening, as we made our way back to camp, he pointed to herdsmen and mentioned that as this was lion country, they were making sure they reached home before nightfall. Later that night, after we had lit a good fire outside our tents, we could now and again make out peering eyes beyond the flames. In such a remote place our only protection against prowling animals was to keep the fire going all night. We eventually fell into fitful sleep in our tents to the sounds of a roaring lion that was just a little too close for comfort!

Our camp at Mui was several hours' drive from the Omo River and Karl Forsmark had promised to drive us across the desert where we could film members of the Murzi tribe. It was a rough, hard drive in the African heat but being young and fit we hardly noticed the discomfort. The Murzi people had their settlement in a clump of forest close to the river and as we approached the location we could see, through the trees, their grass-covered beehive huts, which looked all the world like small haycocks. Karl had met these people on several occasions and he was one of the few white people with whom they had any contact. Before we left the jeep Karl warned us that whenever he gave the signal, we were to get into the vehicle immediately. At different points around the small cluster of huts at the edge of the forest, single warriors sat, each one armed with an old .303 Lee Enfield rifle, and Karl informed us that they would shoot, on sight, members of any other tribe.

The Murzi people were of a much darker colour than the nomad women we had seen at the other end of the country, but they were living in a more severe climate. We were brought to meet the chief, who, like the rest of the tribe, was completely naked, except for a roughly woven cotton cloak thrown over one shoulder and a battered old desert hat, which Karl had presented to him on a previous visit. The three wives who accompanied him were clad in leather skirts and had large discs in their lower lips and ears. The chief kept pushing one of his wives towards me and at the same time pointing at Nóra, making it quite clear that he wanted me to swap her for one of his wives. I don't know what Ruairí's reaction would have been if I had left Nóra with the chief and brought him home a Murzi girl, but at any rate Nóra was not agreeable to the suggested exchange! We went swimming in the beautiful clear waters of the Omo River with the tribespeople. The women kept to themselves in a group away from the men. As we were the only ones wearing swimming togs, I felt quite ridiculous. The women wondered what it was all about and kept pulling at Anja's bikini in an endeavour to see what she was hiding!

After the enjoyment and refreshment of a swim in a clear river, which is a rare enough experience in much of Africa, we continued with our filming. I was just about to begin another sequence showing some of the tribesmen's activities when suddenly, nearby, a small group of tribesmen seemed to become very excited. There was a shout from Karl Forsmark: 'We're leaving! Into the jeep now, hurry, hurry! All in quickly!' We piled in as rapidly as we could and the doors of the jeep had hardly closed when Karl put his foot down and drove up the track, out of the Murzi settlement and away across the desert in the direction of our camp. I never found out what caused the excitement among the tribesmen and it's doubtful if Karl Forsmark quite knew either, but obviously with all his experience he could tell when it was unsafe to hang around without necessarily knowing the cause of the rumpus!

A Hundred Thousand Wings!

Many of Africa's species of wildlife could be termed exotic, but here in Ireland our birds and mammals are, generally speaking, more laid back. The gannet could perhaps be classed as one of the more exotic of our seabirds. It is certainly our largest. I had an opportunity to feature the gannet when in 1976 the Irish Wildbird Conservancy, now better known as Birdwatch Ireland, commissioned me to make a film about Ireland's birds. Many different species of native birds were filmed, including the gannet. Eight and a half miles off the coast of Kerry a spectacular mountain peak known as Little Sceillig sticks up straight out of the sea. It is our largest gannet colony and plays host to an estimated 50,000 birds. In attempting to come up with a title for the film I held this figure and, taking into account that each of those 50,000 birds naturally has a pair of wings, I doubled the gannet population figure and that gave me the name for the film: *A Hundred Thousand Wings!*

Solidarity and support

Filming wildlife is such a specialised area that those of us working in that particular field do not have much contact with filmmakers who work in other areas of filmmaking. Gerrit Van Gelderen and myself were the only people in Ireland regularly making natural history programmes in the 1960s, 1970s and 1980s and even now at the time of writing, the situation has hardly changed except that, sadly, Gerrit is no longer with us.

In February 1976 I received a leaflet in the post announcing that there was to be an International Wildlife Filmmakers' Symposium the following September at the Wildfowl Trust in Slimbridge, on the Severn Estuary near Bristol, and it was being hosted by Jeffery Boswall. At the bottom of the leaflet was a short handwritten note in green ink that read: 'Éamon – Do come!' And it was signed 'Jeffery'. I had never met Jeffery Boswall but I had seen him on BBC films dressed in khaki shirt and shorts, on safari in Africa. He had the reputation of being something of a character and so indeed he proved to be when I met him some months later. It was typical of Jeffery to use green ink when writing to an Irishman.

I made up my mind that a trip to Bristol would be a wonderful opportunity to meet with other wildlife filmmakers. Apart from the symposium, the Wildfowl Trust itself would be worth a visit. It had the largest collection of wildfowl in the world and it was also where Peter Scott lived. Son of Scott of the Antarctic, Peter Scott was regularly to be seen on television. It was he who had discovered that the white-fronted geese wintering on the Sloblands in Wexford were from Greenland and not, as was first thought, the same birds that formed most of the large flocks wintering in England.

The symposium was unlike other film festivals in that it was not a competition. The Oxford English Dictionary describes a symposium as

'A drinking party; a convivial meeting for drinking, conversation, and intellectual entertainment'. But the International Wildlife Filmmakers' Symposium was a lot more than that, with its talks, debates, presentation of films, discussions on particular recent wildlife productions and even a display of the latest camera and sound equipment. It was a great experience to meet for the first time with so many other film people who had the same interest in wildlife as I had – well-known naturalists such as Eric Ashby, famous for his wild badger and fox films, and cameramen Hugh Miles and Maurice Tibbles. Peter Scott attended as did David Attenborough and there were also people from the BBC's Natural History Unit.

The symposium was Jeffery Boswall's brainchild and he ran the event like clockwork. He would appear on the podium every morning, wearing a different colourful bow tie. If he happened to be thirty seconds late, he would apologise profusely! Jeffery Boswall was a full-time producer with the BBC's Natural History Unit and was one of the great characters of that organisation. In the years following, I would meet Jeffery again on many other occasions, as well as a number of the other filmmakers that I came to know at the symposium.

The Killarney safari

It sometimes happens that an opportunity arises to make a documentary film that one had not even thought about. In the mid-1970s, a controversy arose with regard to the red deer in Killarney, when arguments from both sides were flowing to and fro and being aired in the newspapers. The original cause of the problem dates back to 1860 when for the first time, a small group of sika deer were introduced into Ireland by Lord Powerscourt. He imported them from Japan for his large estate in Wicklow. It seems that they hybridised with the red deer, within the confines of the deer park. A few of the imported sika deer were sent to Killarney where the population there soon began to grow. Some people were of the opinion that the sika deer, living in the same mountainous area as the red deer, would inter-breed with them and were therefore a threat to the genetic integrity of the reds. This they felt could eventually result in the hybrid deer replacing the long-resident Killarney red deer herd altogether. As far as is known, hybridisation had not occurred in Killarney, but the suggestion was made that all precautions should be taken and the sika deer should be shot.

The Irish Times is sometimes found in unexpected quarters – Sheikh Mohammed's headquarters in Dubai being just one example. The sheikh was Minister of Defence during the 1970s and although he had purchased bloodstock from time to time in Ireland, he had not yet established what are now his famous racehorse studs. His military aide was a Colonel Eric Mattson, who was seconded to the sheikh from the British Army. Mattson, who hailed from Kinsale in Co. Cork, received a copy of Saturday's *Irish Times* every week. He showed the article regarding the deer to the sheikh, who instructed Mattson to immediately get in touch with the Irish government. The sheikh regarded himself as a conservationist, and felt that he could do something constructive on behalf of both of these species of deer in Kerry. He offered to buy a few hundred of the threatened sika and thereby save them from being shot, a move which would also, in his opinion, be helping to protect the red deer.

There were of course those who regarded the measures being adopted by the government as being the very opposite to proper conservation! Their view was that the sika deer were equally worthy of protection and as their ancestors in Japan had in more recent times become affected by hybridisation, the Killarney herd is now possibly the purest strain of sikas in the world.

Arrangements were made to catch a number of deer for Sheikh Mohammed, and Dr Rory Harrington of the Wildlife Service was appointed to organise the capture. This would have to be done by immobilising the animals with a tranquilliser dart fired from a rifle. It was easier said than done. The first step would be to get fairly close to the deer before any attempt was made to shoot a dart at them. There would be only one opportunity and there was little or no margin for error. Fortunately Rory Harrington was quite experienced and was familiar with both the terrain and the habits of the animals. The operation was carried out under cover of darkness and I was given permission to film all that went on during this 'Killarney safari'. The extra space in the *Amuigh Faoin Spéir* minibus made it possible to carry both the camera and the marksman, and gave me the opportunity to be right up front in

161

the hunt. The deer felt less threatened when their background was surrounded in darkness, even when the foreground was lit up by the car headlights. It took several nights of stalking to capture about forty animals and these were kept temporarily in sheds in the yard of the National Park.

Sheikh Mohammed's private jet, a Boeing named *Falcon*, flew into Cork Airport a few days prior to the departure of the deer. All the seats from a section halfway down the plane to the tail had been removed to facilitate forty wooden crates, each of which contained a single sika deer. The animals had to be tranquillised in preparation for the long journey to Arabia. There were only five or six of us on the plane, plus an air hostess, and rather than being seated in the usual way in normal passenger seats, we relaxed in comfortable sitting-room type couches complete with safety belts. It was a real luxury for us but not so comfortable for the deer, even if they were somewhat in a trance.

The crates containing the deer were transported in army trucks from Dubai airport to the sheikh's private zoo. A special compound had been prepared for them in a desert habitat, complete with wooden structures that would allow them to shelter from the heat of the sun. There was a small army of Pakistanis gathering greens and making sure that there was an adequate supply of water for the animals. The various other specimens of wildlife in the collection were also in open pens, including a couple of ostriches and a water buffalo. The impression I had of the zoo itself was that it seemed to be in the early stages of development. I found Sheikh Mohammed to be friendly and helpful. Apart from his horses, his other great passion was hunting live game with his falcons. He put a military helicopter at our disposal in order to take some aerial pictures.

During our visit I happened to be in the sheikh's outer office where his secretary had his sandle-clad foot resting on a desk littered with dozens of priceless-looking diamond-studded wristwatches. He was arguing with some firm in London about the cost of pigeon-feed, which he was ordering for the sheikh's birds. When the telephone conversation was over I pointed to the watches and enquired if there was an up-and-coming trade show being held in Dubai during that week. He replied that there was no trade show but that the sheikh was going hunting with his falcons in Pakistan at the weekend and that the watches were for his friends. I decided from that moment that if I were to meet Sheikh Mohammed again, I would certainly make it quite obvious that I was not wearing a wristwatch!

In memory of Tommy Kehoe

Since parting with Gerrit Van Gelderen and operating completely independently, there were changes in the titles of the various programmes that I produced, whereas Gerrit kept on working with only one title, *To the Waters and the Wild*. Most of my programmes ran as a series, but there were others such as *Cry of the Mountain* and the Séamus Ennis documentary *Miles and Miles of Music*, which were one-off commissions. Bill Finlay SC was chairman of the Irish Wildbird Conservancy and I had got to know him as a fishing and shooting enthusiast coming in to buy his tackle at Hely's of Dame Street. He was also on the board of directors of the Bank of Ireland and later became governor. He was an excellent chairman and it was he who was largely responsible for my being given the commission to make *Cry of the Mountain*.

One particular bird of prey that I was anxious to feature in the film was the hen harrier, a ground-nesting bird with an owl-like face. It was not at all as common as some of our other birds of prey, such as the sparrow hawk or the kestrel, but in the mid-1970s harriers were found in the mountains of Wicklow. The nesting areas that the hen harriers favoured were on mountain slopes where very young conifer forests were beginning to grow among patches of furze. Heather between the small trees provided cover for the well-hidden nests on the ground. This habitat was in contrast to the one used by nesting hen harriers I filmed in Kerry, where their choice was heather-covered open moorland. Their nests are often difficult to find but I had the assistance of a young and very enthusiastic birdwatcher, Tommy Kehoe.

Tommy knew the mountains much better than I did and spent many hours on his own, taking still photographs of various moorland birds. He was also well practised in putting up hides along the cliff faces, where he would take good pictures of nesting ravens and peregrine falcons. He scared the life out of me the first time he showed me where he had erected a hide opposite a raven's nest. I couldn't identify it at first when he pointed it out to me as we stood below a bracken-covered slope that wound its way towards the high cliffs to the left of a waterfall. Tommy pointed towards a holly bush on a ledge, a little way down from the top of the cliff that looked insignificant because of its distance from us. 'Look through your binoculars and you'll see it beside the holly bush,' he explained. It was so expertly hidden and covered in bits of heather and moor grass that I could barely make out the camouflaged cloth of the canvas hide. 'I hope you're not going up there without a rope!' I remarked. Tommy was like a goat on the mountain and I knew that he hadn't even thought twice about climbing up onto the high ledge when he erected the hide there all by himself. He was actually disappointed that I would see the necessity for a rope but then I did not regard myself as a climber. I only climbed when I had to! There was no climbing involved in filming hen harriers but there was a great deal of searching involved in trying to locate where they were nesting.

A survey of the hen harrier was being carried out in Wicklow by the Irish Wildbird Conservacy, David Scott being the person most involved. He had useful information but I found that Tommy Kehoe seemed to be able to pinpoint the harriers better than anyone. He worked in a camera shop in Dublin and assisted me at weekends and in the evenings during the long days of summer.

There was nothing Tommy Kehoe liked more than to be involved with photographing wildlife all day long. He was more than delighted when eventually I asked him to come and work for me full-time. We had been successfully filming the activities of a pair of peregrine falcons and we had erected a hide close to their eyrie, where I was able to capture sequences of the adults arriving at the nest and feeding their four downy chicks. We were able to follow the youngsters' development over several weeks, up to the point where they were ready to leave the nest. On Tommy's first day in his new job, we set out for the mountains to see how the young falcons were progressing. They must have left the nest that morning at daylight as there was no sign of them at the eyrie when we arrived. Eventually we spotted three of them some distance over to the right of the eyrie, where they had perched on some rocks about halfway up the cliff. It was only a matter of scrambling up the scree at the side of the cliff to reach a point where we were then level with the young peregrines.

When we walked out on to the main cliff, there was a gap in the long sloping slab of rock between ourselves and the birds. They were partly hidden by the cliff-face and getting any closer would have involved making a short jump across the gap, which, though not very wide, involved some risk. When I suggested that we wouldn't bother to try for the shot as the birds were only sitting and it was not all that important, Tommy replied: 'Give me the camera and I'll take the shot!' With that he took the camera, jumped across the crevasse and asked me to pass him over the tripod. He hid behind a jutting rock while he took a picture of one of the young peregrines; the other two had taken off and flown out around the other side of the cliff.

Tommy, who was only a couple of yards from where I stood, then came back and handed me the tripod, before preparing to jump over to my side of the crevasse. I took hold of the tripod and half turned around to lay it on the ground when I was aware of a sudden commotion. I quickly turned around and was barely in time to catch a glimpse of Tommy suddenly disappearing out of sight over the edge of the cliff. All I could do was let out a terrified shout. He had put his foot on a wet rock and had slipped before even attempting to cross back over the gap. Before I eventually found him I knew that he could not possibly have survived the 150-foot fall. The fifteen minutes it took me to locate where he had fallen at the base of the cliff felt like a week. After whispering a prayer in his ear I then made my way across the valley to the gamekeeper's lodge where I was able to make contact with the rescue helicopter. Tommy Kehoe's first day as a full-time assistant wildlife cameraman was the saddest day of my life.

12

Filmmaking
1980s

The film crew – Lesotho – The death of my parents –
More publications – The studio at the end of the garden –
Ó Riada retrospective – Life in the Seanad

The film crew

Shortly before I began the pre-production work on the film *Cry of the Mountain*, Pat Hayes decided that it was time for him to set up his own recording studio. He had worked for me faithfully for eight years and I could hardly expect him to remain in the same job forever. Nevertheless, it came as a shock to realise that from then on I would be without him. Pat's many talents and his imaginative and original ideas were invaluable in the production of the substantial number of programmes we made over the years. To have worked at close quarters with someone for such a long period and never to have had a disagreement or an argument in all that time leaves me with a whole string of pleasant memories. In later years I was glad to be able to use his sound studio to record music and dub my films. When he began working outdoors again I was able to have him record sound in the field for me on an independent basis. I suppose it was fitting that his last sound job was on a film we were making off the coast of Conamara, an area where we had made many programmes in the early years. He had gone to Canada for a week's holiday with his girl-friend Ken, and I had booked him in for the following week. But I was never to see Pat again; he died of a sudden heart attack a few days before he was to return home.

I met Jim Colgan when he was back home on holidays in Dublin. He had been working with the sound effects department in the Abbey

Theatre before joining the BBC's sound department in London. I invited Jim to come and work for me as a sound recordist and after he discussed the matter with Pat Hayes, he decided that moving back to Ireland and working with me would probably be a safe enough move!

Clare Simpson had graduated with a degree in fine arts in England. Her real interest was in films and her relatives in Ireland suggested that she contact me as someone who might assist her in finding work. I had little to offer her at the time, apart from asking her to write a series of articles in the *RTÉ Guide* in relation to my programmes. The editor of the *Guide* at the time encouraged producers to supply an article and photographs for each programme in the series. This weekly article helped to publicise the series and make viewers aware of the content of the particular programme.

By the time I had reached the editing stage of *Cry of the Mountain*, I was in a position to offer Clare a job assisting me in the studio. She had in the meantime been paying visits to editing studios around Dublin, making coffee for free, picking bits of waste film off the floor and playing around on the editing bench with them while the editor was at lunch. I sat her down at the editing machine and began explaining to her how to go about constructing *Cry of the Mountain*. She was an intelligent young woman with a bright sense of humour and she carried out the job very efficiently, even though she was totally unfamiliar with the wildlife of the countryside.

Apart from the birds of prey featured in the film, I had also included some of the ground-nesting mountain birds such as curlew and red grouse. One sequence featured a curlew opening its beak quite wide as it sat on its nest. I had been out of the studio on the morning that Clare was editing the activities of the curlews and on my return she asked me to look through the sequence and to take note of a sound effect that she had just worked into the film and was particularly proud of. She had found the sound of a curlew's lovely liquid whistle in my sound library and had accurately synchronised it with the bird opening its beak. I was sorry to disappoint Clare by telling her that the curlew I had filmed happened to be yawning, not calling!

The music for the film was specially composed by an up-and-coming young composer from Clonmel, Mícheál Ó Súilleabháin, who had studied music at UCD under the direction of Seán Ó Riada. The music was later released on an LP by Gael Linn under the same title as the film.

Clare remained working in the studio for about a year, until she eventually went off to find fame in Hollywood. One night a few years ago, watching the Academy Awards being presented to various winners, I saw Clare on the screen receiving an award for editing the well-known war film *Platoon*. I would like to think that the long road to the Oscars all began for her with the editing of *Cry of the Mountain!*

Lesotho

The films made by my team during the 1970s and 1980s included subjects above and below the water, close to home and in faraway places. We revisited the Red Sea, accompanied by Brendan Keegan and his diving team from UCG. A trip to Africa brought us to Lesotho, where we literally filmed 'on the roof of Africa'. I had Mary McGrath as a production assistant, Jim Colgan operating as a sound recordist and Dáithí Connaughton as camera assistant. Dáithí was a talented traditional flute player and we were therefore never short of good music. Apart from filming the local wildlife, the native Basotho pony was of particular interest to me and to Mary McGrath, who had been involved with horses all her life. Mary had some time previously been given the job of digging up the buried remains of Arkle and reassembling his skeleton for the museum at the National Stud. She was also a talented art restorer.

During the Anglo–Boer war (1899–1902), when the Boers declared war on Britain, horses were in huge demand and well over twenty thousand of the best Basotho ponies were purchased in Lesotho for the war. As a result, the quality of the native breed gradually deteriorated and never fully recovered. In more recent times, the Irish government made finance available through their Foreign Aid Programme to develop a breeding programme for the Basotho pony and to provide support for the establishment of Lesotho's National Stud. Part of the experimental study in this programme included crossing the Conamara pony with the native Basotho pony. This would infuse new blood into the breed and improve the quality of the animals. Arab stallions had already been used for the same purpose.

Those who have watched trotting ponies will have noticed their conspicuous gait. They have been trained to bring both the hind-leg and fore-leg forward on the same side, at the same time. The Basotho ponies do this naturally, with no training. They have learned this method from centuries of stepping their way along very narrow tracks on the edges of high cliffs in the mountains of Lesotho. The particular gait practised by these animals is known as a tripple and it makes riding very comfortable, which is why the Basotho pony is ideal for a rider who spends a long time in the saddle.

In one village where we filmed, a notice had been stuck on the wall of the local school announcing that a musical TV crew were to give a concert that night. We were the only film people around at the time, so obviously they meant us, and as I had no musical instrument with me, I was totally unprepared for a performance. There was no way we could disappoint the local people, however, especially the school children, and I decided that Dáithí and myself would have do something as neither Mary McGrath nor Jim Colgan were musicians.

The evening began with the African children entertaining us with a selection of Lesotho songs. When it came to our turn, Dáithí played on the concert flute while I accompanied him on a tom-tom, which was the nearest I could find to a bodhrán. By the time Dáithí had played his third reel, 'The Limestone Rock', I could see that the children were not really relating to our kind of music. There was one sound, however, that I knew all the village children would appreciate and I planned to give it a try as soon as Dáithí finished his third tune. Animal sounds usually appeal to young people. Imitating various animals was something I had used for children at home and there was no reason to believe that it wouldn't work here. Most families in the village kept a pig and I decided to imitate the sounds that a pig makes when it becomes over-excited. Cupping my hands together and pursing my lips, I drew my breath backwards, making a squealing sound in my throat. The African children screeched in delight. They related to the sounds immediately and it was even more successful than I had first thought. As soon as I finished the performance the children themselves began having a go at imitating pigs as well and, leaving the school hall, the sound of dozens of pigs was still ringing in our ears. The following morning on our way to do some more filming, we passed by the school and I could hardly believe my ears. The sound of dozens of little squealing pigs was coming from the classrooms. The children had obviously been practising all night!

There are only two ways in which the locals travel up into the mountain villages in Lesotho – either by horseback or in a light Cessna aircraft. I was surprised to learn that there were many old people in Lesotho who had never been on a bus but who had flown regularly in an aeroplane. We were fortunate in meeting Ireland's man in Lesotho, Martin Greene from the Department of Foreign Affairs, whose office was in the capital Maseru. Martin had a real understanding of the local community and was of great assistance to us in organising whatever was necessary by way of getting us to locations for filming. I was quite happy that our own government's participation in the various schemes being undertaken in Lesotho would be given publicity in my series of programmes to be transmitted on RTÉ. One of the areas I wanted to visit was the National Park. It had been established in 1970, only eight years earlier. Martin Greene wished to see the area for himself and I was delighted when he offered to accompany us there.

Sehlabathebe National Park is about 2,400 metres above sea level and occupies an area of approximately 65 square kilometres, at the source of the Tsoelikane River. We flew in a small plane from Maseru to an airstrip some 12 kilometres from the park. I knew that the rest of the journey would have to be covered on horseback and I thought that Martin was aware of this. He really didn't believe me when I mentioned that this would be the only way of travelling up that last stretch of the mountain. As we circled over the airstrip in preparation for landing, I could see below us an African sitting astride his mount with a group of horses close by. I counted a mount for each of us, Martin included, and a pack horse for our gear. Martin protested that he couldn't possibly travel by this method and that he had never even sat on a horse, let alone ridden one! Our pilot was quite sympathetic and as soon as we got out of the plane, he proceeded to give Martin Greene a riding lesson on the grassy airstrip. The best-qualified rider among us was Mary McGrath, who had plenty of experience where she lived in the Curragh. Jim Colgan and Dáithí Connaughton were not horsemen and I had not ridden for years, but we enjoyed the fairly rough mountain ride, which was led by our

African guide. Martin, however, hated every moment of it and promised that he would never again sit on a horse.

As the park was only in its infancy, various kinds of game were gradually being established. There were several species of antelope, the largest being the eland, which is more like an ox than an antelope. There was also the blesbok, once in danger of extinction, and the wildebeest, also known as a gnu. The oribi, a dwarf antelope standing 60 cm high at the shoulder, had also reappeared in the park. A feature of so much of the African landscape is the rich population of birds, and Sehlabathebe National Park was no exception. The most spectacular bird, which was to be seen soaring overhead, was the lammergeyer or bearded vulture, which drops bones of large mammals from a height in order to smash them on the rocks below. It can swallow bones the size of a lamb's femur.

We stayed in a small rest-house in the park, where we catered for ourselves. I was glad that I had included my fishing rod with the equipment, and I caught a nice trout in a nearby lake. We were due to fly back to Maseru the following morning, so we didn't have a great deal of time to spend in the National Park. Trying to convince Martin to ride all the way back was not easy, especially as the guide had disappeared overnight with no explanation as to where he had gone. 'How on earth are you going to find your way back?' Martin asked. 'You're not familiar with this area.' He was quite right: to find my own way back would have been extremely difficult. 'Don't worry about getting back. Just follow me,' was my reply, hoping that I was correct in thinking that it would only be a matter of mounting the horses, giving them free rein and letting them find their own way home. We headed away from the park with my pony in the lead, followed by Martin and the rest of the crew. They were intelligent animals and obviously had no wish to spend another night in the mountains. They brought us along much the same track that we had travelled previously and, just a short distance from the airstrip, there was our guide sitting on his pony as if he was expecting us all along.

The death of my parents

Back home it was sad to observe my father's general health deteriorating by degrees. For someone whose life was so occupied with books in a whole variety of ways, not being able to read must have been particularly hard for him to bear. His doctor probably never knew what the real state of his health was at any stage. Even when he was not feeling well and my mother insisted on him going to visit his GP, he informed the doctor that things were fine! He died on 6 August 1981.

The army gave my father full military honours. The hearse, draped in the tricolour and accompanied by an army motorcycle escort, travelled the few miles from the church in Bray to the graveyard at Kilmacanogue. The picturesque location in the shadow of the Great Sugarloaf Mountain was a location my mother had chosen for their burial many years previously. During the ceremony, as I stood at the graveside with my mother, I could see on the brow of a hilly field a short distance away, looking in our direction, a pony standing as if to attention. At the sound of the firing party he ran off. Somehow I managed to hold back my emotion until the army bugler sounded the last post, and then, as the tears flowed down my cheeks, I bade him a whispered 'Slán, a Dhaidín!'

My mother had always been concerned that she might die first and that my father would then be left to fend for himself. She had confided in a friend that she would not be around for very long after he went. Mother always meant what she said and in December of that year, when she caught a cold, the doctor thought it better to send her to hospital. Nothing very serious, we all thought, but it seems that she had no wish to continue living any longer. She died on 19 December 1981, a little over four months after my father.

More publications

The publication of three books for the Bank of Ireland as part the celebration of their bicentenary in 1982 was something with which my father would have loved to be involved. Bill Finlay SC, Governor of the bank, saw the need for books on Irish wildlife for children, and the bicentenary, in his view, provided an ideal opportunity to do something about it. The title I used for the publishing company was Amach Faoin Aer Publishing, a slight change from the title of our early television series *Amuigh Faoin Spéir*. The company had already published a whole series of film-strips for use in primary schools. They seem quite out of date nowadays, compared with the visual technology of the twenty-first century, but in 1980 teachers all around the country were delighted to have them. Grants were available from the Department of Education for the purchase of projectors and film-strips. The titles ranged across a number of interesting subjects which included nature stories, studies of pets, domestic and wild animals, birds, hibernation, migration, basic ecology and plant life. During those years a very good zoologist, Ruth Gallagher, worked for me. Ruth was extremely enthusiastic and had a great understanding of how to make the environment interesting for children. We used hundreds of my own colour slides to reproduce the pictures, and a whole series of booklets was published as a complement to the film-strips. The subject matter was carefully chosen from the Social and Environmental section of the Primary Curriculum and the text was given in both Irish and English.

The three books for the Bank of Ireland were *Coinín the Rabbit*, *Detective in the Wild* and *Wild in the Garden*. They were aimed at children of different ages. *Coinín the Rabbit* and *Detective in the Wild* were bilingual and all three books were highly successful and enjoyed by children all over the country. Many more books in relation to wildlife and the countryside were published in the following years under the Amach Faoin Aer and Country House labels. One of these was *Wild Ireland*, which the botanist David Bellamy launched in Dublin in 1984. The title was the same as the one I had used for a programme commissioned by the BBC's Natural History Unit for their series *The World About Us* and transmitted on RTÉ and the BBC. Being involved with the best natural history unit in the world in the making of *Wild Ireland* was a very exciting and worthwhile experience. My associate producer and commentator was Barry Paine, whose voice I had so often heard on wildlife programmes. Síle Fullom was Barry's production assistant and had been working at the BBC for years. Both had connections with Ireland through a grandparent, which gave them a more than usual interest in the production. Barry loves Ireland and still comes to visit on the slightest excuse!

The studio at the end of the garden

Our own children had acting parts in *Amuigh Faoin Spéir* when they were very young, and now they were never far away from where they could observe filmmaking as a daily occupation. All the pre-production and post-production work happened in the studio at the end of our garden. At the early stages of their various careers, each of the children became involved in programmes of one kind or another, the only exception being our eldest daughter Aoife, who was always more interested in matters of a medical nature and, instead of filmmaking, concentrated on becoming a successful nutritionist. In later life she has featured regularly on Raidió na Gaeltachta, where advice is sought on matters relating to diets and dieting. Éanna, who was next in line, operated as a sound recordist on *Wild Ireland* and subsequently for a while on my RTÉ series *Island Wildlife*. That was before he decided to make his living working with wood, like his grand-uncle Mick, who was a master cabinet-maker. Róisín joined the team as a production assistant on a later series, *Exploring the Landscape*. That was during a period when she was on holidays from the National College of Art, where she was studying to become a designer in glass. Cian began by recording sound for various programmes, including *Why Watch Birds, My Forgotten River* and *Tír na mBádóirí* (Land of the Boatmen, 1986). He then spent a period as an assistant to the film editor Dáibhí Doran, who was editing *Tír na mBádóirí*. Working in an editing room is very good training for any young person interested in film, especially with an editor of Dáibhí's standard. Cian had to do everything from making coffee and keeping Dáibhí in good humour, to dealing entirely with the colour laboratories in London. Finally there was our youngest daughter Doireann, who worked very efficiently on my most recent series for RTÉ, *A Life in the Wild,* and also on the BBC series *Ballykissangel*. Doireann enjoys working full-time in the production end of TV programme-making rather than spending time behind a camera or sitting beside a recording machine.

Ó Riada retrospective

It was while I was in the studio working on a script for one of my television programmes that I received a call from impresario Noel Pearson. I was familiar with the name but I had never met the man. Speaking with a Dublin accent, he came to the point immediately: 'I'm organising a retrospective concert for Seán Ó Riada, and I'd like to meet you to talk about it.' 'When do you want to meet?' I asked. 'Well, where do ye live?' he queried. 'Outside Bray, on the road to Enniskerry'. 'Aw, Jaysus, it's a f----n' pen friend you want!' was Pearson's colourful reply. He was obviously of the opinion that I lived out in 'the back of beyond', so I decided that meeting him in town would be less complicated and we arranged to meet in Dublin the following day.

Noel Pearson did not believe in doing things by halves. He had booked the National Concert Hall for three consecutive nights where he planned to stage a weekend of Ó Riada's music. It would begin on Friday 24 April 1987 with a Film Score Night. This would include the various compositions for the many films with which Ó Riada was involved, including *Mise Éire, Saoirse* and *An Tine Bheo*. Both the RTÉ Concert Orchestra and the RTÉ Symphony Orchestra were to take part in the performances. The Film Score Night would be followed on the Saturday by a Traditional Night and the weekend would come to a close with a Symphonic Night on the Sunday. It was interesting to observe how Pearson operated and how he could immediately hand over responsibility to others, once he felt they were capable of handling the situation. I made a few suggestions as to what might be done music-wise when Ceoltóirí Chualann would be playing. Almost before I realised it, Pearson had given me the task of practically running the first half of the concert for the Traditional Night on Saturday! He could see that if he left that part of the concert to me he would have half a concert less to worry about.

The ideal situation would be to have all the members of Ó Riada's original group Ceoltóirí Chualann present for the concert, but as Paddy Moloney, Martin Fay and Seán Keane were away playing with The Chieftains, that was not possible. I was fortunate, however, in being able to call on two excellent fiddle players, Paddy and Séamus Glackin, who had been members of my own group Ceoltóirí Laighean. They were familiar with Ceoltóirí Chualann's style of playing and were accustomed to performing on the concert stage. Peadar Mercier, Michael Tubridy, John Kelly, Seán Potts and Ronnie McShane, all original members of Ceoltóirí Chualann, were available to play on the night. Organising the musicians reminded me of how John Kelly had described Ceoltóirí Chualann in the early days when he said, 'We're not a band! We're a crowd!' Although the concert would not be taking place for several weeks

I realised that there would be a great deal of work involved in gathering the musicians together and arranging rehearsals. At the same time I also had to look after my filmmaking in order to earn a living.

In the midst of a lot of frenetic activity, a telephone call came from the Taoiseach's office. It was Mr Haughey's secretary announcing that the Taoiseach wished to speak to me. I had received a call from his secretary on previous occasions, once when I wanted to arrange to have the writer Deirdre Purcell interview Charlie Haughey for one of my books for children, *Wildlife* Book 3. There was another occasion when Mr Haughey had a query in relation to some aspect of wildlife. And I had also contacted his office about filming on Inis Icealáin, Mr Haughey's island off the Kerry coast. Although I had been to Inis Icealáin before he had ever set foot on it, I felt it was only proper that I should inform him whenever I wished to go there. Strangely enough we were never on the island at the same time.

The phone call on this particular occasion related to the Ó Riada concert. 'Charlie Haughey here,' said the voice on the other end of the phone. 'Good morning Taoiseach!' I said. 'You know that I am officiating at this Ó Riada concert,' he announced, as if I should have known about it all along. 'Actually I didn't,' was my surprised reply. 'Can you give me any information on Seán Ó Riada?' he asked. 'Yes of course.' 'You'll bring it in to me. Thank you!' And he put down the phone. Telephone conversations with Charlie Haughey always seemed to end very suddenly. It was if he regarded the phone as an instrument that was only for short, abrupt messages.

That particular week was a busy one for me in the studio and as there was no special reason for travelling into Dublin, I had not yet brought the Ó Riada material into the Taoiseach's office. The concert, after all, was several weeks away and there could hardly be any great urgency about the information he required. On Monday morning of the following week, there was another telephone call from the Taoiseach's office and again it was the secretary announcing that Mr Haughey wished to have a word with me. 'Good morning Taoiseach!' 'When are you coming in to see me?' I thought it just a little strange that he was asking me to come in and see him. 'Well, I cannot come in today as I have a producer from the BBC with me here at the moment,' I replied. 'Can you not come in at any time today?' he asked a little impatiently. 'Well, I'll try and make it at lunch-time.' I could not understand why he was in such a hurry, but knowing how Charlie Haughey liked to have things done well, I took it that he wished to familiarise himself with the Ó Riada material well in advance of the opening night of the concert.

I managed to reach town just after lunch and I was ushered up to the Taoiseach's office where he welcomed me cordially. We chatted for a while, about little or nothing. I had my large envelope of Ó Riada material in my hand and I kept wondering if he was ever going to mention the concert. Then came the bombshell: 'If I were to offer you a seat in the Senate would you accept it?' I could hardly believe what I was hearing. 'The Senate?' I replied. 'But I'm not a politician. I know nothing about politics!' 'I know that,' answered the Taoiseach, 'but I would like to have you in there'. 'Why are you offering me the seat?' I asked, stunned. 'Because if you were to accept it I would be seen to be serious about the environment,' he answered quickly. 'I would really have to think about this,' I said. 'How long do I have?' 'Five minutes!' he snapped. 'I will have to think about it! I said, at the same time feeling that there was a sense of unreality about the whole situation. He gave me his telephone number and asked me to get back to him urgently.

This was a very serious situation for me and one that I would have to resolve pretty quickly. I eventually tracked down a friend who, like myself, had no political connections and, after a lot of discussion with him, I made a decision. Later that afternoon I telephoned the Taoiseach, thanked him for his offer and accepted a seat in Seanad Éireann. His response was brief as usual and he asked me to keep the news of the appointment to myself for the time being.

Whatever about being suddenly catapulted into the political arena, there was the urgent matter of music and musicians to contend with just then. Noel Pearson had never met Ó Riada, but to quote from his introduction in the elaborate concert souvenir programme: 'Throughout the months of preparation for this weekend I heard stories of Ó Riada the film director, Ó Riada the angler, Ó Riada the hunter, Ó Riada the laird, Ó Riada the lad and Ó Riada the odd man out. This weekend is not about any of those Ó Riadas. This weekend is about Ó Riada the musician, the composer, the artist.'

Pearson's talent as an impresario was evident in the distinguished group of people he had assembled to honour Ó Riada. In paying tribute to some of them, Pearson wrote at the end of his introduction: 'What better accomplices to join in the celebrations than Thomas Kinsella, Seamus Heaney, John Montague and Louis le Brocquy. For their poetry and painting of Ó Riada we're all indebted; for their participation in this Retrospective, I am extremely pleased and grateful. Finally, of all the productions I have been involved in, this surely has been one of the happiest for me and I hope it will be for you too.'

On the opening night of the *Ó Riada Retrospective*, the host was actor Joe Lynch but the task of introducing the Taoiseach was left to me. After I introduced him from the stage, the Taoiseach, who stood at the podium at the far side to my left, turned towards me and said: 'Go raibh maith agat, a Sheanadóir!' This was the first time my appointment to the Senate had been made public. The weekend, as expected, was a great success and the Concert Hall was full for all three concerts. The Traditional Night was quite nostalgic for those of us who had been members of Ceoltóirí Chualann. The last time we had played together was sixteen years previously at Seán Ó Riada's funeral in Cúil Aodha, and coming together for the concert was our first time appearing on stage without him. The guest artists on the night included the piper Liam O'Flynn, traditional singer Darach Ó Catháin, virtuoso whistle player Mary Bergin, Julia and Billy Clifford on fiddles, *seancahaí* Éamon Kelly, Peadar Ó Riada and the singer Seán Ó Sé. After the interval Donal Lunny introduced his new band and the concert came to a close with a performance from Cór Chúil Aodha under the direction of Peadar Ó Riada.

Life in the Seanad

The Seanad consists of sixty members. Eleven are nominated by the Taoiseach, three each are elected by the National University of Ireland and the University of Dublin and forty-three are elected from panels of candidates having knowledge and practical experience of a variety of interests and services. It is most unusual for a Taoiseach to nominate to the Seanad five members who are not politicians. The five nominees nominated by Charlie Haughey were: Sir John Robb, an eminent surgeon from Northern Ireland who was renowned for his skill in treating bomb victims during his period at the Royal Victoria Hospital; Professor George Eogan, whom Charlie Haughey had on occasions described as his favourite archaeologist; John Magnier, the well-known bloodstock breeder, owner and trainer; the playwright Brian Friel, and myself. John Robb was the only one of the five newly nominated senators who had any political experience. He was first nominated by Charlie Haughey in 1982 and he was re-appointed by Garret FitzGerald when he became Taoiseach the following year.

With the exception of John Robb, we were all totally unfamiliar with the business of the Seanad. Practically all Bills brought before the Seanad are Government Bills and motions. These are Bills that have been initiated in the Seanad by the Leader of the House or have been initiated in and passed by the Dáil. As a majority of the Bills would not have been of interest to the independent senators, most of them did not take part in the debates. That is not to say that the arguments for or against particular Bills were not interesting. The contributions from the other elected senators, including Mary Robinson, John A. Murphy, David Norris, Brendan Ryan and Joe O'Toole, to name but a few, were at times quite lively. The independent senators who sat on the government side of the House would have been expected to support the government, but whenever I thought a motion coming from the opposite side of the House deserved support, I voted in favour of it.

I was in the studio when I received a further phone call from the Taoiseach's office. 'Mr Haughey wishes to have a word with you, Senator.' 'A Sheanadóir!' It was the Taoiseach's voice. 'I'm establishing a National Heritage Council and I'm putting you on it. The chairman will be Lord Killanin. My office will be in touch with you shortly.' And that was it. I suppose it is nice to be asked. But then I wasn't asked. It seems that I was on the Heritage Council before I even knew it! Another member, the botanist Ann Quinn, learned about her place on the Council when she read it in *The Irish Times*! When Lord Killanin, who was over seventy, was asked by Mr Haughey if he would take charge of the Council, he responded by saying, 'If I am to be chairman of the National Heritage Council, Taoiseach, I think that you should first slap a preservation order on me!' But whatever about making a joke about his age, there was nothing wrong with the chairman's mind – he was most astute and very perceptive. Establishing a National Heritage Council was another example of Charlie Haughey's imaginative ideas.

The National Heritage Council came into being on 5 September 1988, the date on which it was formally launched by the Taoiseach. After the Taoiseach departed, we all sat down for our first inaugural meeting. Lord Killanin was at the head of the long, polished table holding some official papers, his small half-set of reading glasses perched on the end of his nose. Addressing us in his Anglo-Irish accent he said, 'The situation in Ireland is that we do not have an Honour's List as such, and when the government thinks rather highly of you, they bang you on to some committee or other!' He had a good sense of humour and the more I came to know the chairman the better I liked him. Our meetings were held in the Taoiseach's Department for as long as Charlie Haughey was in office.

There were occasions when members of the Council travelled out of Dublin to have meetings at different venues, or to visit a particular place that might be of interest to the Council. This was necessary as we had been given the responsibility of distributing National Lottery Funds to heritage projects in various parts of the country, subject to the approval of the Taoiseach. Travelling with the chairman in the company of Council members Maurice Craig and the architect Austin Dunphy was an education in itself, as we hardly passed a building that they did not have some interesting information to share with us about.

I am sometimes asked if I knew at the time that Charlie Haughey was receiving money from certain benefactors. I knew nothing about his private affairs and, like many others, was under the impression that he had made his money from his former accounting practice and from selling some of his land. Whenever we happened to meet he always addressed me, 'Ah! a chara.' I was never invited to any of his functions or parties and the only time I saw the inside of his house was when I attended a meeting in relation to the re-introduction of the sea eagle. I did ask a Fianna Fáil senator on one occasion why the Taoiseach always had some suspect individuals around him, and his reply was, 'Oh, he has to have these people around him!' I still don't really know what he meant.

Mr Haughey was a man of action who wanted things to happen quickly. He was not a patient individual and when he wished to re-introduce the sea eagle to the coast of Kerry, he imagined that the birds would be flying around the Blasket Islands sooner than was physically possible. He had formed a small committee for the sea eagle project, of which I was a member, but when we explained that it would be a long-term operation such as the successful programme carried out in Scotland, he went against our recommendations. He wasn't prepared to wait. He took somebody else's advice and the project then ended in failure. It was a similar situation in the case of the interpretative centres in Co. Wicklow and in the Burren in Co. Clare. The Heritage Council's balanced view of the situation with regard to both counties was ignored. But it should be remembered that Charlie Haughey was not alone in refusing to listen to the recommendations of the Heritage Council. Subsequent Taoisigh were to follow suit in relation to the interpretative centres, at an eventual cost to the taxpayer of millions of pounds.

13

Conservation Matters
1990s

*The history of the landscape – Conserving the boglands – The Burren
saga – Leaving the Dargle – Leaving the Seanad – The battle of
the stoat – Ireland's Wild Countryside – The Wild Islands Series –
The king of fishes – The otter family*

The history of the landscape

The vehicle was conveniently parked between Buswell's Hotel and the gates of Leinster House in Kildare Street and it was my first experience of standing on the back of a lorry as a form of protest. It was part of a demonstration objecting to the government's plan to cap RTÉ's advertising revenue. Most people regarded the strategy as Fianna Fáil's way of getting back at RTÉ, and the person whom they were blaming most for it was Ray Burke, Minister for Justice and Communications. I was still a member of the Seanad and it must have been unusual to have a Taoiseach's nominee on a truck outside Dáil Éireann, condemning one of the government's own senior ministers! In spite of a wave of objections to the imposition of the cap, however, it seemed to have had little effect on the members of the government as they went ahead with their decision to penalise RTÉ.

I had been considering making a series of films in 1988 on the history of the landscape of Ireland. It was to be a change from my usual form of programmes, which had dealt specifically with wildlife. I had intended that Cian would be the sole cameraman on the job, should it be commissioned. Having discussed the subject with Cian we decided to approach John Feehan, an up-and-coming geologist who in the 1980s was engaged in research in Trinity College, Dublin. His home was on the doorstep of the Sliabh Bloom Mountains, in Co. Offaly, about which he had written an interesting book. Apart from his expertise in geology, he was also very knowledgeable in relation to botany and entomology. When I met John Feehan at his home in Birr and suggested the idea to him, he was very enthusiastic and agreed to be involved. I then explained to him that RTÉ would first have to be persuaded that the idea was worthwhile.

John was a great admirer of Frank Mitchell, also of Trinity College and former President of the Royal Irish Academy. In his book *Reading the Irish Landscape*, which was published in 1986, Frank told the story of the shaping of the land from the beginning of time to the present day, by all the varying forces: nature, sea, climate, man and machine. This was the approach we wished to take with the new series and when I submitted the proposal to RTÉ under the title *Exploring the Landscape*, it was accepted. We spent many weeks filming for the series and included areas of the countryside in the north, east, south and west. John Feehan presented the series. This was a first venture for John but Cian is well able to put his subjects at ease while filming them, and as a result John appeared as if he had been presenting programmes all his life! Images of the land-scape can often appear dead and uninteresting and this is especially true in the case of rocks. In order to add a variety of movement and a touch of imagination to the pictures, we had a special crane built for the camera, and this, along with a dolly and tracks, really brought life to the photography. The series received wonderful reviews and earned John Feehan a coveted Jacob's Award.

Conserving the boglands

Bogs once covered one-sixth of Ireland but due to drainage, peat extraction and commercial developments, less than one-fifth of the original area remains. Were it not for the watchful eye of the Irish Peatland Conservation Council (IPCC), many more of our peatland areas would have been lost long ago. The importance of conserving Irish peatlands had been recognised by the European Community, and in the early 1980s the European Parliament passed a resolution stressing the need for bog conservation in Ireland. This resulted from a Dutch member repeatedly pointing out the international importance of the remaining Irish bogs. In

1987 I was invited to Holland to attend a Peatlands Symposium. The travelling party included the Minister of State, Noel Tracey, Mary Banotti MEP, Dr Catherine O'Connell and Peter Foss of the IPCC, as well as several other botanists who had an interest in peatlands.

The Dutch botanist Dr Matthijs Schouten was largely responsible for the Dutch interest in Irish bogs and for organising the trip to Holland. At the conference, His Royal Highness, Prince Bernhard, handed over to the Irish government the title of Scragh Bog in Co. Westmeath, to show the Dutch commitment to assisting Ireland in its bog conservation efforts – a clever move on the part of the Dutch, I thought, towards persuading our government to take a far more serious view of conservation in Ireland! It was on the trip to Holland that I first met Mary Banotti, whom I would see taking part in a variety of conservation campaigns on many future occasions. She had a great personality and a good sense of humour and made her presence felt in every company.

The Burren saga

Our peatland areas were not the only places that were a cause for concern. Plans had been drawn up by the Office of Public Works in the late 1980s for an interpretative centre in the Burren National Park in Co. Clare and another interpretative centre at Lugalla in Co. Wicklow. A team from the Office of Public Works (OPW) had already made a presentation to the National Heritage Council, after which the Council members visited both sites. The OPW proposal had received the approval of the Taoiseach but it seemed to many of us on the Council that the cart was being put very much before the horse. Here was an elaborate building plan for each of the centres but no thought whatsoever had been given either to a conservation strategy or a management plan. Both sites were sensitive conservation areas. This was particularly so in the case of the Burren, and no farmer, for example, would have been allowed to erect a building in either location. In the case of the site in Wicklow, on the side of a mountain, it would not have been possible to use the centre in winter because of weather conditions and even during the summer there were times when the area was often covered in mist. Many people were of the opinion that it would have been far more sensible to locate the interpretative centres close to a village where they would be used on a regular basis by the local communities. The main attraction of the scheme as far as the government was concerned was that money had become available from Europe and their feeling was that, come what may, no effort should be spared in applying for it.

I arranged a meeting with Noel Tracey, Minister of State at the Office of Public Works and with whom I had several conversations on the trip to Holland. The President of the Association for National Parks in the United States accompanied me to the meeting. He informed the minister that thirty years earlier, in the United States, they had abandoned the policy of building interpretative centres close to nature. He also issued a personal invitation to Noel Treacy to visit America, adding that he would accompany him to locations where they were actually pulling back the centres to populated areas. The minister was very cordial but the invitation to the United States was not accepted and the government's view of the situation did not change. I later learned that the minister was having some doubts about OPW's policy but that he was persuaded by senior civil servants that they would win out in the end.

As the arguments for and against the location of the interpretative centres continued, the controversy began to make headlines both in the press and on the airwaves. Early in 1991 the Burren Action Group (BAG) was formed. BAG evolved as a local response to oppose plans by the Irish National Parks and Wildlife Service to develop a large-scale interpretative centre at Mullaghmore in the Burren. The members planned to campaign for the relocation of the centre to a suitable site in or near a village. Their argument was that the Burren, being the largest karstic limestone area in western Europe, was known internationally for both its unique flora and its spectacular archaeology. The Mullaghmore area, for which the interpretative centre was planned, is widely regarded as one of the most interesting, diverse and sensitive parts of the Burren. The Burren Action Group consistently argued that visitor facilities should be sited in villages – where there are already existing services and where economic benefits can accrue to the local populations – and not in the sensitive core area of the Burren National Park.

An Taisce criticised the approach of the OPW in acting under Section 84 of the 1963 Planning Act, which facilitates developments needed for urgent government use, thus by-passing the normal planning process. They were not the only group to criticise the government's policy in relation to the interpretative centres. Every conservation organisation in the country was opposed to it, including the Irish Peatland Conservation Council, the Mountaineering Council of Ireland, World Wide Fund for Nature, Plantlife International, the Conservation Foundation and a large number of individuals from the north Clare area. But officialdom dug in its heels and refused to budge. On 22 April 1991 plans for the Burren National Park, with an interpretative centre at Mullaghmore, were announced by Vincent Brady TD in Lisdoonvarna, Co. Clare. It had reached the point where local politicians had become involved and unfair promises were being made to certain individuals in the area, with the result that some local people were left with the impression that they were going to make a good deal of money. The Fianna Fáil politician Brendan Daly TD, on turning the first sod, held it aloft and exclaimed in a loud voice, 'Solid gold!' Fine Gael politicians were also getting in on the act.

In July 1991 a joint submission was presented to the EU Directorate General XI (Environment) by the Burren Action Group, An Taisce, the World Wide Fund for Nature and Plantlife International. It was entitled 'The case for an independent and comprehensive environmental impact assessment of a visitor/interpretation centre at Mullaghmore for the Burren National Park in Co. Clare, Ireland'. The main concerns of the report related to: (i) potential impacts on the freshwater systems (on-site sewage treatment; water abstraction), (ii) trampling pressure and disturbance in a wider area around the proposed site, (iii) creation of a development precedent and subsequent development pressures, (iv) impact of traffic generation in an as yet undeveloped area.

Dr Ludwig Kraemer, a senior official in the EU Commission's environmental directorate, acting on behalf of Commissioner Carlo Ripa di Meana, stated in a letter to Michael D. Higgins TD that 'an environmental impact assessment would be warranted' for the centre and that assistance under the Structural Funds should only be forthcoming 'if it is satisfactorily demonstrated that there will be no significant adverse effects'. He also stated, 'the Commission has received an unusually high level of correspondence' on the subject.

On 7 October 1991 Vincent Brady TD, Minister of State, announced that the OPW would commission an environmental impact survey (EIS) dealing with 'the proposal to provide a visitor centre on the site selected by the OPW'. One would have hardly expected the result to be anything but favourable to the Department and, as everybody had guessed, in March 1992 the EIS concluded that the interpretative centre should go ahead! The study was condemned by BAG, An Taisce and various international environmental groups as 'woefully inadequate'. In May 1992 the Director General of the IUCN (International Union for the Conservation of Nature and Natural Resources), Dr Martin Holdgate, expressed serious reservations about the proposed development in response to the EIS and suggested that an alternative location be sought. In December 1992 the Burren Action Group sought a High Court injunction restraining the OPW from further development at Mullaghmore and although this was refused they were granted a Judicial Review, set for 28 January 1993.

In the meantime a new government had been voted in by the Oireachtas. The Fianna Fáil/Labour Coalition negotiations for government had been delayed by a row over who should have control over developments at Mullaghmore, but Fianna Fáil's Noel Dempsey (Minister of State with Responsibility for the OPW) won control of the future of the project, despite Labour's attempts to bring it under the jurisdiction of Michael D. Higgins (Department of Arts, Culture and the Gaeltacht).

On 12 February 1993 the High Court ordered work on the partially completed centre at Mullaghmore to cease on the grounds that: (i) the OPW actions were *ultra vires*; (ii) the OPW could not, as was previously believed, be considered exempt from the requirement to seek planning permission for its developments. This rendered many previous developments carried out by the OPW illegal and on 16 February 1993 the government introduced legislation retrospectively legitimising OPW developments and decided to appeal the planning element of the High Court judgement to the Supreme Court. On 26 May 1993 the Supreme Court rejected the government appeal. The fact that a voluntary organisation had succeeded in changing the law of the land was a historic occasion for the Burren Action Group and for the country as a whole.

Noel Dempsey was now the minister in charge of OPW, and Dr Emer Colleran of UCG, who was a prominent member of the Burren Action

Group, requested a meeting with him to which I was invited. Our discussions went on for quite some time but we had no indication as to what the eventual outcome would be or if we had made any impression at all on the minister. In November 1994 An Bord Pleanála refused the OPW permission to develop an interpretative centre planned for the Wicklow National Park at Luggala in Co. Wicklow. Garech de Brún, whose property would have been overlooked by the centre, had put a lot of time and effort into fighting that development. But west of the Shannon, the construction of an interpretative centre in the Burren had already begun.

The following December Labour withdrew from the Coalition government in a row over the appointment of a new Attorney General. The new government formed by Labour, Fine Gael and the Democratic Left gave unequivocal responsibility for the current and future policy on national parks to the Department of Arts, Culture and the Gaeltacht under Minister Michael D. Higgins. On 28 March 1995 Michael D. Higgins announced that 'the partially completed buildings (at Mullaghmore) are to be dismantled' and he invited interested parties to participate in a 'management plan for the Burren before decisions are made to the site or sites of visitor centres for the National Park'.

The uncompleted structures, however, were not dismantled. In July 1996 Minister Higgins announced that he would apply for planning permission to retain one-sixth of the originally proposed and partially constructed centre for use as an access point but without interpretation facilities. This announcement went solidly against his earlier pronunciations on the subject. On 5 December 1996 The Heritage Council submitted a detailed series of observations on the planning application, which included the following: 'The Heritage Council is severely critical of the quality of the materials submitted by the OPW in support of its planning application for the "Entry Point" at Mullaghmore.'

To make this ten-year saga a little shorter, An Bord Pleanála held a ten-day oral hearing in Ennis in July 1999. It was interesting to observe the contrast between the government's apparently unlimited resources in relation to the barristers, higher civil servants and various experts who were present at the hearing in support of the OPW and the limited funds available to a voluntary organisation such as the Burren Action Group, the majority of whose supporters were paying for it all out of their own pockets. The general feeling after the hearing was that we had done well but the possibility of preventing the OPW going ahead with their plans looked slim.

It was in March 2000 that An Bord Pleanála announced their decision, which was to refuse the OPW permission for the development. In July the Burren Action Group sought a High Court order to have the site at Mullaghmore on the Burren restored to the condition it was in before the development began. The judge in the case was Justice Flood, of tribunal fame, and this was to be his last case. Justice Flood's ruling was in favour of the Burren Action Group. They had finally won the battle and secured a High Court order to have the site at Mullaghmore restored! The cases brought before the courts were known as Howard & Others vs. the Commissioners of Public Works and there were seven plaintiffs – Emer Colleran, P.J. Curtis, Lelia Doolan, Patrick McCormack, Finola McNamara, James Howard and John O'Donoghue. There were hundreds of people in the wider group but the plaintiffs actually stood to lose their houses if they had been sued for costs. In May 2001 the rehabilitation work at Mullaghmore was completed.

A huge amount of money was squandered by the Office of Public Works during that ten-year campaign. Many of its own personnel were totally opposed to the locations chosen for the interpretative centres, as were other civil servants outside that department. Some of them had even encouraged me in private to keep up the pressure, stating that they were not in a position to say anything. Time and resources that should have gone into protecting our environment and our wildlife was wasted in fighting what became a very bitter political campaign. The only prominent elected politician from the three largest parties to come out in public in support of our campaign was MEP Mary Banotti who, as a result, had to suffer insults from other politicians including members of her own Fine Gael party.

Leaving the Dargle

Regardless of what county one cares to visit, it is plain that the changes to the Irish landscape in the last forty years have been quite dramatic. Co.

Wicklow, situated as it is on the doorstep of our capital city, suffers huge pressures. The demand for building land has been immense in the 'Garden of Ireland' and is certain to continue. Miles of new roadways have swallowed up important habitats, not alone for terrestrial wildlife but also for aquatic life. Countless numbers of important nursery streams which have been culverted have lost their value as aquatic habitats for many varieties of plants and animals and especially for important wild populations of very young trout and salmon. Developers will look for any excuse to culvert streams through a pipe in order to gain a few extra metres of land for either roads or houses. Unfortunately the public is often not aware of this until it is too late to take any action. The Fisheries Boards who look after those valuable habitats are completely understaffed and underfunded and are totally frustrated in their attempts to protect our populations of wild fish.

When it became apparent in 1989 that the N11 dual carriageway was to come within yards of my studio in the Dargle Valley, I knew then that the time had come to leave my beloved River Dargle and find somewhere else to live. I was only a toddler when we relocated there from Galway and apart from that I had never moved house more than a few hundred yards. On that basis, therefore, my most recent move of six miles further south, in May 1989, could be classified as a major upheaval, even though I had not gone outside of the county boundary! Waving goodbye to the river was difficult enough but to leave Co. Wicklow. How could I?

Leaving the Seanad

On 15 June 1989 a General Election was held. When the Dáil assembled on 29 June, all candidates for the office of Taoiseach were defeated. It was the first time in the history of the state that the Dáil had failed to elect a Taoiseach. Charles Haughey then resigned but continued to act as Taoiseach, and when the Dáil re-assembled at the beginning of July, no further votes for Taoiseach were taken. Charles Haughey's Cabinet continued as Acting Ministers until his re-election on 12 July of that year. The election of the 26th Dáil and Seanad that resulted in a two-party government of Fianna Fáil and the Progressive Democrats changed the political scene completely and perhaps forever. Whoever had advised

Charles Haughey to call an election after a little over two years in office had made a major miscalculation. The Senate elections took place on 16 August 1989 but it was obvious that there was little chance of any non-politicians being offered a seat, especially as there was an agreement with the PDs that the Taoiseach's nominees would have to include three members from that party. My career as a senator was over.

The battle of the stoat

In 1990 I had the opportunity to make another film for the BBC's Natural History Unit. My associate producer for the programme was Pelham Aldritch-Blake, an angling enthusiast who had a particular interest in any river that offered him the possibility of catching a wild salmon or two. My previous producer Barry Paine had in the meantime retired from the BBC, but Síle Fullom, Barry's production assistant, chose to work on my film as her final job before retiring from the BBC. I was particularly keen to capture some good footage of stoat behaviour and, having a good field assistant in Neil Stronach, a zoology student from Trinity College, we were able to carry out some worthwhile research prior to filming. Many years before that I had filmed Neil's father Brian, also a zoologist, when he was studying wildfowl in Mayo.

We came upon the stoat when we were researching the sand martin. A typical habitat for sand martins is an undisturbed sandpit with a soft, sandy cliff-face. But we discovered a colony in a midland cut-away bog where the birds were nesting in a turf bank. While I was in my hide, concentrating on the sand martins, a stoat suddenly appeared as if out of nowhere. It bounded along the top of the bank, its arched back so typical of its cousins, the pine marten and the otter. These little animals can travel very fast – about 20 miles an hour when they are in a hurry. This stoat looked very much as if it meant business and was obviously intent on chasing something. Just as I was beginning to wonder what it had on its mind, it headed straight for the bank where the sand martins had their nesting burrows. I could tell by the alarmed, harsh twittering chorus of the martins that the birds had already spotted the little animal as they flew rapidly to and fro above the bank in helpless panic. The stoat paid no heed to their aerial stampede. It flipped down over the edge of the turf bank and into one of the small nest holes. In a matter of seconds it was out again, a young fledgling sand martin in its mouth. As it bounded over the bank and disappeared, five or six of the sand martins followed overhead, their rasping chirr-chirr-chirr calls filling the air. I couldn't quite see from my hide where the stoat had gone but it was back again as suddenly as it had vanished. Down the bank it went again and into another hole. As it poked its head out, it had another youngster dangling from its mouth.

The stoat paused for only a moment at the entrance, as if to see if the coast was clear and then over the bank it went again. It bounded over some loose sods of turf and headed off towards the clump of furze and disappeared. There was obviously a family of kits nearby in a well-hidden nest, possibly in one of several turf ricks at the edge of the bog. The stoat repeated the exercise four times, each trip ending with one young fledgling less for the sand martin colony. Later I wondered if any fledglings survived in the colony that week. It was early June, time enough for the sand martins to rear a second brood. By that time the family of stoats may have left the nest and moved further afield.

Ireland's Wild Countryside

I would have wished to study zoology, but my life did not flow in that path. There were some generous academics, however, who were obviously of the opinion that it was still not too late for me to have a science degree, and in 1991, on the recommendation of Professor Frank Convery, the National University of Ireland conferred on me an Honorary Doctorate in Science (D.Sc.). I was delighted to receive it from the Chancellor, Dr T.K. Whitaker, for whom I had great admiration. In the following year I was granted the UCD (University College Dublin) Lifetime Environmental Achievement Award, 'In recognition of a lifetime devoted to the achievement of the conservation and wise use of Ireland's environmental endowment.'

Then one day I received a telephone call from Sarah Mahaffy at Boxtree, a publishing company in London. She said she would like to commission me to write a book about Ireland's wildlife. It was quite a busy period for me and she could sense that I was not over-enthusiastic about her offer. However, she was a determined person and said that she would like to fly to Dublin to see me. When we met we discussed the format and the content of the book and agreed that there would be plenty of space for colour photographs, many of which would be from my own library. I knew that I could depend on Richard Mills, the wildlife photographer from Cork, to supply me with whatever might be missing from my own collection. There was less than a year for the project to be completed and I sought the co-operation of Richard Nairn, a local biologist who had an excellent knowledge of Irish wildlife. Richard was at hand whenever his assistance was required and the book would never have been finished within the year were it not for him. There was no difficulty with the title, which I took from the current series I was working on for RTÉ and which I had called *Ireland's Wild Countryside*.

The first programme in the series of *Ireland's Wild Countryside* was transmitted on RTÉ 1 on 23 April 1994. The series had five half-hour documentaries about different personalities who were involved with the wildlife of the countryside. *An Offering of Swans*, the first programme in the series, was devoted to Richard Collins's study of the mute swan, Ireland's largest wild bird. Richard had to date captured and ringed over 1,300 swans and he had logged 64,000 sightings of ringed swans during his study period. He was amusing in his narration, describing the swan as a giraffe duck. He explained that, based on his research, the tales of fidelity and devotion to family values among swans were more or less true. However, according to Richard, marital difficulties did occur and the divorce rate among Dublin swans was about 3 per cent! During the programme, he was to be seen taking to the water on several occasions, following and expertly capturing some of the swans as part of his fascinating study.

The other programmes in the series included personalities such as John Feehan in *Animals in Folklore* and Chris Wilson in *Birds of the Cold Wind*, telling his audience about the Wildfowl Reserve in Wexford. The film *Helena's Deer* featured Helena Harrington, who originally came to Ireland from Finland and lived in Waterford. The programme included sequences of Helena's large herd of sika deer as well as the other species of deer that occur in this country. Readers of *The Irish Times* are familiar with the name Lorna Siggins, the newspaper's environment correspondent. In the final programme, *Reporting on Nature*, Lorna was to be seen observing both wildlife and people while she gathered information in various parts of the country for the feature page of the newspaper. The series was cleverly edited by James Dalton, who is more familiar than anyone with every sound tape in my library. Cian and myself were the photographers and we used three soundmen for natural effects – Brendan Deasy, Pat Hayes and Simon Willis.

A second series followed, using the same format but with different personalities. They included Cathryn Hannon, a young ornithologist who had taken part in a recent nationwide survey of those most graceful of seabirds – terns or sea swallows; Maryangela Keane, who could recognise almost every rock and plant in the Burren in Co. Clare; Rory Harrington, a scientist who had studied the many changes in the land-scape of Ireland down through the centuries and who demonstrated how agriculture and forestry have a major role to play in how this country will look in the future; Michael Gibbons, an archaelogist who had made many exciting discoveries in his native Co. Galway but where one particular valley had to be avoided because according to the locals, 'it's polluted with fairies'; and lastly, Declan Dooge, a zoologist and primary school teacher who believed that future generations would have an understand-ing and a real love of their countryside if they were encouraged to take a closer look at the fascinating wildlife of their own particular area.

The Wild Islands Series

The commissioning editor in the Independent Film Unit at RTÉ, Claire Duignan, wrote to me at the beginning of January 1996 in relation to a twelve-part film series being proposed by S4C International and Scottish Television Enterprises. The series, *Wild Islands*, was to feature the wildlife of Ireland, England, Scotland and Wales. The executive producer was to be David Rolfe of Performance Films in Buckinghamshire. I had already sent in a proposal to RTÉ for a different series but Claire was very enthusiastic about the approach she had received from the two British broadcasters and suggested that I might like to consider the *Wild Islands* series instead. They had originally given it the title of *Wild Britain* even though Ireland was to be a very large part of it!

Having discussed the project at length with David Rolfe, I told Claire Duignan that I would be happy to work on the *Wild Islands* series. There were to be twelve half-hour films, three each from Ireland, England, Scotland and Wales. I was to supply the three Irish films, featuring a particular species of animal in two programmes, and a third programme illustrating a specific area or habitat in which a variety of wildlife would feature. I had only a year to complete the three films – a very short time to capture good animal behaviour sequences.

I had a very good team for the series, which included an energetic field assistant who had been working with me on other programmes before I began filming *Wild Islands*. My first contact with him had been in the 1980s when I had a telephone call from a young man who asked if he could come and show me some photographs he had taken of a peregrine falcon's eyrie. The mention of a peregrine's nest by someone who had been close enough to take pictures of the birds and who was obviously inexperienced, immediately set off alarm bells. I told the caller that I would very much like to see the pictures. He came to the studio that afternoon, extremely enthusiastic about the photographs he had taken of three or four very young peregrine chicks. Not wanting to crush his eagerness, I explained to him as gently as I could that although he had only been taking pictures, he might well have been arrested had a wildlife ranger found him up at the highly protected falcon's eyrie. It was actually more serious than that, as I found out some months later. On the day he was up at the eyrie one of the chicks appeared to be a bit poorly, so he took it home and nursed it for a few days and then when it looked health- ier he returned it to its nest! I can still visualise the look on a ranger's face if a culprit had told him that he was only borrowing the nestling to nurse it for a while but that he was eventually going to return it to its mother! The boy's name was Frank Doyle and, whatever about his unfamiliarity with the Wildlife Act, his concern for the peregrine chick was a sign that he really cared for the welfare of animals in the wild.

Frank was at the time working as a storeman at Hallmark, the picture- card firm, but he spent all his spare time outdoors. After his visit to the studio I contacted a good friend of mine, Jim Haine, who had been a birdwatcher since his schooldays and who had accompanied me on many filming trips. Jim had been carrying out a survey of the peregrine falcon population in the Wicklow area and he was very familiar with their eyries. Jim agreed to take Frank under his wing and bring him with him on his survey work in the mountains. He was as good as his word and brought Frank with him on many of his trips. I then began to train Frank as a wildlife camera assistant. His enthusiasm was boundless and he was prepared to do anything and go anywhere. He had worked with me on a number of films prior to the *Wild Islands* series and he had also done a course in mountain climbing. Frank eventually left his old job at Hallmark to devote more time to wildlife filmmaking.

The king of fishes

A film about a particular species of mammal is, on average, more likely to appeal to the public than for example a programme about a fish or an insect. Perhaps we see mammals as bearing more of a resemblance to ourselves and as a result we relate more easily to them. If I were to be asked to choose a particular fish instead of a mammal as a subject for a film, one that would immediately come to mind would be a fish whose superb leaping power has earned it the Latin name of Salmo, meaning leaper. Since its appearance some 10,000 years ago in the cold, glacial streams gushing from the retreating ice caps, people have been fascinated by this wonderful fish. It is of course the salmon, which, because of its fine taste and nutritional qualities, has been a favourite food for many generations.

When I chose to make a film called *The Wild Atlantic Salmon* for the *Wild Islands* series, I knew that its success would be very dependent on the weather. Salmon choose the middle of winter for their spawning activities, when days are at their shortest and the rivers are very often affected by seasonal floods. It would appear that their choice of the winter period is no mere accident; in fact it is the perfect time of year for the salmon to spawn. Both the extra hours of darkness and high water offer the fish some badly needed extra protection. The disadvantages are on the side of the filmmaker, whose work is made far more difficult by these conditions. Although I had an excellent adviser in Dr Ken Whelan, who was in charge of the Salmon Research Agency in Co. Mayo, there was nothing he could do to control the elements. But Ken was almost on first-name terms with the salmon, and with his expertise in all stages of the life-cycle of the fish, we were able to plan our shooting schedule far more accurately.

A very important section of the film was to include the salmon arriving on the gravel beds, where the male fish patrol their area and attempt to take control as the females prepare for spawning. My hope was that I would be able to film much of this fascinating behaviour provided the conditions were favourable. We carried out a great deal of research prior to filming and although it actually snowed during the eventual spawning sequences, fortunately the water was clear at the time and we were able to capture some dramatic salmon behaviour. Cian did most of the filming and his experience with the underwater gear really paid off. In the springtime we filmed the young salmon smolts on their journey downriver, as they prepared for their first trip to the sea. The little fish measure only five inches or so at this stage and miraculously turn from a golden, yellow-brown colour with little red and brown spots, to a beautiful silver. They had in fact donned silver sea-suits in preparation for their arrival in what would be for them a much more expansive and dangerous environment.

The otter family

The otter is also a difficult subject to film but is such an interesting animal that I really wanted to include it as the main actor in one of the programmes. Having introduced Frank Doyle to the ways of otters, I knew that I could depend on him when it came to making a film about them. An otter family would be essential for the story I had in mind for my second film, *The Land of the Wild Otter*, but finding a mother with young cubs could not by any means be guaranteed. I decided, however, that it would be worth the risk and the effort, although the situation could be quite complicated if we were to have too many weeks of bad weather. With a transmission date fast approaching, it could in fact become an absolute disaster if we were to finish up with little or no film of otters! The third film I planned for the series, *A Bay of Birds*, was to be about the many species of seabirds living and nesting in the vicinity of Dublin Bay.

The location I chose for the otter film was on the west coast where the open landscape offers good opportunities for watching coastal otters during daylight hours. Although our coastal otters are sometimes referred to as sea otters, this is incorrect. We have only one species of otter in Ireland and it is found both in fresh water and in the sea. Our animal is the Eurasian otter *Lutra lutra*, and it has a larger geographical range than any other species of otter. It is found from the Atlantic Ocean to the Pacific and from Siberia to Northern Africa, India and Indonesia.

Capturing good behaviour sequences of otters on film usually means many hours and days of patient watching. The otter keeps moving while it fishes, and a knowledge of the territory by the photographer is a very definite advantage if he or she wishes to keep up with the animal. Having a trained assistant familiar with the habits of otters makes the lot of a cameraman a good deal easier. Two pairs of eyes make all the difference when trying to locate an animal that constantly manages to vanish into thin air! I had made an arrangement with a local boatman, Paddy Quinn, to bring Frank and myself and our camera gear up along an isolated stretch of coastline, where we had regularly seen otters. This would be the pattern for three or four days every week over many months while we attempted to familiarise ourselves with the daily routine of individual otters in the area. The intention was to obtain good film material whenever possible during these visits.

One morning we stood above a pebble shore, scanning the shoreline of a small island a few hundred yards directly across from us. The tide was rising fast but there were still quite a number of large rocks showing themselves above the water, their damp mantles of untidy wrack beginning to float about their necks. We had seen an otter in among the seaweed but it had disappeared out of view, which is nothing unusual – you only have to blink and they suddenly melt away. It couldn't possibly have seen us. We weren't moving about and we had been absolutely silent. The question was where had it gone? We were still searching the shoreline with our binoculars when Frank signalled that he thought he had seen some movement behind a rock. When you keep staring for long periods every odd lump of wrack takes on the shape of an otter, especially when the incoming tide creates a see-saw movement between the rocks. We then saw what we had hoped and prayed for and neither Frank nor I could believe our luck: it was an adult otter with at least one cub.

There was no time for another look; the dingy was on the shore and we got to it as quickly and as quietly as was possible. We had to make a detour in order to move downwind and head for the south tip of the island. As we headed away, we knew we would lose sight of the otters briefly and our hope was that we would find them again soon after we landed on the other side of the island. We came in on a stony beach that led up to a sandy bank, above which a grassy slope ran twenty feet or so up to the ridge. We literally crawled halfway up the slope and around the point to where we had an overview of the shoreline that we had seen across the water from the far side. Had we attempted to make our approach lower down along the beach, there would not have been a clear view and there was the likelihood of suddenly coming upon the otter and causing her to panic.

We had only crawled another five yards along the grassy sheep-track when without warning she came from behind a seaweed-covered rock, followed by two very young cubs. The track was nine feet above the otters and we were downwind. At a given signal Frank crawled up abreast of me and gently placed the short tripod legs in position. It only took a moment to line up the shot and have the three otters in my lens. There is an indescribable thrill in having a wild animal and her youngsters framed in close-up in your camera, especially when they are totally unaware of your presence. The two cubs were so small they were only able to swim along the surface of the water and they looked comical in their attempts to follow their mother. They were unable to even wriggle under the rafts of seaweed, let alone dive. Their mother caught each one of them in turn in her mouth and delivered them, first one and then the other, to a clearing beyond the patch of floating seaweed.

Having discovered this otter family, we realised that we should film as much as was possible of their activities while they were around. Although we had discovered the holt the female otter was using as a resting place for herself and the cubs, there was every possibility that she could disappear with them without warning. We returned as often as we could, whenever tides and weather allowed us to do so. Young otters face many threats at this period of their lives, the elements being only one of them. When north-westerly winds occur on that area of coast where we were filming, storms build up very quickly and in all the noise and confusion cubs may lose contact with their mother. She can only tell where they are when she hears their voices, and if they become separated by too great a distance, she may be unable to make out the cubs' high-pitched contact calls amid crashing waves and howling winds. The youngsters then lose their way and the female otter never sees them again.

We had been following the otter family for a few days when the coast was suddenly hit by a north-westerly gale. Filming had to be postponed for a day or two before we could make a return trip to continue the work. On taking up our usual observation point along the sheep-track, we eventually came upon the female otter swimming across the sound on her own. Just below us we could see one cub but there was no sign of the second one. When she returned to our side again she ran past us up along the shore and back down again, still searching. If the otter had felt threatened, her first impulse would have been to take to the water. She finally gave up and returned to where her single cub was and lay down beside it.

Later that same day, while filming some distance further up along the shoreline, Frank drew my attention to something on the surface of the water, just a few feet from the edge of the shore. When I waded over I could see in the middle of a patch of floating bladderwrack, the body of a small otter cub. There was little doubt but that this was the second cub the female had been anxiously searching for earlier in the day. It was a sad spectacle but there was nothing we could do about it. Losing a cub in a storm is all part of the animal's struggle for existence in a very tough environment. The otter female had only one cub to look after now.

After the success of the first series of *Wild Islands* a further series of twelve programmes was commissioned in 1998. I recorded twenty-four commentaries in English for transmission on RTÉ. There were also commentaries recorded in Welsh for S4C and in Scots Gaelic for STV. By the time the second series was under way, however, the production company, Performance Films, who were responsible for the programmes, ran into financial trouble. This was a pity as they had built up a very good team and for a period during the making of *Wild Islands*, the future had looked very promising for them. The series then came to an end.

14

Final Frames

A Life in the Wild – The Islandman – Chance meetings –
Water is life – Back to earth

A Life in the Wild

As we were approaching the end of 1999, I encountered difficulties in getting new commissions from RTÉ. Claire Duignan, Head of the Independent Production Unit, then suggested a retrospective that would look back at all my programmes from the earliest days. So we devised a new six-part series that was to be called *A Life in the Wild*.

The plan was to revisit old locations, including the Blasket Islands where we had been marooned for five days some thirty years previously, the River Dargle where I spent my childhood, Conamara where I first came in contact with West of Ireland boatmen, and the Island of Terceira in the Azores, which had a connection with the mythical island of Hy-Brasail off our west coast and was the location for our first overseas safari. The black-and-white film that I had taken during the 1960s was incorporated into the programmes, and Cian filmed me returning to those locations.

A Life in the Wild proved to be immensely popular and as there was a lot more material available from the archives of *Amuigh Faoin Spéir* I had hoped that RTÉ would commission a follow-up. However, submissions for a new series were rejected.

The Islandman

Nevertheless, when one door closes another opens. We had been planning a documentary on Johnny Bailey, a popular Conamara boatman who owned a famous craft called *An Capall*. Johnny, according to himself, was the last of the *bád mór* skippers. He had worked on his father's boat since he was a schoolboy, and he took over as skipper when his father died. All through the 1940s and 1950s and right up until the 1960s, Johnny had been sailing his craft on a commercial basis to the Aran Islands, to Galway and across to Clare. He is the only one left of all those skippers who sailed during that period, and he is still sailing his own boat, albeit for racing and not for commercial purposes. The film we had planned was an hour long, with the title *Islandman – Máistir Báid Mhór*.

The *Islandman* project depended on extra funding from both Bord Scannán na hÉireann/The Irish Film Board and Foras na Gaeilge. It was only when that particular funding was confirmed that *Islandman* finally got the go-ahead from RTÉ.

The filming of *Islandman* was almost like working on a feature film. There were sailing boats, crews, safety precautions to consider, photographic and recording equipment to be organised, and a lot of food to supply all the participants. Most of the filming was done during the spring and summer months. Cian was Director of Photography and took most of the pictures, but there were occasions when we had as many as five cameras operating. As I mentioned in an earlier chapter, my soundman of many years, Pat Hayes, went to Canada on a short holiday prior to the week of the last shoot. We booked him for the following week and he was very much looking forward to another spell of sailing. Sadly, he was never to return; he died in Canada. We dedicated *Islandman* to his memory.

Once the film-shoot was over we began organising the music. It's always great fun when musicians gather together, especially when Philip King is involved. The group included Máire Breathnach, Alex Finn, Breandán Ó Beaglaoich, Philip King, myself and the traditional singer Pádraic Ó Conghaile. The final music soundtrack added just the right atmosphere to the film, which was launched at Béal an Daingin in Conamara, quite close to where Johnny Bailey was born. The hall was crammed with locals who formed an enthusiastic audience.

Islandman – Máistir Báid Mhór was transmitted on RTÉ on Easter Monday, 21 April 2003.

A film on the history of the Galway hookers, *Húicéirí*, which was commissioned by Mícheál Ó Maillí of TG4, was transmitted on St Stephen's

Day, 2003. It was a particularly important film as it featured boat builders who had never before appeared on a programme, and it included Gaelic sailing terminology that was in danger of being lost and forgotten. The programme was filmed by Cian and presented by an experienced Conamara sailor, John Deairbe Ó Fláitheartaigh.

Húicéirí won the overall prize in the John Healy National TV and Radio Awards in May 2004.

Chance meetings

It always fascinates me how chance meetings can affect one's life forever. Were it not for deciding on that particular day to stroll into Garnett & Keegan's in Parliament Street, my meeting with the entomologist Dick Harris would not have ended up with a job. And all those characters who were regular customers of that wonderful establishment would never have crossed my path. The experience I had gained in Parliament Street eventually led to another job offer in Hely's of Dame Street. It was there that I received the invitation to present my first radio programmes from a fishing customer, Fachtna Ó Hanracháin. My meeting with Seán Ó Riada took place at the same shop counter when he called in to purchase a shotgun. If it were not for Hely's, would I ever have met Ó Riada? Probably not, and Ceoltóirí Chualann would certainly not have been a part of my life.

To be told by young zoologists on many occasions that they had taken up their profession because of my television programmes is extremely satisfying, but I can hardly claim all the credit. Apart from the people involved in the production of a programme, there are also others who have been involved behind the scenes and they also deserve some praise. In striving for accuracy in programmes that feature particular plants or animals, there is often a need for some extra expert advice. An endless list of wildlife people, both professional and amateur, are due a special debt of gratitude for their assistance to me in the making of hundreds of programmes over the years.

How does one set out to be a wildlife filmmaker? It is a question I am often asked. There is really no easy answer and if you have read this book you will know by now how it all began for me, but for a young person starting off today, the way I began would hardly be the normal route to travel. Most wildlife filmmakers began by first having a real interest in wildlife; the filming followed later. Although every filmmaker has a different story to tell, I have noticed that nowadays almost all the young people who begin working with the BBC's Natural History Unit in Bristol have a degree in either zoology or science. There are others of course, people like Hugh Miles, one of the world's best-known wildlife cameramen, who began training at the BBC as a cameraman and worked on programmes that had nothing to do with wildlife. Hugh always had an interest in the countryside and he is an excellent field naturalist.

In some respects it is easier to make a film today than it was when I began. Advances in modern technology make it possible to obtain excellent pictures, which can be viewed as soon as they are taken. Until quite recently there was the drudgery and expense of having to send film over to London for processing and then having to wait for its return. There is no processing with video and there is the added advantage of stock costs being much cheaper than they are for film. Programmes where good animal behaviour sequences are required need a lot of time spent in the field and that is what drives up the overall cost.

Water is life

Attempting to produce TV programmes that illustrate environmental problems, and at the same time hoping to hold the attention of a general audience, can be quite daunting. Nobody wishes to be bored, and if a programme begins to sound like a lecture, the viewer will quickly switch over to another channel. As pressure on our environment increases, protecting the landscape and its wildlife becomes an almost permanent occupation for the natural history filmmaker. Trying to create awareness among the public as to what is happening to the countryside is a constant challenge.

A slogan used by the ESB some years ago was 'Water is Life', but trying to get the meaning of that message home to a wide public can be very difficult. It's only when the quality of our drinking water is threatened that the lesson is finally understood. There are times when I am close to tears thinking about our waterways and the number of rivers we have destroyed in recent years. Many of those rivers had extended wetlands occupying one or two fields up from the riverbank. Those patches of grassland acted as a store capable of holding a great deal of water, but this capacity to retain water was not well favoured by the farming community, who mounted an incessant campaign in the 1960s and 1970s to have these watercourses drained, with devastating effects on the aquatic and terrestrial wildlife. Unfortunately, the unique environment contained in those rivers cannot now be restored. Perversely, draining them has also resulted in the lowering of water storage capacity in the giant limestone aquifers feeding these unique systems. We are now facing a situation where Ireland will doubtless have to spend millions of euros constructing expensive and highly disruptive dams to retain and store water to replace the natural stores that previously were provided by nature, free of charge.

On a more hopeful note: in the absence of a viable national water policy, a community in Co. Waterford are attempting to do something about the environment in their own areas of Dunhill and Annestown. The scheme that has been devised could provide a blueprint for future national policy and a means in many instances by which Ireland can cope with EU water directives.

At present, in many parts of the country, untreated or partially treated water from various sources issues straight into the local watercourse. In the method being used in Co. Waterford, polluted water is intercepted by shallow, vegetated, constructed wetlands. The vegetation in the ponds supports the microbial activity, which cleanses the water. These constructed wetlands are at last gaining much-deserved recognition and could solve many of the pollution problems being suffered in other parts of the country. The creation of the ponds at Dunhill and Annestown are also proving very attractive to wildlife and there has been a dramatic increase in the number of species in the area as a result of those imaginative new habitats.

Back to earth

On a recent occasion I was invited to a local primary school to talk to the children. I was brought into the classroom by an enthusiastic young teacher who explained to me how overjoyed the children would be when they saw me. As I stood at the front of the classroom facing about thirty bright-faced little ones, all curiously looking at this ancient individual beside their young teacher, she began to address them.

'Now children, you are all delighted, I am sure, to see who has come to speak to you this morning.' They all did look delighted, but anything to break the routine would have had the same effect. The teacher continued: 'Now children, I want you to put up your hands, those of you who know who this is.' Thirty hands shot up. The teacher pointed at a brown-eyed little fellow with rosy cheeks. 'Yes Séamus, tell me who it is?' 'The inspector!' shouted the little lad enthusiastically. For both the teacher and myself it was a quick return back down to earth!

Index